KAUFMAN FOCUS GUIDES

MAMMALS
OF
NORTH
AMERICA

**NORA BOWERS,
RICK BOWERS,
and
KENN KAUFMAN**

special consultants
Christine C. Hass,
Nancy Mann,
and Ronnie Sidner

Illustrated with
more than 1,200 images
digitally edited
by the authors
and based on photos
by more than
50 top photographers

HOUGHTON MIFFLIN COMPANY

RABBITS, HARES, PIKAS

TREE SQUIRRELS AND CHIPMUNKS

GROUND SQUIRRELS AND MARMOTS

MEDIUM-SIZED MAMMALS

DOGS, CATS, BEARS

HOOFED MAMMALS

MICE AND RATS

KANGAROO RATS

POCKET MICE AND JUMPING MICE

VOLES AND LEMMINGS

SMALL BURROWERS

SHREWS

BATS

SEALS, WALRUS, MANATEE

DOLPHINS, PORPOISES, WHALES

PICTORIAL TABLE OF CONTENTS

WHEN YOU SEE AN UNFAMILIAR MAMMAL:

1. Try to place it in one of the groups shown on the next four pages.
2. Refer to the page numbers or color tabs and go to that section of the book. Find the pictures that match your animal most closely.
3. Always check the range maps to see which of the animals shown is likely to be found where you are. In some cases there are several species that look very much alike. In these cases, range may be the best way to tell them apart.
4. Read the text for additional pointers on habitat, behavior, seasonal variations, and comparisons to other species.

RABBITS, HARES, AND PIKAS, pages 22–37
Rabbits and hares have big ears; pikas do not.

TREE SQUIRRELS AND CHIPMUNKS, pages 38–67
In trees or on the ground, mostly in wooded areas.

GROUND SQUIRRELS AND MARMOTS, pages 68–95
Usually on the ground, usually in open country.

Dotted line: rare stray in this area

Pale green: uncommon in this area

Dark green: common to fairly common here

Dark blue: common range at sea

Pale blue: uncommon range at sea

Pale orange: formerly found in this area

MEDIUM-SIZED MAMMALS, pages 96–123

A catch-all group of mammals that do not fit neatly into other categories. The largest rodents and smallest carnivores are here.

DOGS, CATS, AND BEARS, pages 124–147

Carnivores, medium-small to very large.

HOOFED MAMMALS, pages 148–173

Grazers and browsers, mostly large.

MICE AND RATS, pages 174–197
The most familiar small rodents. Most have long tails.

KANGAROO RATS AND KANGAROO MICE, pages 198–207
Great jumpers, with big hind feet. Mostly in dry country.

POCKET MICE AND JUMPING MICE, pages 208–217
Pretty good jumpers also. Small. Most with small ears and long tails.

VOLES AND LEMMINGS, pages 218–231
Small, fuzzy, with blunt noses and usually short tails.

SMALL BURROWERS, pages 232–245
These gophers and moles are usually underground.

SHREWS, pages 246–259
Hyperactive little predators with pointed snouts and small eyes.

BATS, pages 260–285
The only flying mammals. Active mostly at night.

SEALS, WALRUS, AND MANATEE, pages 286–301
Bulky aquatic mammals. Seals and walruses haul out on land to rest; manatees never leave the water.

DOLPHINS, PORPOISES, AND WHALES, pages 302–341
Ocean mammals, ranging in size from moderate to massive.

To Beth Greenland
and to Dick and Joan Bowers
for all their love and support
of Nora and Rick

For information about permission to reproduce selections from
this book, write to Permissions, Houghton Mifflin Company,
215 Park Avenue South, New York, New York 10003.

Visit our Web site: www.houghtonmifflinbooks.com.

*Library of Congress Cataloging-in-Publication Data
is available.*

ISBN 0-618-15313-6 (cloth)
ISBN 0-618-38296-8 (flexi)

Book design by Anne Chalmers
Typefaces: Minion, Univers Condensed

Illustrations and maps for this guide were produced in
Tucson, Arizona, by Hillstar Editions L.C. and Bowers Photo.

Printed in Singapore

TWP 10 9 8 7 6 5 4 3 2 1

DISCOVERING WILD MAMMALS
A Note from Kenn Kaufman

Mammals, as a group, might seem to be lacking a constituency. Many other groups of living things are centers of attention for thriving communities of hobbyists. There are reptile clubs and fish clubs and orchid clubs. Tidepool walks and wildflower hikes are popular. Mushroom festivals and dragon-fly festivals have appeared. More and more people identify themselves as butterflyers today, and of course the birders are legion. But no one is a "mammaler."

Or, perhaps, everyone is. I have seen hints of this time after time while leading groups in the field. The stated purpose of a trip might be to look for birds or plants or butterflies, but that pursuit is suspended if a wild mammal appears. Let a fox or deer cross the path, let even a chipmunk approach the group, and it will become the center of attention. The mammal trumps everything else. Maybe we feel a visceral sense of connection (since we are mammals ourselves), but the attraction is undeniable. Ask anyone, "Are you excited about mammals?" and you may get a tepid response. Ask, "Would you be excited to see a jaguar, moose, bear, whale, fox, badger, dolphin, or wolverine?" and you're likely to hear a lot more enthusiasm. The average person may not think much about mammals as a group, but for the most part, mammals are what we have in mind when we think about the thrill of seeing *wild animals.*

My own fascination with wild animals goes back to childhood, and some of the most vivid experiences of my life have been mammal encounters — first view of a badger, first lynx, first wolf, first Killer Whale. I had long wanted to do a book focused on mammals, but it was a particular pleasure to work on this project with my longtime friends Nora and Rick Bowers. These two are best known for their excellent nature photography — images from Bowers Photo have been published widely, including the hundreds that formed the backbone of the two previous Focus Guides, to birds and butterflies — but they are also trained biologists and superb field naturalists. In working on this guide, they were able to draw on their own photographs of (and experiences with) bears in Canada, bats in Texas, seals in Alaska, whales in the Atlantic, marmots in Montana, and of course scores of mammals here in Arizona, where we all live. We hope that the sense of immediacy and of direct observation and experience comes across throughout this guide.

Mammals are often challenging to observe, and sometimes challenging to identify, but they are always worth watching. Take this Focus Guide with you when you go exploring in the outdoors, and see what you can discover for yourself about the world of these quintessential wild animals.

Identifying mammals is not the same as identifying birds. Virtually all North American birds can be recognized at a distance, by sight or sound, or both. By contrast, some of our mammals are genuinely impossible to recognize on sight and can be distinguished only by details of the teeth or skull. Most birds have distinctive color patterns, allowing us to point to specific field marks for recognizing them. By contrast, most mammals lack obvious markings; those with strong patterns, such as the skunks, are exceptions. To identify mammals, therefore, we must focus on things like the size and shape of the animal and its habitat, range, and behavior.

Variation: No two individual mammals look exactly the same, and even the same one will look different at different times of year, so you should not expect any animal to look *exactly* like its picture in this book. Individual variation in color may be extreme, as with the variants of Black Bear and Red Fox (often neither black nor red), or they may be subtle. Some mammals vary from place to place, as described under "Subspecies" on p. 16. Seasonal variations occur also. Most mammals molt their pelage (fur) at least once a year, with the old fur being shed a little at a time and new fur growing in, and they may look quite scruffy while the molt is in process. Some mammals molt twice per year and have dramatically different seasonal colors, as with Snowshoe Hares, which are brown in summer and white in winter.

Terminology: This guide is intended for a general audience, so we have avoided technical jargon as much as possible. A few terms are essential for describing mammals; most of them are obvious (like *tail* or *ears*), but we have diagrammed a few of the more useful terms in this illustration of a Mexican Gray Wolf.

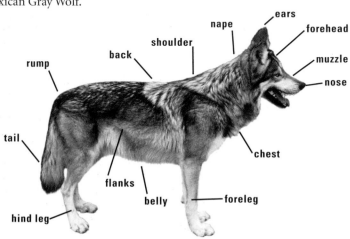

Marine mammals (like this White-beaked Dolphin) are so different in structure that they require their own set of terms. Details of their *dorsal* (back) *fin* and flippers are often important in identification. On many dolphins and small whales, the *melon* (enlarged forehead region) has a distinctive shape.

Sizes and weights: Size is undoubtedly a factor in identifying mammals. (The Grizzly Bear and the Meadow Vole may have similar colors, for example, but no one is likely to confuse the two.) Illustrations in this book are in correct scale relative to the others on the same page but not necessarily to those on other pages. Be sure to check the measurements given each time you turn the page to get an idea whether the animals shown are actually big, medium-sized, or small.

Describing sizes of these animals can be surprisingly tricky. When we say in the text that a particular mammal is large or small, for example, we mean that only by comparison to related species: even a very small whale, for example, will be much bigger than a very large mouse. But even giving measurements for each species can be problematic. Other species of mammals vary in size as much as humans do. It might seem simplistic just to give the height and weight of the average human, but citing the extremes would be misleading also. In this guide, in most cases, we have presented average lengths and weights for each species, and these should be taken as very approximate figures.

Scientists describe the length of an animal by measuring from the tip of its nose to the tip of its tail, and we have followed that convention here. By this method, a slender, long-tailed squirrel might have the same length as a stocky, short-tailed marmot; so to give a clearer idea of the relative sizes of the animals, we also indicate the weight of each. These figures are even rougher and more approximate than those given for length. For many mammals, the full range of weights has not been recorded. Variation is often extreme: some hibernating mammals weigh almost twice as much when they enter their dens in fall as they do after emerging the following spring, and we have often averaged the available figures and rounded them off. Still, we hope that these very approximate figures for length and weight will give you an idea of the sizes of the animals in this book.

Shape: Many mammals can be easily grouped by their shape and overall gestalt. Wolves, Coyotes, and foxes all are shaped somewhat like the familiar domestic dog. Deer, Pronghorn, bison, and Moose all have hooves. The shape of an animal is more important and less variable than color. Note especially the length of the tail relative to the rest of the body, the size and shape of the ears, and the shape of the muzzle.

The importance of studying the range maps: Many of us, when looking at an identification guide, have a natural tendency to focus on illustrations above all else. But for identifying most kinds of mammals, after we have arrived in the right general group, it's actually best to narrow down the possibilities by looking at the maps. In several groups — small rodents, bats, shrews, etc. — there are many species that look essentially the same, but only a few of these are found in any one place. Develop the habit of scanning the maps first, to narrow down the possibilities.

We compiled our maps from a wide array of sources, and we believe they represent the most accurate set of maps currently available for North American mammals. If you think you are seeing one of these animals outside the range we have mapped for it, you should identify it with caution, and try to photograph it if possible.

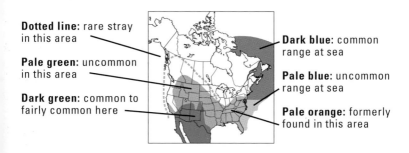

Dotted line: rare stray in this area

Pale green: uncommon in this area

Dark green: common to fairly common here

Dark blue: common range at sea

Pale blue: uncommon range at sea

Pale orange: formerly found in this area

We use darker colors (dark green on land, dark blue at sea) for most maps. Where the range is mapped in a paler shade, we are signaling that the animal is relatively rare. For a few species we use pale orange to show an area where it no longer occurs, but there are many more cases of animals that have retreated from areas where they once lived. On the other hand, some animals (such as the Nine-banded Armadillo) have expanded their ranges in recent times; we have attempted to map the most current range, and if space permits we mention the range expansion in the text.

Birds often wander outside their normal ranges, but mammals seldom do, except for a few mobile creatures such as bats and marine mammals. In a few cases we have put dotted lines on the maps to indicate the extent of wandering. Some bats actually have regular migrations, but we have not mapped summer and winter ranges, because in some cases there are questions as to how much of the population hibernates instead of migrating.

Habitat: After checking the maps to determine which species of a group are likely to occur where you are, the next thing to consider is the habitat. Most mammals are choosy about where they live, and their preferences can provide good clues for identification. For example, pikas generally will be in rock piles in the mountains, muskrats will be in or very near marshy waters, and prairie dogs will be in wide-open country. Even among groups of related species, habitat preferences can be helpful. In the interior of the west, for example, the Montane Vole favors damp meadows, streamsides, and the undergrowth of forests, while the Sagebrush Vole is usually on dry open flats dominated by big sagebrush.

Behavior: Along with habitat, the animal's behavior within that habitat provides major clues to its identity. In the west, for example, the Rock Squirrel has a much larger, bushier tail than most other ground squirrels. Superficially it looks a lot like the tree squirrels, but it doesn't act like them. It lives on the ground, scampering about on rocks, and when it climbs in bushes or trees it looks quite clumsy there. If danger threatens it will dash for its underground burrow rather than dash up a tree. Likewise, in the southeast, the Marsh Rice Rat is separated from other rats not only by its habitat (marshes) but by its behavior, diving and swimming gracefully underwater. We have tried to describe all of these distinctive behaviors, so be sure to read the text for each species that you are considering.

Seasonal occurrence: Most mammals are sedentary, rarely migrating south in fall like birds or butterflies, with the exception of some bats and marine mammals. Season is still important to consider, however, as many mammals hibernate through winter, being active only for a limited time in spring and summer. Of course, the actual dates of a season vary quite a bit with latitude, so an animal described as coming aboveground in early spring might emerge in January in Arizona and in June in Canada.

The impossible: This book probably should come with a label saying something like, "Warning: some mammals cannot be identified in the field." When we have had a good look at an animal, it is tempting to look through a guide to find a picture that looks right and identify the creature on that basis alone. Despite any differences that may appear in the illustrations, however, some species can be separated only by obscure features such as the number of grooves on the front teeth or the bumps on the skull, and some are separable only by chromosome number — a bit hard to ascertain in the field. If you have matched an observation to a picture in this guide, please follow up by reading the text for that species to see if it really is identifiable. In many cases the best that a field naturalist can do is to identify a mammal to the correct group: to say that that small rodent was one of four possible species of pocket mice, for example, or that that chipmunk was one of three local possibilities. This kind of knowledge is satisfying in itself and better than the false precision of putting a specific name on an unidentifiable animal.

TIPS FOR OBSERVING MAMMALS IN THE WILD

It's a fact: the average wild mammal is much more difficult to observe than the average bird, butterfly, or wildflower. Although there are conspicuous exceptions — for example, squirrels bounding across urban lawns or seals lounging on harborside rocks — most mammals are elusive. Many are active only at night, many are relatively silent, and many actively avoid humans. Because of the challenges involved, going out to look for mammals can rightly be regarded as an adventure.

Some of the best opportunities for watching wild animals can be found at the magnificent national parks in the United States and Canada. After decades of complete protection, many of the large mammals in these parks are not only numerous but also somewhat accustomed to humans, making them relatively easy to observe. Generations of visitors have been thrilled by the bears and bison of Yellowstone, the Elk and bighorns of Banff and Jasper, and other such glamorous mammals. But if you don't live near a national park, you can still have mammal encounters just about anywhere.

Some mammals are regularly active by day, including some that may thrive around the edges of cities, such as chipmunks, tree squirrels (except for flying squirrels), and ground squirrels (including the largest of all ground squirrels, the Woodchuck). Some rabbits and hares and some small rodents may be out in daylight as well as at night. Seeing animals like these is largely just a matter of paying attention. The antics of squirrels in city parks are well worth observing, and even small children may be fascinated by the chance to watch these animals up close.

Looking for mammals at night: The nocturnal activity of many mammals makes them more difficult to observe but not impossible. Naturalists who venture out at night may have spectacular encounters with mammals.

One simple approach for seeking nocturnal mammals is just to watch for them in the headlights while driving slowly on quiet back roads at night. Another approach is to walk quietly on a trail or deserted road with a flashlight. Either way, some mammals will be spotted first by their *eyeshine.* In many mammals that are active in low light conditions, the back of the eye has an additional reflective layer, the *tapetum lucidum,* which lies behind the receptor layer of the retina. If light passes through the receptor layer without being absorbed, the *tapetum lucidum* reflects it back, so that it might be picked up by the receptors on the second pass. This reflection creates the eyeshine that may be visible from a great distance. In order to see the eyeshine, however, your own eyes must be lined up more or less directly with the source of the light, or the reflection will not come back to you. It happens automatically when you are driving, as you will be looking rather directly along the beam of the car's headlights. If you are walking, hold the flashlight up near the level of your eyes, not down at your waist. A headlamp is a good piece of equipment for nocturnal mammal searches, leaving your hands free for taking notes on what you are seeing.

Most nocturnal mammals seem particularly sensitive to sound, so your chances of seeing them are greatly increased if you can be as quiet as possible.

Some naturalists have been experimenting recently with night-vision scopes, which operate on available light. These instruments give an odd blurry green cast to the scene, but after one has adjusted to that, they may offer a great opportunity to watch the animals going about their activities undisturbed by any artificial light.

**Ringtail:
Common in many
western habitats
but active only
at night**

Stalking mammals: Techniques used by hunters to get close to game can also be used by observers who just want to watch the same kinds of animals. (Of course, many hunters are excellent naturalists and do spend time watching all manner of wild creatures in addition to their quarry.) Waiting and watching along a well-traveled game trail may produce good views. Watching at a waterhole may work well, especially in dry country. Remember that most mammals have a much keener sense of smell than we do. If you are upwind from a trail or waterhole, any approaching mammal will know you are there and will be much more wary.

In wilderness areas, actively stalking large mammals for closer views can be exciting, but it is important to exercise common sense and respect for the animals. Moose, bison, and other large mammals can be dangerous if startled. Even with non-dangerous animals, stalking too close and then scaring them can constitute harassment. If in doubt, don't get any closer.

Observing marine mammals: In some places, whales and dolphins can be watched from shore, as when Gray Whales are migrating along the Pacific Coast. But close observation usually requires going offshore by boat. Regular whale-watching trips are now being offered from many ports on the east and west coasts, and these provide the chance to see whales, dolphins, and other sea creatures in their own element.

Feeding wild mammals: In some cases, we can attract mammals for observation by putting out food for them. Many a homeowner has discovered that it is all too easy to attract squirrels, simply by putting up a bird feeder. At night, that same bird feeder may be visited by flying squirrels or other more exotic creatures. In the southwest, nectar-feeding bats may come to hummingbird feeders at night. In general it is not a good idea to feed larger mammals; animals such as bears, Coyotes, and peccaries that have been fed by people are likely to lose their natural fear of humans and become dangerous (and besides, the junk food that people give to wild animals is often bad for their health).

DETECTING MAMMALS BY TRACKS AND SIGNS

Many wild mammals are good at staying out of sight, so the naturalist who goes looking for them may spend most of the time looking for signs of their presence rather than watching the animals themselves. Tracking mammals is an art and a science, worthy of a whole book of its own (and in fact a number of good books are available; see "Sources of Further Information" on p. 342). In this section we give only a few general pointers.

Tracks are often the easiest signs to find, identify, and interpret. The appearance of a mammal's tracks is determined by the shape of its feet; the way it walks, hops, or runs; its weight; and the kind of surface on which it is moving. Some species have such distinctive feet that their tracks are easily recognized (for example, the Virginia Opossum, p. 102, with the big toe oddly askew on the hind foot). In many cases, however, the shape of the track will take us only to the right general group, and then we must rely on more subtle details and on clues relating to size and habitat. For many species, we have illustrated typical tracks (in the margin, below the range maps), but these diagrams should be taken only as general guides. If the forefoot and hind foot are substantially different in shape (as they often are), and if we have room, we have illustrated both, with the diagram of the forefoot above that of the hind foot. With all of these track diagrams we have given an *average* measurement for the length of the track, but please keep in mind that all of these mammals show a lot of individual variation in size. The typical Grizzly Bear, for example, is bigger than the typical Black Bear, but some small Grizzlies are smaller (with smaller tracks) than some large Black Bears.

**Bobcat tracks
in the snow**

Droppings: An expert tracker learns to recognize many mammals by the droppings (scats) that they leave, and is even able to make judgments about what the animals have been eating. Some generalizations are possible: the scats of predatory mammals are frequently rather long and twisted, often with traces of fur or feathers showing, while hoofed mammals often leave pelleted scats that are remarkably small for the size of the animal. In our experience there is so much variation in scats that it would be misleading for us to illustrate just a few, and space did not allow for us to show the full range of variation for each species. If you wish to pursue this means of learning more about the mammals that you are following, see the references on tracking listed on p. 342.

Signs of mammals feeding: Telltale signs of the feeding behavior of mammals are everywhere in the outdoors. Some are obvious, such as the conical pointed stump left when an American Beaver has chewed down a tree. Some are more subtle, such as the little piles of clipped green grass left by voles. Some can be downright irritating, as when a Red Squirrel has used the attic of your cabin as a place to store its midden of spruce cones.

Animal trails: Just like human hikers, many other mammals tend to take the easiest path, and over time they establish well-worn trails. In some undisturbed forests there are deer trails that probably have been used for decades. But many smaller mammals also use regular trails. The "runways" of cotton rats, voles, and some other small rodents are easy to pick out in areas of dense grass.

**sign of a master builder:
the lodge of an American Beaver**

Dens: Some mammals build their own homes, making rather elaborate nests or dens out of sticks and other materials. Tree squirrel nests among the high branches often look like masses of twigs and dead leaves. Some deermice and other mice build neat little nests woven of dry grass. The remarkable lodges built by beavers and muskrats are often conspicuous features in marshes or ponds.

Diggings: A great many mammals make their homes underground. A few, such as moles and pocket gophers, are so adapted to the burrowing (or *fossorial)* lifestyle that they seldom come out on the surface. The mounds and ridges they create may be all that we see of them. Many other mammals, from kangaroo rats to ground squirrels to foxes, do their foraging aboveground but retreat to their holes to rest, raise their young, or hibernate. If we know what burrowing mammals occur in our area, we can make good guesses as to what has made a particular hole. But if a burrow entrance appears to have been used recently — with fresh scratch marks or diggings — it may be worthwhile to spend some time watching it from a distance, to see if the current tenant will come out in the open.

Mole diggings

HOW MAMMALS ARE CLASSIFIED AND NAMED

The sheer variety of nature is wonderful, but it can also be very confusing. To make sense of this diversity, scientists classify living things in categories such as order, family, subfamily, genus, and species. The color-coded sections in this guide are mostly built around orders and families of mammals (although in some cases we have grouped unrelated animals together because they are superficially similar). For most of us, the most interesting category is the species — the basic "kind" of mammal that we can relate to most easily.

Species of mammals: Whole books have been written to define exactly what a species is. No definition will fit perfectly, because there are many borderline cases: things that appear to be in the process of becoming species but are not quite distinct enough (yet). In general, however, members of a species are isolated from members of other species in terms of reproduction. Different species often can interbreed (and may even produce fertile offspring), but they generally don't. And distinct species don't necessarily look different to us. For example, the Hispid Cotton Rat and Arizona Cotton Rat are so similar that an expert can tell them apart only by measuring their hind feet (or determining their chromosome number), but they apparently do not interbreed in places where they overlap, so they must be classified as separate species.

Subspecies: Members of a species do not all look the same. In addition to the variations among individuals, they may vary consistently from one place to another. These regional variations, if they are well marked, may be formally described by scientists as subspecies. Subspecies within a species will interbreed with each other if their ranges come in contact, so the divisions between them are often not precise. In some cases, the appearance of a species will change gradually over a broad area (becoming gradually larger and darker from south to north, for example), and dividing this kind of clinal variation into subspecies is arbitrary and not very useful. But if a subspecies has an isolated range and is not in contact with other populations of its species, it may be quite distinctive, and it may eventually evolve into a full species.

Differences among subspecies of mammals are seldom obvious in the field, so we have mostly ignored them in this guide, but in some cases we mention subspecies that are either well marked or endangered.

Scientific names are applied to every known species. Mainly Latin or Latinized Greek, these names are recognized by scientists working in any language. The names are written in italics: *Sylvilagus palustris* is the Marsh Rabbit. The first word of this name, *Sylvilagus,* is the genus to which this species belongs. The Desert Cottontail, *Sylvilagus audubonii,* belongs to this same genus, so it is related to the Marsh Rabbit even if its English name might suggest otherwise. The second word of the scientific name identifies the species. If the scientific name consists of three words, the third identifies the subspecies: *Sylvilagus palustris hefneri* is a subspecies of Marsh Rabbit limited to the Florida Keys.

Standardized names: If you look at older books about mammals, you may find different names used for many of the species. The Sewellel has been called Aplodontia and Mountain Beaver, the Round-tailed Muskrat has been called Florida Water Rat, and there are many other examples. When these alternate names have been used widely and recently, we try to mention them in this guide, usually in parentheses in the header for a species.

Harris's Antelope Squirrel: older books called it Yuma Antelope Squirrel or Harris's Ground Squirrel

Scientific names for mammals have varied as well, making it hard to trace just what species is being discussed. Fortunately, the American Society of Mammalogists has worked for a number of years to provide a standardized classification of all the world's mammals. The most recent edition of their work, *Mammal Species of the World,* published in 1993, gives the recommended scientific name for every known species. The next edition is due to be published shortly, and it will include standardized English names as well. In the meantime, the best source for English names is *Common Names of Mammals of the World* (Wilson and Cole 2000, Smithsonian Institution Press). Don E. Wilson, a world-renowned mammalogist at the Smithsonian, has been a leader in this move to provide standardized names and classification. We salute him for his work in this regard, since it will greatly improve communication among scientists and the public, help promote public interest in mammals, and ultimately help provide more support for their conservation.

In this book we have followed these standardized names in almost all cases. Some of the English names that we use are different from those in *Common Names of Mammals of the World,* based on information about what these species are probably going to be called in the next edition of *Mammal Species of the World.*

The unknown: Although we have tried to present information that is as up-to-date as possible, the classification of mammal species is an ongoing process. There are borderline cases on which even the experts differ: for example, whether to treat the Kit Fox and Swift Fox as one species or two. New techniques of study in recent years have revealed the existence of cryptic species, especially among small mammals, which may look almost identical but are quite different genetically. Even among large animals there are still mysteries out at sea: one whale illustrated in this guide was just described to science in 2002! And, of course, the habits of many mammals are still largely unknown. Scientists who study mammals still have plenty of exciting work to do.

CONSERVATION

Ever since our human ancestors arrived in North America more than 10,000 years ago, we have been having an impact on many of our fellow mammals. Scientists are still divided on the question of whether early human settlers had a hand in wiping out the "megafauna" of this continent. We know that early Americans hunted mammoths and mastodons, but no one knows whether such hunting pressure could have hastened the extinction of these big brutes, or of others, such as saber-toothed cats or giant ground sloths, which disappeared at about the same time.

We do know with certainty that the arrival of Europeans starting about 500 years ago had a major impact on many mammals. Some species prospered and spread: the adaptable Coyote, for example, may be more numerous now than it ever was in the past. Others have not fared so well. Because mammals are so diverse, it is difficult to generalize, but a few points are worth making about particular groups of mammals.

Predators: In an earlier era, all predators were regarded as "bad," since they sometimes took livestock and often were thought to compete with humans for game. Today there is wider appreciation for the fact that predators play an essential role in natural ecosystems and that they actually benefit the overall health of the populations that they prey upon by taking out the sick and the weak individuals. Still, animals such as Pumas, Gray Wolves, and Grizzly Bears are now absent from large areas of North America where they once lived. Efforts to reintroduce these animals still run into resistance from people who remember childhood nursery stories a little too clearly and who can't imagine wanting to bring back the "big bad wolf." An example of an organization that is doing fine work to educate the public about these magnificent animals and the need for their conservation is the North American Wolf Foundation, Inc., Route 133, Ipswich, MA 01938; www.wolfhollowipswich.org.

Grazing or browsing mammals: Many of the large hoofed mammals lost a lot of ground as European settlers spread across this continent. The most shocking example involves the American Bison, which became the target for massive commercial hunting in the 1870s and 1880s, reducing its total population from the millions or tens of millions to just a few thousand before legal protection saved it from extinction. Other hoofed mammals, such as Elk, Caribou, Pronghorn, and Bighorn Sheep, also disappeared from large areas where they had once occurred. Today, however, most of these animals are doing well, and efforts to reintroduce them into former haunts have had some success. Hunters' organizations are often at the forefront of conservation efforts for these animals; they understand that to maintain sport hunting they must maintain healthy populations of the game animals. By taking responsibility in this way, hunters often set a good example for other naturalists to follow.

A different kind of conservation problem involves areas where deer have become too numerous for their own good. In urban edges where large predators are lacking and where hunting would be difficult at best, deer may increase to the point of being garden pests, road hazards, and destroyers of the understory of woodlands, eventually becoming stunted and starving themselves. State, provincial, and local agencies are struggling with such situations in a number of areas.

Bats: At one time, bats were maligned and persecuted for purely superstitious reasons. Because many species roost and nest in concentrations in caves and other shelters, they were especially vulnerable to being disturbed or killed. In recent decades we have seen much progress in public attitudes toward bats. Much of the credit for educating the public must go to Bat Conservation International, P.O. Box 162603, Austin, TX 78716 (on the Web at www.batcon.org). Another excellent group that is working for the good of the bats is the Organization for Bat Conservation, P.O. Box 801, Bloomfield Hills, MI 48303 (www.batconservation.org). There are also several state and local bat organizations that do excellent work.

Marine mammals: In North American waters and worldwide, populations of many marine mammals have been severely depleted by human activities. Guadalupe Fur Seal and Northern Elephant Seal were both hunted almost to extinction by about 1900 (although both have made good recoveries since), and the Caribbean Monk Seal is apparently extinct. Large-scale commercial whaling, which continued through much of the 20th century, drove several whale populations to the brink. Blue Whales, probably the largest animals that have ever lived, were hunted intensively; more than one-third of a million were killed in the Southern Hemisphere, where the fragmentary remaining populations show little sign of recovery. Northern Right Whales (the name literally comes from having been considered the "right" ones to kill) exist as remnant populations, and the ones in the Pacific may be too few for them ever to rebound.

Even without direct hunting, marine mammal populations are affected in negative ways. There are several types of deep-sea commercial fishing operations that accidentally take dolphins and small whales in their nets. The extent of this "bycatch" problem is difficult to measure. Another threat, a new and serious one, comes from the U.S. Navy, which is killing and maiming whales and dolphins through the use of high-intensity sonar: blasts of incredibly powerful sound broadcast through the water. Tests have resulted in whales stranding on beaches, dying there, bleeding from their ears and eyes and brains. Some politicians, apparently unmoved, are working to exempt the military from all environmental laws, making it likely that this torture and killing of marine mammals will continue. The organization that has done the most to try to stop this threat is the Natural Resources Defense Council, 40 W. 20th Street, New York, NY 10011 (www.nrdc.org). The NRDC has also worked to protect Grizzly Bears and other mammals, and it deserves support from anyone who cares about wildlife, at sea or on land.

Endangered species: Under some accounts in this guide, we mention that the species is listed as endangered or threatened. A species is regarded as *endangered* when it is in danger of extinction within the foreseeable future throughout all or a significant portion of its range. It is regarded as *threatened* when it is likely to become endangered within the foreseeable future throughout all or a significant portion of its range.

Some endangered mammals have been at the center of major efforts. The Black-footed Ferret, for example, was thought extinct until a few were rediscovered in Wyoming in 1981. A captive breeding program has pro-

duced enough offspring for release in several states, and there is hope for the ferret's future. Similar reintroduction programs are under way for Red Wolf and some other mammals. We applaud these heroic efforts to pull species back from the brink; but most conservationists agree that the best time to save a species is before it is reduced to such dire scarcity.

Space: the final problem. Animals need space — enough living space, in the right kinds of habitat. This is basic to their survival. One organization that understands this very well is the Nature Conservancy (TNC), 1815 Lynn Street, Arlington, VA 22209. TNC has succeeded in protecting more than 90 million acres of habitat worldwide, mostly through the non-controversial approach of buying the land; they deserve support.

The mention of living space does lead us into controversial territory, however. Animals need living space. People do too. The human population is increasing at a rapid rate. As the world's human population continues to grow, there will be less and less space left over for other living things.

Many conservationists shy away from talking about the population problem, because the issue is charged with emotion. But the facts speak for themselves. World population has almost tripled in the last 50 years, from just over 2 billion to 6.1 billion. Every year there are another 85 million mouths to feed. We are now the most numerous species of mammal, and we affect the planet far more than any other. The growth of human population exacerbates many social problems (poverty, crime, the spread of diseases) and most environmental problems (air and water pollution, destruction of forests, spread of deserts, loss of biodiversity). The earth has only so much land, water, and air, and if we continue to increase, eventually we will outstrip the carrying capacity of the planet.

There are no easy answers. No one should be forced to have fewer children than they want (although there are millions of people in particular social groups who are, in effect, forced to have more children than they really want). The idea of "population control" is abhorrent, but so is the idea of a crowded and subdued world with no wild animals. We who care about nature must address the population issue for the good of all species, including our own.

ACKNOWLEDGMENTS

In working on this guide, we were repeatedly struck by the generous and helpful nature of scientists who study mammals. Many busy professionals (and former professionals) went out of their way to provide information, answer our questions, or help us to obtain photographs.

Particular thanks to our three technical reviewers, Dr. Christine C. Hass, Nancy Mann, and Dr. Ronnie Sidner. Each of them gave us information and advice that improved our approach, and did detailed reviews of material (Hass particularly on carnivores and ungulates, Mann on marine mammals, and Sidner on bats). Any errors that slipped through, of course, are the responsibility of the authors. Another consummate professional, Don E. Wilson, graciously allowed us to follow the nomenclature used in the fine *Princeton Guide to Mammals of North America* (Roland W. Kays and Don E. Wilson, 2002) as a likely indication of the names to be adopted soon by the American Society of Mammalogists (see p. 17). Robert and Virginia Rausch went out of their way to help us on several issues.

Photographs of rare mammals are often very challenging to find. The following individuals went to great lengths to help us track down photos: Robert S. Sikes and Elmer J. Finck (American Society of Mammalogists), Orcilia and Bryan Forbes (photos by the late Richard Forbes), Sherry Johnson (photos by the late Murray Johnson), Keri Lodge (National Marine Mammal Laboratory), William Rossiter, Sue Ruff, C. Gregory Schmitt, and Betsy Webb.

Thanks to the following for extra information: Jane Church, Eric R. Eaton, North American Wolf Foundation, Alison Sheehey, Paul Sherman, South Dakota Department of Game, Fish, & Parks, and John and Gloria Tveten. Greg Lasley helped with color issues. Bruce Hayward and Owen and Arlene McCaffrey assisted Rick and Nora with photographing bats.

In the task of assembling this book at Hillstar Editions, Stacy M. Fobar again did an outstanding job of organization, design, editing, and tracking myriad details. Digital-graphics guru Eric Powell worked wonders on the most challenging of photographs and went on to clean up most of the other images, greatly improving the appearance of the book. Thanks also to Leslie Holmes and Juliet Niehaus for help with graphics.

As always, it was a privilege to work with the professionals at Houghton Mifflin. Editor Lisa White and designer Anne Chalmers were with us every step of the way, and we also had essential help from Harry Foster, Nancy Grant, Martha Kennedy, Beth Kluckhohn, Larry Mallach, Becky Saikia-Wilson, and Michaela Sullivan. Special thanks to Wendy Strothman for guidance and help throughout, and to Megan Butler for advising on how best to communicate with the public about mammals.

Finally, thanks to Joseph Neal, Doug James, and the late Charlie Wooten for introducing Nora to the study of ecology, and thanks to Ronnie Sidner and Wendel Cochran for Rick's and Nora's introduction to mammalogy.

RABBITS, HARES, AND PIKAS

make up the order **Lagomorpha**. Rabbits and hares (family **Leporidae**) are among the most familiar wild mammals in most regions of North America. Pikas (family **Ochotonidae**) are restricted to the mountains of the west and northwest. All members of this order (called Lagomorphs for short) are herbivores, grazing and browsing on a wide variety of plant material. They all have two pairs of incisors, the front pair being the chisel-like "buck teeth" typified by the cartoon character Bugs Bunny.

Swamp Rabbit

Rabbits and hares (family **Leporidae**): pp. 24–34. These animals are adapted to their habitats by the size of their ears and legs. Hares include jackrabbits of the west and Snowshoe, Arctic, and Alaskan Hares of cooler climates. Jackrabbits and Arctic Hares lives in more open country, while Snowshoe and Alaskan Hares are found in forested areas. Their relatively long ears and large eyes help them to detect predators and other sources of danger, and their large hind legs give them the speed to escape. Rabbits, by comparison, tend to live in areas of dense vegetation. Not as long-eared or long-legged as the hares, they depend more on concealment for protection. When danger threatens, rather than running away in the open as hares may do, rabbits typically dive into cover.

The big ears of rabbits and hares have another function besides listening for danger: they aid in regulating body temperature. The jackrabbits and cottontails that live in the hottest desert climates tend to have very large ears that are mostly hairless. Convection of heat from the veins in these relatively naked ears can help to lower the overall body temperature and cool the entire body of the animal. By contrast, rabbits and hares that live in colder climates tend to have smaller, densely furred ears that help to conserve heat rather than radiating it away.

Black-tailed Jackrabbit

The young of hares and jackrabbits are born well furred, with their eyes open, and are capable of running shortly after birth. Their nests, which are generally occupied for only a very short time, are simple scrapes, with or without some simple lining material. The young of rabbits are born naked and helpless, with their eyes closed, so they are raised in nests that are more carefully constructed: cup-shaped hollows lined with grass, other plant materials, and the mother's fur, often with a plug of material on top to conceal the young during the day while the mother is away. Rabbits tend to visit the nest to nurse the young at dawn or dusk or at night. Although young rabbits do grow quickly, they stay in the nest longer than hares and jackrabbits.

baby cottontails in nest

Rabbits and hares are coprophagic, eating rapidly and chewing less thoroughly in order to decrease their exposure in the open, then seeking cover to rest while eating their own partially digested and pelleted green feces. This allows better assimilation of unused nutrients.

SIGNS OF RABBITS AND HARES: To detect rabbits and hares when the animals themselves are out of sight, watch for signs like the following. Their droppings are usually seen as piles of dark brown and slightly flattened pellets. Their tracks are typically in clusters of two pairs, with the two rounded foreprints showing up *behind* the pair of elongated hindprints (because these animals plant their forefeet and swing their hind legs through past their forefeet when hopping). Hares frequently leave flattened areas in the grass where they rest, and rabbits frequently make runs (tunnels through dense vegetation or deep snow). A few species construct their own burrows, but most borrow the burrows of other animals.

tracks of Black-tailed Jackrabbit

American Pika

Pikas (family **Ochotonidae**): p. 36. These are found mainly in the mountains of Asia. Only two species live in North America, around rockpiles and talus slopes of the mountains of the west. Pikas have much shorter ears and hind legs than rabbits or hares, and they are active by day, gathering food and storing it for the winter. They are also much more vocal than rabbits or hares, and their sharp whistled calls are often heard before the pikas themselves are spotted.

Widespread and familiar, cottontails are found almost throughout the lower 48 states, barely extending into southern Canada.

EASTERN COTTONTAIL   *Sylvilagus floridanus*

typical track pattern, with hind feet (up to 3″ long) hitting in front of front feet

Our most widely distributed cottontail, even more so since it has been introduced into areas outside its original range. Now common in farmland, parks, and other manmade habitats, but historically occurred in natural clearings, forests, deserts, swamps, and prairies. Feeds usually at dawn and dusk — on grasses and forbs in summer, woody twigs and bark in winter. Tends to run for cover in a zigzag pattern when startled. Females have three to seven litters per year, averaging three to five young. Baby cottontails, born naked and helpless, are sheltered in a nest on the ground, lined with leaves, grasses, and fur from the mother. ► Medium-sized with dense rusty-brown fur on body mottled with black, white underneath. Ears, from base to tip, are equal to or shorter than the length of the head from nose to neck. Tail dark on top, cottony white underneath. Rusty nape patch, whitish feet, sometimes a distinct white spot on forehead. Compare to species below, also other cottontails on following pages.

NEW ENGLAND COTTONTAIL   *Sylvilagus transitionalis*

Very secretive and localized in northeastern boreal forests, especially where there is an understory of mountain laurel and blueberry. This cottontail is declining in numbers and disappearing from some areas, probably owing to loss of habitat and introduction of other species of rabbits. Rarely far from cover, it feeds mainly on grasses and clovers in summer and on twigs in winter. ► Very similar to Eastern Cottontail, only safely identified by skull measurements or DNA. This species tends to be slightly smaller with shorter ears. Usually has a black patch between the eyes and black leading edges on the ears (only about 40 percent of Eastern Cottontails show either).

APPALACHIAN COTTONTAIL   *Sylvilagus obscurus*

Recently described as a separate species from the New England Cottontail, this rabbit occurs in dense forests of conifers and in the cover of montane shrubs in the Appalachians from Pennsylvania to Alabama. Feeds on grasses, forbs, shrubs, and conifer needles. ► Almost identical to New England Cottontail, separated by range. Very similar to Eastern Cottontail, but more often shows a black spot on the forehead and black front edges of ears; usually occurs at higher elevations.

COTTONTAILS OF THE EAST

young in
grass nest

**Eastern
Cottontail**

L 17″   W 2¹/₂ lbs

**Appalachian
Cottontail
and
New England
Cottontail
(almost identical)**

L 16″   W 2 lbs

SWAMP RABBIT   *Sylvilagus aquaticus*

Our largest cottontail, frequenting marshy lowlands from the Gulf Coast north into the central midwest. Common in the southern part of its range, but its range in the north is decreasing. Swimming comes naturally to this rabbit, and it is seldom seen any distance from water. Feeds on aquatic and terrestrial plants such as cane, sedges, grass, tree seedlings, corn, and blackberry. Unlike most other cottontails, Swamp Rabbits defend territories (of up to nearly 20 acres), and males mark their territories with scent from a chin gland. Common resting spots, above water on stumps or logs, are easily spotted by their piles of fecal pellets. Females average two litters per year of three young. ▶ Large for a cottontail. Short, coarse fur, ranging from yellowish brown to brownish gray, streaked with black. A darker brown wash on head outlines a lighter cinnamon-buff eyering. Similar to Eastern Cottontail (previous page) but larger, with feet usually reddish brown, not whitish. Marsh Rabbit, mostly found farther east, is smaller and has underside of tail brownish, not white.

MARSH RABBIT   *Sylvilagus palustris*

In the southeastern corner of the U.S., this cottontail lives in very wet places — mostly brackish cattail marshes but also freshwater marshes, and sometimes swamps with sweet gum and tupelo. With shorter legs than most rabbits, it is less agile on land, mostly walking rather than hopping (and sometimes walking upright on its hind legs). However, it swims readily, hiding from predators by floating with only its eyes and nose exposed. Mostly nocturnal, it feeds on leaves and bulbs of marsh plants such as cattails, rushes, and water hyacinths, and leaves and twigs of trees. Females have several litters per year, usually of two or three young, nurtured in a large covered nest of grasses and leaves. ▶ A small, dark brown rabbit with short, broad ears and small, slender, dark reddish feet. Rusty or chestnut wash on upperparts and hind legs. Belly and chest redbrown, with white only on the lower abdomen. Tail is small and usually dingy gray-brown underneath. Distinguished from Swamp Rabbit by its smaller size and by its dingy undertail; from Eastern Cottontail by habitat, red-brown feet, and dingy undertail. A subspecies (*S. p. hefneri*) in the Florida Keys is endangered.

juveniles in nest

one week
old

**Swamp
Rabbit**

L 20″   W 4³/₄ lbs

Marsh Rabbit

L 17″   W 3³/₄ lbs

juveniles
in nest

DESERT COTTONTAIL   *Sylvilagus audubonii*

Widespread in the west, in pinyon-juniper woodland and riverside brush as well as deserts. Most active at dawn and dusk. Tends to freeze motionless rather than run when startled. ▶ Has larger ears than other cottontails (longer than length of head), only sparsely furred inside. Note the lack of dense hair on the feet. Whiskers are mostly black. Tail dark gray above with bases of hairs black and a broad fringe of light gray, white underneath. Compare to the three species below and to Eastern Cottontail (p. 24), which overlaps in the southwest.

MOUNTAIN COTTONTAIL   *Sylvilagus nuttallii*

A rabbit of the intermountain west. Usually in sagebrush deserts, but also in wooded areas to the south. Browses on grasses, sagebrush, juniper berries, and other plants, usually near dense cover. In sparsely vegetated areas, may seek shelter in rock crevices. ▶ Similar to Desert Cottontail but ears are slightly smaller, more rounded, more heavily furred inside. Feet are densely covered with long hair. Whiskers are mostly whitish. Where they occur together, this species is usually at higher elevations than Desert Cottontail.

BRUSH RABBIT   *Sylvilagus bachmani*

Native to the far west, in dense brushy areas from sea level up to over 6,000 feet. Secretive, leaving cover only cautiously to feed or bask in the sun. Feeds mostly on grasses. Uses burrows of other animals and travels in runs hollowed out in dense vegetation. When pursued, will climb up onto low branches to escape. ▶ Small and dark, with shorter ears, legs, and tail than Desert Cottontail, the only other cottontail that shares its range.

PYGMY RABBIT   *Brachylagus idahoensis*

Our smallest rabbit. Limited to big sagebrush flats of the Great Basin region, a disappearing habitat. Feeds mainly on big sagebrush, even climbing into the tops of bushes to feed. Unlike other rabbits, digs a complex system of burrows and gives a sharp buzzing squeal when alarmed; also has a pika-like bark. ▶ Very small. Pinkish gray to blackish gray above; underside of tail buff, not white. Ears very short, densely furred inside, edged with buff. Moves with a unique scurrying or scampering gait. Might be confused with young of other species, but note habitat, buff underside of tail.

Desert Cottontail

**L 15"
W 27–44 oz**

young

Mountain Cottontail

**L 14"
W 22–31 oz**

Brush Rabbit

**L 13"
W 18–32 oz**

Pygmy Rabbit

**L 9–12"
W 13–16 oz**

JACKRABBITS

are big, fast-running hares with long legs and long ears.

BLACK-TAILED JACKRABBIT *Lepus californicus*

A familiar sight in open country over much of the west, from sea level to high in the mountains, although it is most common in arid rangeland and farm country. It also has been introduced into several eastern states and is established in some locales. Mostly active at night, it feeds on a wide variety of grasses, weeds, shrubs, and sometimes agricultural crops. It can survive in very dry country, obtaining the water that it needs from its food. Females average four to seven litters per year of two to five young each; in the north (where summers are shorter) they usually have fewer litters with more young in each. Populations go through cycles, and jackrabbits can reach densities of more than 1,000 per square mile. ▶ Large, with very long ears and legs. Tail mostly black above, with black continuing as a stripe up lower back; ears tipped with black. The two species below lack black ear tips and have more white on the sides. See White-tailed Jackrabbit (next page).

typical track pattern, with hind feet (up to 3″ long) hitting in front of front feet

ANTELOPE JACKRABBIT *Lepus alleni*

Possibly the fastest of the hares, running at speeds of up to 40 miles per hour. When it runs, the flashing of white on its rump recalls the effect made by a running Pronghorn Antelope, hence the name. Still locally common in southern Arizona, in open desert with grasses and mesquites, but disappearing from some areas that have been taken over by exotic grasses. Mostly active at night, feeding on grasses, leaves, and even cacti; will stand up on hind legs to reach food. ▶ Very large, with huge ears. Has contrasting gray on sides and *white* on rump, hips, and sides of legs. Tail may be black on upperside. Often found with Black-tailed Jackrabbit, but recognized by *lack* of black tips on ears, and by gray and white on sides.

WHITE-SIDED JACKRABBIT *Lepus callotis*

This Mexican hare crosses the border only in Hidalgo County, New Mexico. It favors flat plains with native grasses and is disappearing as grasslands are degraded by overgrazing and invasion of shrubs; may be endangered throughout its range. Unlike most rabbits and hares, male and female White-sided Jackrabbits form strong pair bonds. ▶ In its limited U.S. range, easily separated from Black-tailed Jackrabbit by *extensive white* on sides and *lack* of black tips on ears.

young

Black-tailed Jackrabbit

L 22" W 5 lbs

running

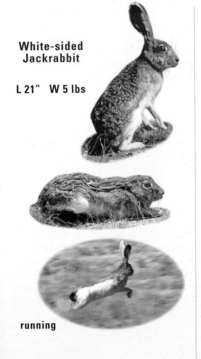

White-sided Jackrabbit

L 21" W 5 lbs

running

Antelope Jackrabbit

L 25" W 8²/₅ lbs

running and flashing white rump from side to side

VARIABLE HARES

molt into a white pelage (fur) in winter, helping to camouflage them in open snow-covered country.

SNOWSHOE HARE   *Lepus americanus*

typical track pattern, with large hind feet (up to 4½" long) hitting in front of front feet

Smaller and shyer than most hares, the Snowshoe hides in thickets during the day, coming out to feed mostly at night. It is widespread in boreal forests of Canada and Alaska, extending southward in the mountains in alder swamps, aspen groves, and hardwood forests. Feeds mostly on grasses, leaves, and berries in summer, bark and conifer buds in winter, but will also eat carrion. Named for its large and densely furred hind feet, which act as snowshoes, allowing the hare to traverse the surface of snow. Snowshoe Hares in the northern forest go through population cycles, peaking and then crashing at about ten-year intervals, affecting populations of some northern predators. ▶ In summer, reddish brown to grayish brown above. Tail is small, brown above and white below; feet can be either brownish or white. In winter (except in western Washington and Oregon), all white with black-tipped ears. Mottled brown and white while molting. Jackrabbits (below and previous page) are larger, with much longer ears. Arctic and Alaskan Hares (next page) are larger and slightly longer-eared; they mostly live on tundra, not in forest.

WHITE-TAILED JACKRABBIT   *Lepus townsendii*

Widespread in open grassy areas of west-central North America, from the plains up to high mountains. It has expanded its range northward in some areas as forests have been cleared; at the same time, it has decreased in some southern areas, as degradation of grassland habitat has favored the more adaptable Black-tailed Jackrabbit. Solitary and mostly active at night, it feeds on grasses, weeds, and shrubs. Young are born in nests lined with grasses and fur; they are born fully furred and can hop within 30 minutes. Averages four or five young per litter, one to four litters per year. ▶ Seems intermediate between the more southerly jackrabbits (previous page) and the northern hares (above and next page). Upperparts yellowish brown (on Great Plains) or grayish brown (intermountain west); in northern and high-elevation parts of its range, it turns white with buff tinges in winter. Tail conspicuously white above and below, sometimes with dusky stripe above. Black-tailed Jackrabbit (previous page) has tail black above, often with black stripe extending up back. Compare to Snowshoe Hare.

VARIABLE HARES

autumn

summer

Snowshoe Hare

L 18″
W 3½ lbs

tracks

winter (most of range)

summer

autumn

White-tailed Jackrabbit

L 24″
W 6–9 lbs

winter (in cold regions)

ARCTIC HARE *Lepus arcticus*

Northernmost hare in North America, reaching islands of the Canadian high Arctic. Lives mostly on tundra beyond treeline, sometimes out on ice up to three miles from land; in winter, may drift south into timber. Feeds mainly on the bark, buds, and roots of willows at all seasons, but also eats grasses, mosses, lichens, and berries, using its front claws to dig through snow to find food. When resting or foraging, it always faces uphill. Females have one litter per year of two to eight young. ► In most of its range, the only hare present. Mostly grayish brown in summer, white in winter, with black-tipped ears; northernmost populations remain white all year. Snowshoe Hare (previous page), which overlaps southern edge of range of Arctic Hare, is smaller, with shorter ears, and is usually darker and richer brown in summer.

ALASKAN HARE *Lepus othus*

Largest hare in North America, found only on tundra and coastal lowlands of western Alaska. Very large body and relatively short ears help it to conserve warmth in extremely cold weather. In summer, often spends midday hiding in dense thickets of willow or alder. Feeds on bark, buds, and leaves of many plants, especially willow and crowberry. Recent studies suggest that Alaskan and Arctic Hares belong to the same species. ► In summer, reddish brown or grayish brown above, with tail white or gray; in winter, white with black-tipped ears. Separated from Arctic Hare by range. Snowshoe Hare (previous page) is smaller, with shorter ears, and with the tail partly brown in summer.

EUROPEAN RABBIT *Oryctolagus cuniculus* (not illustrated)

Our common domestic rabbit, this species has been deliberately introduced or escaped in a number of areas and is established locally, such as on the San Juan Islands, Washington. Has six or more litters per year of up to 12 young, builds extensive underground connecting burrows (called warrens), and can become a serious pest. ► Larger than native cottontails, gray-brown with tail dark above and white below, but variable and can come in many other colors.

CAPE OR EUROPEAN HARE *Lepus sp.* (not illustrated)

Introduced into North America in the 1890s, large hares from the Old World are still locally established in open fields and low hills of Ontario, New York, and New England. ► Reddish brown above in summer, gray in winter. Twice the size of Snowshoe Hares or cottontails, with larger ears.

winter

summer

autumn

Arctic Hare

L 24″ W 10 lbs

Alaskan Hare

L 24″ W 11 lbs

winter

summer

PIKAS

(family **Ochotonidae**) are related to rabbits and hares, but their ears are short and their hindlegs are barely longer than their forelegs. They differ in habits as well: they are active by day, they store food for the winter, and they are very vocal. Tracks are more like those of a rodent than those of a rabbit, with the hind feet not elongated and the front prints preceding the hindprints.

AMERICAN PIKA *Ochotona princeps*

Fairly common on rockpiles and talus slopes in the mountains throughout western North America, where their sharp whistled or bleating calls are often heard before the pikas are seen. Each individual pika defends its own territory among the rocks and spends much time sitting motionless at a high vantage point from which it can watch for intruders or predators. Pikas will scamper out to adjacent meadows to eat grasses and other plants. They harvest grasses and carry them back to their territories for storage, to feed on during winter; the presence of piles of "hay" among the rocks is a good sign that pikas are in residence. Pikas do not hibernate, remaining active in their burrows in winter, and may be seen sunning atop the rocks on clear winter days. Males emit a long call, like a song, probably to attract females. At its southern limits this species lives mostly at elevations above 7,500 feet, although farther north it may be found at lower elevations. Recent surveys show that this pika is dying out at some of its southernmost colonies. It may be a victim of climate change: isolated on these peaks, it cannot escape uphill to cooler temperatures as the climate warms up. ▶ Grayish or buffy brown, underparts washed with buff, with small rounded ears edged in white and no visible tail. Fur is much longer and somewhat grayer in winter. Lacks grayish collar of Collared Pika, but most easily separated by range.

COLLARED PIKA *Ochotona collaris*

Similar in appearance and behavior to American Pika. Active during the day on talus slopes in southeastern Alaska and northwestern Canada. Feeds on grasses and other green vegetation, which it gathers for winter stores. Frequently gives loud, short, high-pitched calls. Females produce one litter per year of up to six young. ▶ Small rounded ears with buffy edges, no visible tail. Dark gray-brown on back with indistinct grayish collar on shoulders, light gray on sides, creamy white underparts. Fur is longer in winter.

PIKAS

calling

American Pika

L 7½″
W 5¼ oz

drying haystacks

harvesting grass

Collared Pika

L 7½″
W 4½ oz

belong to the family **Sciuridae,** which also includes the ground squirrels, treated in the next chapter. This family is classified within the order **Rodentia,** the rodents, the most diverse and numerous category of mammals on earth. Tree squirrels and chipmunks are probably the most familiar rodents over most of North America: most of them are active in the daytime, conspicuously out in the open or up in trees, and several species have become common in suburbs or city parks.

Tree squirrels and chipmunks generally have a lot of variety in their diets. Nuts and seeds are often at the top of their menu, but they also eat berries, buds, bark, fungus, insects, birds' eggs, and sometimes odd items such as smaller rodents, lizards, or carrion. Fast moving and agile, most of them feed both on the ground and in trees. They have very keen eyesight with good depth perception, allowing them to judge distances as they leap through the treetops; their eyesight and excellent hearing also help them to detect the approach of predators. Most species in this group are quite vocal, with a variety of calls to express alarm, aggression, or simple contact.

The animals in this section fall into four groups:

Typical tree squirrels (genus *Sciurus*), pp. 40–46. Found mostly in deciduous or mixed forests, at temperate or tropical latitudes. Agile climbers, they are able to run down tree trunks headfirst and to leap from branch to branch among the treetops. Their dens are often in hollows in tree trunks, but they also build bulky nests of leaves and sticks among the open branches of trees.

Reddish squirrels (genus *Tamiasciurus*), p. 48. These small noisy squirrels live mostly in coniferous forest. Just as acrobatic as the typical tree squirrels but more hyperactive, they may be seen anywhere up in the trees or bouncing across an open clearing on the ground. Our two species both feed heavily on the seeds of conifers, harvesting unripe cones in summer  and storing them in middens in sheltered spots. These middens may be used for years, and their accumulated mounds of peeled-off cone scales (in a hollow log, in the attic of a woodland cabin, etc.) make a telltale sign that these squirrels have been at work.

Flying squirrels (genus *Glaucomys*), p. 50. They don't truly fly, but these squirrels are very impressive gliders. Along each side of their body, an extended membrane, called the *patagium,* stretches from the front legs to the hind legs. When the squirrel leaps from a high branch it adopts a spread-eagled position, with the patagium fully outstretched and the wide, flat tail spread out behind, giving it a large surface area for gliding. Using its tail as a rudder and adjusting the position of the patagium, it can direct its glides with precision, aiming for a landing spot that may be more than 200 feet away. Just before reaching its destination, the flying squirrel swoops upward, slowing itself for a gentle landing. Flying squirrels are active at night, spending the day roosting in a tree hole or other sheltered spot.

Chipmunks (genus *Tamias*), pp. 52–66. Most species spend the majority of their time on the ground, but all are capable of climbing and some clamber about high in trees. All chipmunks have stripes on their faces, lacking on all other squirrels. They have cheek pouches that they use for carrying seeds and other food, caching large amounts of food in their dens, especially in fall. Hibernation does not seem to be as deep in chipmunks as in many ground squirrels (next section); the chipmunks may be asleep for much of the time in winter, but they probably awaken periodically to feed on their stored supplies. In warm climates, some chipmunks apparently do not hibernate at all.

Only one species of chipmunk occurs in most of eastern North America, but there are twenty-one species in the west, and identifying them in the field is difficult or sometimes impossible. Many of these western chipmunks are extremely similar to each other not only in appearance but also in their ecological requirements. As a general rule in nature, we don't find two species with exactly the same habitat choice and habits living in the same place, because competition will result in one species excluding the other. There are many situations among western chipmunks when the ranges of two species meet but do not overlap. Where two or more species in this group are found in the same area, they usually differ in size, food habits, or preferred habitat.

When identifying western chipmunks, your first step always should be to know exactly where you are on the map, and then study the range maps in this book to see which species are possible where you are.

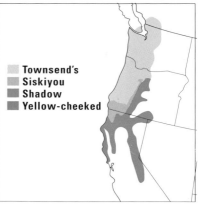

Townsend's
Siskiyou
Shadow
Yellow-cheeked

In the Pacific Northwest, the ranges of these four species of chipmunks fit together like the pieces of a jigsaw puzzle, meeting but not overlapping.

EASTERN GRAY SQUIRREL   *Sciurus carolinensis*

**hind track
2¼″ long**

Common in eastern North America, especially east of the Mississippi, in deciduous and mixed forests; there are also introduced colonies in cities in California, Washington, Oregon, and British Columbia. Probably the best known mammal over much of its range, active by day and able to thrive in suburbs and city parks, wherever there are good-sized trees. It builds bushel-sized nests of sticks and leaves high in trees, but seeks out tree hollows for its winter dens and for places to raise its young. The varied diet of Eastern Gray Squirrels includes many acorns and nuts, but they also eat flowers, buds, bark, fungi, insects, birds' eggs, and carrion, and they chew on bones and deer antlers for calcium. They cache nuts for winter in the ground and in tree hollows. As many people have learned, these squirrels are also very good at raiding bird feeders. The most frequent call is a hoarse bark. ▶ Usually gray above, whitish below, with brownish wash on head, back, and tail. Compare to Eastern Fox Squirrel (next page), the only similar species over most of its range. Black forms of Gray Squirrels can be numerous in northern areas and in Washington, D.C.; albinos are rare in most areas but locally common in a few towns such as Olney, Illinois, and Greenwood, South Carolina.

WESTERN GRAY SQUIRREL   *Sciurus griseus*

This big squirrel of western oak-conifer forests seems shyer than its eastern cousin, and it has not adapted as well to civilization. It has become rare in parts of its range as introduced Eastern Gray Squirrels and Eastern Fox Squirrels have taken over parts of the available habitat. It feeds mainly on acorns and on cones of conifers, but also eats berries, fungi, bark, and insects. In fall it caches many acorns in the ground, finding and eating them later when food is scarce. For sleeping and for raising young, it uses natural cavities in trees or builds large rounded stick nests high in the branches. Most frequent call is a hoarse bark. ▶ Silver-gray above, whitish below. Eastern Gray Squirrel, introduced into its range, averages smaller, has smaller ears, and usually has a brownish tinge in the tail. See Eastern Fox Squirrel (next page), also introduced into range of Western Gray Squirrel.

GRAY SQUIRRELS

ready for
winter

typical

**Eastern
Gray Squirrel**

L 19″
W 12–26 oz

albino

melanistic

**Western
Gray Squirrel**

L 20–24″
W 18–33 oz

EASTERN FOX SQUIRREL   *Sciurus niger*

**hind track
to 2½″ long**

Very common in many areas east of the Rockies, in open woods and parklike areas with large scattered trees and an open understory. It is often found in the same forests as the Eastern Gray Squirrel, but because it favors more open habitats, it is more numerous in the midwest and in the south. The Eastern Fox Squirrel has expanded its range in the midwest as people have planted more trees there, but farther east it has declined in numbers with changes in habitat, and in some areas along the Atlantic seaboard it is now confined to small local colonies. (The subspecies on the eastern shore of Maryland, *S. n. cinereus,* is considered endangered.) Meanwhile, the species has been introduced into the west and is thriving in a number of cities in California, Washington, Oregon, and Colorado. Less arboreal than some of its relatives, this squirrel spends a lot of time foraging on the ground, even venturing out into open fields. It usually travels from tree to tree by running across the ground, rather than leaping from branch to branch. For shelter, however, it builds bulky nests of leaves and twigs high in tree branches or chooses a hollow in a tree trunk.

Like most tree squirrels, Eastern Fox Squirrels have a varied diet. Acorns and other nuts are staple items, but they also eat flowers, buds, seeds, bark, fungi, birds' eggs, insects, and sometimes carrion. They also raid bird feeders, but because they are not as agile as Eastern Gray Squirrels, they are more easily foiled by strategic placement of feeders in places they can't reach. Their most commonly heard call is an alarm bark.

▶ A very large squirrel (averaging twice the bulk of the Eastern Gray Squirrel) with a large bushy tail, suggesting the tail of a fox. Quite *variable* in overall color. Those showing the typical pattern are brownish gray on the back, bright rusty orange on the belly and edges of the tail, and brown on the face. (Compare to Eastern Gray Squirrel, preceding page, which can show a prominent reddish brown tinge.) Some individuals have the legs rusty orange and the top of the head black, while some are mostly black. A common pattern in parts of the southeast features a blackish body and big white patches on the face.

EASTERN FOX SQUIRREL

eastern form

**Eastern
Fox Squirrel**

L 23″
W 28 oz

southeastern
variation

Texas

hairless babies in nest

immature of
black form

ARIZONA GRAY SQUIRREL *Sciurus arizonensis*

Usually rather uncommon in its limited range in the southwest. Found mainly along streams and canyons at middle elevations, in areas just below the Mogollon Rim and in isolated ranges of southeastern Arizona, in forests of cottonwood, sycamore, walnut, oak, and pine. Similar in habits to the Eastern Gray Squirrel (p. 40), the Arizona Gray Squirrel is generally more secretive. It seems less tolerant of people, and it often reacts to humans by freezing motionless on a high tree branch until the intruders have departed. In a few places, however, where it lives close to humans, it becomes tamer and even becomes a brazen raider of bird feeders. Like other squirrels, it has a varied diet. Walnuts are a favored item, but it also eats acorns and other nuts, juniper berries, flowers, fungi, and other items. Females produce no more than one litter per year of an average of three young. ▶ Gray above, often with a wash of brown or yellow; white below. Tail is dark gray to black with some buff beneath. The only other tree squirrels in its range are Abert's Squirrel (next page), which has the tail all white below, and Red Squirrel (p. 48), much smaller and usually at higher elevations. Compare also to Rock Squirrel (p. 76).

MEXICAN FOX SQUIRREL *Sciurus nayaritensis*

Widespread in the mountains of western Mexico, this colorful creature extends north across the border only to the Chiricahua Mountains of Arizona, where it is the only tree squirrel. In the Chiricahuas it lives in pine-oak forests of canyons, mostly between 5,000 and 7,000 feet. Less agile than most tree squirrels when aloft, it spends much of its time on the ground. It forages for a wide variety of nuts and seeds, as well as roots, bulbs, and buds. Unlike many squirrels, it does not usually cache or bury food for later retrieval. For shelter it builds leaf nests or uses tree hollows of oaks and pines. Often silent, but gives gruff alarm barks. ▶ Large and colorful, bright *rusty orange below,* grayer on the back, with more contrast in winter. Tail is very large and bushy and edged with white or yellow. No other tree squirrels occur in the Chiricahua Mountains, but compare to the duller Rock Squirrel (p. 76).

Arizona Gray Squirrel

L 20″ W 23 oz

Mexican Fox Squirrel

L 22″ W 24 oz

ABERT'S SQUIRREL *Sciurus aberti* (Tassel-eared Squirrel)

In the southwest and western Mexico, this handsome squirrel is closely tied to ponderosa pine forests, although it also ranges down into pinyon-juniper woods and into mixed coniferous forest at higher elevations. Ponderosa pine furnishes much of its food: the squirrel feeds on its seeds, buds, and the inner bark of the tips of its branches. In summer, this squirrel also eats many fungi, which it helps to propagate throughout the forest floor. Abert's Squirrel usually builds its nest of sticks high in a pine, but it will also take shelter in tree hollows and even birdhouses. Females usually raise one litter of two to four young per year. When alarmed, this squirrel stamps its front feet and gives a fast, loud chatter. ▶ Large and colorful. The ears are *large* and have a unique long fringe (or "tassel") of hair along the top edge, most evident in late fall and winter (may be mostly worn away by summer). Over most of its range, Abert's Squirrel is gray above with a rusty stripe down the middle of the back, whitish below, with a long bushy tail that is dark above and *white below*. North of the Grand Canyon, the subspecies *S. a. kaibabensis* ("Kaibab Squirrel") has the body mostly dark gray, the tail *all white*. Some individuals anywhere in the range may be mostly blackish, and in Colorado some are all dark brown. These dark individuals may be best identified by ear shape.

RED-BELLIED SQUIRREL *Sciurus aureogaster* (Mexican Gray Squirrel)

This relative of the Eastern Gray Squirrel is a common resident of forests in southern Mexico and Guatemala. Introduced into the U.S. in 1938, it has successfully colonized dense subtropical forest on Elliot Key and nearby small keys a short distance south of Miami, Florida. It builds nests of leaves and twigs among the branches of trees or sometimes uses natural cavities in tree trunks. Feeds on a wide variety of nuts, fruits, and seeds. Litters of one or two young may be born at any time of year. ▶ Larger than the Eastern Gray Squirrel (p. 40), gray above with brighter *chestnut belly and flanks,* or can be black all over. Litters can contain both color forms.

summer

winter

black form

Abert's Squirrel

L 21″ W 22 oz

Kaibab form

Red-bellied Squirrel

L 20″ W 19 oz

47

RED SQUIRREL   *Tamiasciurus hudsonicus* (Pine Squirrel)

This bouncy, noisy little squirrel is abundant in evergreen forest across Alaska, Canada, and the northeastern U.S., extending south in the mountains to Arizona, New Mexico, and the Carolinas. It favors conifers such as pine, spruce, fir, and hemlock, but also occurs in mixed forest of conifers and hardwoods. In typical habitat, Red Squirrels dash about harvesting unripe cones from conifers in summer and store them in central middens to feed on them later. These middens may be used for years by different squirrels, with the scales from the cones eventually forming large mounds. The squirrels also feed on many other items, including various nuts and seeds, insects, birds' eggs, and flowing sap. Mushrooms are often important in their diet, and the squirrels may hang up certain types of mushrooms to dry and then store them for later consumption. Nests are usually in tree hollows but may be up in the branches or even in a ground burrow. Loud and almost continuously vocal — most often a bark-and-chatter territorial call and a loud descending trill. Courtship includes wild chases through the trees, accompanied by harsh buzzing calls. The subspecies isolated on Mount Graham, Arizona *(T. h. grahamensis)* is listed as endangered. ▶ Rusty brown above, whitish below, with a white eye-ring. A *blackish line along the sides* may be less obvious in winter. Redder above and much smaller than most tree squirrels, but in far west, compare to next species.

**hind track
about 2″ long**

DOUGLAS'S SQUIRREL   *Tamiasciurus douglasii* (Chickaree)

A noisy, active little squirrel of conifer forests of the far west. Like its relative the Red Squirrel, it harvests unripe cones from conifers in summer and stores them in middens to feed on throughout the winter. It also feeds on many other items, including acorns, berries, insects, birds' eggs, and many mushrooms. It has a variety of callnotes, including a sharp staccato bark and a rough trill. ▶ Small, rusty brown above, with a *buff eye-ring* and a darker stripe down center of back; dull *orange-buff below.* Has small black ear tufts in winter. Redder above and much smaller than most tree squirrels in its range; see Western Gray Squirrel and the introduced Eastern Gray Squirrel and Eastern Fox Squirrel (pp. 40–42). In limited area of overlap with Red Squirrel, note color of underparts and eye-ring.

Red Squirrel

L 11–14"
W 5–9 oz

western type

Douglas's Squirrel

L 11–14"
W 5–11 oz

49

FLYING SQUIRRELS

are slightly misnamed: rather than truly flying, they "hang glide" from tree to tree. They are equipped with a loose flap of skin, called the *patagium*, along each side of their body, stretching from the front legs to the hind legs. When a flying squirrel launches from a high perch, it splays its legs out to the side so that the patagium is fully extended, and the long flat tail spread out behind it adds to the gliding surface. An extension of cartilage from the squirrel's wrist along the edge of the patagium gives it more control, and with the use of its tail as a rudder, it can direct its glides with precision. Most glides by flying squirrels are in the range of 20 to 60 feet, but they have been known to go more than 250 feet in a single glide. Unfortunately, it takes a special effort to watch these performances, because flying squirrels are active mostly at night.

SOUTHERN FLYING SQUIRREL   *Glaucomys volans*

Common in lowland forests of the eastern U.S. and locally in the mountains of Mexico and Central America. Prefers deciduous forest, but also found in mixed and coniferous forest in some areas. It may be common in well-wooded suburbs and even city parks but is often overlooked because of its nocturnal nature. It usually spends the day inside a tree hollow, old woodpecker hole, or birdhouse; in winter, several may den together, perhaps to share warmth. Its varied diet includes many fungi and lichens, also nuts, seeds, berries, buds, sap, insects, birds' eggs, smaller rodents, and carrion. In fall it gathers many acorns and other nuts and stores them in a tree cavity or other sheltered spot. ▶ Smaller than other tree squirrels, with large black eyes. Folds of extra skin along its sides may or may not be obvious as it moves about. Very silky fur, gray-brown above, whitish below. Compare to next species.

NORTHERN FLYING SQUIRREL   *Glaucomys sabrinus*

Widespread and common in coniferous forest of the north, extending south in the mountains; less common in mixed or deciduous forest. Where their ranges overlap, Northern Flying Squirrels are generally at higher elevations than Southerns. Even in the far north, this species apparently does not hibernate, remaining active through the winter. Similar in habits to the Southern Flying Squirrel, spending the day in tree cavities or other sheltered spots, foraging at night, sometimes coming to bird feeders in the dark. Some populations in the southern Appalachians are considered endangered. ▶ Very similar to Southern Flying Squirrel but averages larger, and tail is often darker toward the tip.

**Southern
Flying Squirrel**

L 8–10"
W 2–3 oz

**Northern
Flying Squirrel**

L 11–14"
W 3–5 oz

EASTERN CHIPMUNK   *Tamias striatus*

**tracks less than
1″ long**

**most chipmunk
tracks are similar**

The largest chipmunk in North America, and the only one in most of the east. Common in deciduous forests, it also adapts readily to well-wooded suburbs and even city parks. This chipmunk spends most of its time on the ground, running with its tail held straight up. It favors areas with rocks, stumps, and fallen logs, using them for shelter and for perches; it also digs extensive systems of burrows underground. Like other chipmunks and squirrels, the Eastern Chipmunk has a varied diet, including acorns and other nuts, berries, seeds, flowers, roots, fungi, snails, and sometimes carrion. It hoards food in chambers in its burrow, and this food is essential to its winter survival: unlike some ground squirrels that hibernate and survive on accumulated body fat, this chipmunk merely enters a torpid state in winter, awakening every few days to feed on its stored food. Its callnotes include a sharp, birdlike chip and a low, repetitive clucking. ▶ Easily identified in many areas as it is the only chipmunk present (see maps). Where it overlaps with Least Chipmunk, in the Great Lakes region and parts of the upper midwest, the Eastern Chipmunk is recognized by its much *larger size, reddish rump,* and less distinct face stripes.

LEAST CHIPMUNK   *Tamias minimus*

One of the smallest chipmunks, and the one with the largest range. Lives in a wide variety of habitats — most numerous in open coniferous forest, but occurs from above treeline in the mountains to sagebrush desert. Sometimes climbs trees and may nest there, but mostly seen on the ground. Has a varied diet like its relatives, feeding on acorns, conifer seeds, buds, berries, flowers, fungi, and insects, and it stores food in its burrow to get it through the winter. Very vocal; callnotes include a birdlike chip, a low cluck, and a dry trill. Flicks tail up and down when calling. ▶ Variable. Tends to be darker in moist climates, grayer in far west, paler and browner in southwest. In eastern part of range, compare to Eastern Chipmunk. Farther west, overlaps with at least 10 other chipmunks; see illustrations and maps on following pages. Least Chipmunk is often *duller* than others in its range. It is always at least slightly smaller than others (except Alpine Chipmunk, p. 62), and its proportions differ, with a relatively shorter muzzle and longer tail for its size than other chipmunks.

Eastern Chipmunk

L 10"   W 4½ oz

pale desert form

Least Chipmunk

L 8"   W 1½ oz

typical

eastern form

53

As with all chipmunks in the west, these should be compared not only to other chipmunks but also to Golden-mantled Ground Squirrel (p. 72).

YELLOW-PINE CHIPMUNK   *Tamias amoenus*

Common and widespread in the northwest, extending south in the Sierras as far as Mammoth Pass, California. Found mainly at middle and upper elevations of the mountains, from around 3,000 feet up to treeline. Favored habitats include the edges of open pine or juniper woodland, chaparral, and meadows with rocky outcrops. This chipmunk tends to forage out in open areas, but usually with some kind of cover nearby. Like its relatives, it has a varied diet, including many plant materials and fungi but also some insects, birds' eggs, and other items. It also stores up food for the winter, passing the colder months in periods of torpor, awakening every few days to eat. Its nest is usually in an underground burrow, but it is known to build grass nests up in trees, as high as 60 feet above the ground. ▶ A fairly small chipmunk. Overall color varies in different regions, but usually *fairly bright yellowish or cinnamon on the sides.* The five dark stripes on the back are all well defined. Most chipmunks in its range are larger, except for Least Chipmunk (preceding page) and Alpine Chipmunk (p. 62). Least Chipmunk is duller and its tail averages a bit longer. Alpine Chipmunk is found only at highest elevations of the Sierras, and its tail is tipped with black. Lodgepole Chipmunk (p. 62) averages larger and has the outermost dark stripes on the back poorly defined. Long-eared Chipmunk (p. 62) is larger, more distinctly striped, and has longer ears.

RED-TAILED CHIPMUNK   *Tamias ruficaudus*

This colorful chipmunk is common in its limited range in the northwest. It favors the shrubby edges of clearings in dense coniferous forest, in zones of Engelmann spruce, hemlock, Douglas-fir, or western red cedar. It feeds on a wide variety of seeds, fruits, leaves, and flowers. Although it usually nests in underground burrows or under boulders or logs, it will also build nests up in trees. During the winter it stays in its den. ▶ A medium-sized, brightly colored chipmunk. Range is one of the best clues, as it overlaps only with Least Chipmunk (preceding page) and Yellow-pine Chipmunk. Red-tailed Chipmunk averages larger than either of those and is more colorful, especially on the tail.

Yellow-pine Chipmunk

L 8³/₁₀"   W 1¹/₂ oz

Red-tailed Chipmunk

L 9¹/₄"   W 2 oz

UINTA CHIPMUNK   *Tamias umbrinus*

Although this chipmunk occurs in parts of eight western states, its range is broken up into fragments, with populations isolated on mountain ranges surrounded by desert. It appears to prefer ponderosa pine forest but also occurs in other conifers such as Douglas-fir, juniper, and pinyon pine. It spends more time up in trees than most chipmunks, foraging there and often nesting and sleeping in tree hollows, but spends the winter in the underground burrows, where it stores food. Has a varied diet like other chipmunks but feeds mainly on seeds. ► A medium-sized chipmunk with a brownish look. Overlaps with several other chipmunk species and is hard to distinguish from some of them. Larger than Least Chipmunk (p. 52) and holds its tail horizontally while running, not vertically. Averages larger and browner than Yellow-pine Chipmunk (preceding page). Cliff Chipmunk is duller, has less distinct stripes, and lives at lower elevations. Panamint Chipmunk (p. 60) is more contrasting reddish and gray. Colorado Chipmunk (next page) is a more colorful reddish brown and has more distinct back stripes, extending all the way to the base of the tail (those of Uinta Chipmunk end on the rump).

CLIFF CHIPMUNK   *Tamias dorsalis*

This grayish chipmunk is often found in relatively dry country. Its typical habitat involves rocky areas and cliffs in open woodland of juniper and pinyon pine, but it also occurs out into sagebrush desert and into cooler coniferous forests. Over most of its range, where it overlaps with other chipmunks, it lives at lower elevations than the others; in southern Arizona and extreme southwestern New Mexico, where it is the only chipmunk, it occurs all the way up to the mountaintops. This species has a long breeding season, from spring to fall, but each female apparently has only one litter per year, usually of five or six young. ► Usually rather easy to separate from other chipmunks because it is so *gray* and because the stripes on its back are relatively *indistinct*. Range and habitat are also good clues. In dry open habitats at lower elevations, compare to the various antelope squirrels (p. 70).

**Uinta
Chipmunk**

L 9″ W 2 oz

**Cliff
Chipmunk**

L 8²/₃″ W 2 oz

COLORADO CHIPMUNK   *Tamias quadrivittatus*

Common in parts of Colorado and some adjacent states, especially around rocky areas in ponderosa pine forest or pinyon-juniper woodland. Where it meets the range of the Uinta Chipmunk, it is apparently kept out of the higher-elevation forest by competition with the Uinta, but it overlaps freely with the Least Chipmunk. Vocal like other chipmunks, with a repeated chipping call; flicks its tail slowly sideways while calling, rather than up and down. ▶ Medium-sized and brightly marked, showing *strong contrast* between the dark and light stripes on the back. Uinta Chipmunk (preceding page) is somewhat duller, and its back stripes end on the lower rump (those of Colorado Chipmunk extend to the base of the tail). Least Chipmunk (p. 52) is smaller and holds its tail vertically while running, not horizontally as in this species. Also compare to the two species below.

HOPI CHIPMUNK   *Tamias rufus*

Formerly considered to belong to same species as Colorado Chipmunk, and replaces it to the west. Favors rocky areas in woodland of juniper and pinyon. Seeds and flowers make up much of its diet, but like other chipmunks it will feed on a wide variety of items, and it stores up food in its underground burrow to survive on during the winter. ▶ Averages smaller, paler, and more buffy than Colorado Chipmunk, with back stripes that are not as dark. Least Chipmunk (p. 52) usually occurs at higher elevations than Hopi Chipmunk where their ranges overlap; it averages smaller still, the underside of its tail is dull yellowish (not reddish), and it runs with its tail held vertically (not horizontally).

GRAY-COLLARED CHIPMUNK   *Tamias cinereicollis*

Limited to mountains of central Arizona and southwestern New Mexico, mostly in coniferous forest of upper elevations. Has a varied diet like other chipmunks but especially favors acorns and the cones of Douglas-fir, climbing high into trees to forage. ▶ Distinctive color pattern. Clear *gray areas* on cheeks, neck, shoulders, and lower back contrast with pale *orange-buff* on the sides; the dark back stripes are bold; pale stripes are rather dingy. Colorado Chipmunk has brighter white stripes on back, dull orange on shoulders. Cliff Chipmunk (preceding page) usually occurs at lower elevations and has back stripes much less distinct.

**Colorado
Chipmunk**

L 9″ W 2⅓ oz

**Hopi
Chipmunk**
L 8¼″ W 2 oz

**Gray-collared
Chipmunk**

L 9″ W 2⅕ oz

GRAY-FOOTED CHIPMUNK   *Tamias canipes*

The heart of this species' small range is the Guadalupe Mountains of Texas, where it is one of the most numerous mammals, but it also extends south to the nearby Sierra Diablo and north in New Mexico as far as the Sacramento, Capitan, and Jicarilla Mountains. It lives in a variety of wooded habitats but appears to be most common in forests of Douglas-fir and ponderosa pine. ▶ Medium-sized, with gray nape and shoulders. Tops of hindfeet are uniquely gray. Best identified by *range*, as it apparently does not overlap with other chipmunks. Gray-collared Chipmunk (preceding page), which occurs just to the west, has gray cheeks, darker back stripes, and oranger sides.

PANAMINT CHIPMUNK   *Tamias panamintinus*

This chipmunk straddles the California-Nevada border. It lives mainly in dry pinyon-juniper woods at middle elevations on the east slope of the Sierras and in the Panamint, White, Grapevine, Kingston, and Inyo Mountains of California, plus the Spring Mountains, Nevada. Prefers rocky crevices to nest, but also builds nests in pines. Calls from tops of rocks: chatters, chucks and whistles. ▶ Medium-sized, relatively pale, with gray on the head and rump. Uinta Chipmunk (p. 56) is duller. Least Chipmunk (p. 52) and Alpine Chipmunk (next page) are distinctly smaller, and Alpine mostly occurs at higher elevations. Long-eared Chipmunk (next page) has big white patches behind the noticeably long ears. In the Spring Mountains, compare to next species.

PALMER'S CHIPMUNK   *Tamias palmeri*

Found only in the Spring and Potosi Mountains of Clark County, Nevada, above 6,500 feet, in forests of pinyon and juniper or white fir and ponderosa pine. May be a close relative of Uinta Chipmunk (p. 56), which does not occur in those mountains. ▶ Gray-brown, with only three brown back stripes; the four paler stripes are gray in the middle and creamy white on the outer pair. The only other chipmunk in its limited range is Panamint Chipmunk; the two may be found together, but Panamint is most numerous around 7,000 feet, while Palmer's is most numerous above 7,800 feet.

LOCALIZED CHIPMUNKS

Gray-footed Chipmunk

L 9¹/₃" W 2¹/₂ oz

Panamint Chipmunk

L 8" W 1⁴/₅ oz

Palmer's Chipmunk

L 8²/₃" W 2 oz

When identifying any western chipmunk, always start by checking the range maps to see which species are possible where you are.

LODGEPOLE CHIPMUNK   *Tamias speciosus*

This chipmunk is widespread in the Sierra Nevada and also occurs in isolated ranges of southern California, including the Mount Piños area and the San Bernardino, San Jacinto, and Piute Mountains. As its name implies, it may be found in open forests of lodgepole pines, but it also lives in other coniferous forests with undergrowth of manzanita and other brush. It has a varied diet like other chipmunks, including flowers and berries of manzanita, insects, nuts, and many seeds and fungi. ▶ Brightly marked, with the outer stripes on the back relatively *wide* and *bright white.* Underside of tail reddish, with black tip. Overlaps with several other chipmunk species. Yellow-pine Chipmunk (p. 54) averages smaller and has the outermost dark stripes on the back more distinct. Least Chipmunk (p. 52) averages smaller and duller. Compare to next two species.

LONG-EARED CHIPMUNK   *Tamias quadrimaculatus*

A distinctive chipmunk of middle elevations in the northern and central Sierras. Favors open coniferous forest as well as chaparral and logged areas. It forages on the ground and in shrubs and regularly climbs trees, even nesting there. ▶ Warmly colored overall, and has very distinct stripes on back and face, but best known by its *large ears,* with a large conspicuous *white patch* behind each. Yellow-pine Chipmunk (p. 54) is shorter-eared, smaller, and less distinctly striped. Lodgepole Chipmunk has shorter ears and tail. Shadow Chipmunk (next page) is the most similar species; its ears (and white patches behind them) average smaller, but it may not always be separable in the field.

ALPINE CHIPMUNK   *Tamias alpinus*

Lives at higher elevations than any other chipmunk in the Sierra Nevada, in subalpine forest, talus slopes, and meadows at timberline. Unlike most chipmunks, it puts on a great deal of fat for hibernation. Its common callnote is a thin *weeet,* repeated. ▶ Our *smallest* chipmunk, averaging even smaller than Least Chipmunk (p. 52). *Pale and rather dull overall.* Least Chipmunk averages a little larger and darker and has a longer tail. Lodgepole Chipmunk is larger and usually more colorful. Habitat and elevation are often good clues for Alpine Chipmunk.

CHIPMUNKS OF THE SIERRAS

Lodgepole Chipmunk

L 8″   W 2 oz

Long-eared Chipmunk

L 9″   W 3 oz

Alpine Chipmunk

L 7″   W 1¼ oz

These four were formerly all classified as one species under the name of Townsend's Chipmunk. They are virtually indistinguishable by sight, although their voices differ. They are mostly separated by range, but where they do meet, they apparently do not interbreed.

TOWNSEND'S CHIPMUNK *Tamias townsendii*

A chipmunk of dense forest, its behavior varying by location. The inland form is often tame and conspicuous, calling as it runs about on the ground; the coastal form tends to be quieter, shyer, and more arboreal. Callnote a high *chi-chip* or *ch-ch-chip*. ▶ Large. Fairly dark brown on the coast, with relatively indistinct back stripes; paler orange-brown inland, with back stripes a little more obvious. Identified by range on the Oregon-Washington coast, as no other chipmunks occur there. Inland in the Cascades, compare to the smaller Least Chipmunk (p. 52) and Yellow-pine Chipmunk (p. 54).

SHADOW CHIPMUNK *Tamias senex* (Allen's Chipmunk)

This stocky chipmunk inhabits both wet coastal redwood forests and drier forests of inland mountains, spending much time up in trees. Its usual callnote is a quick barking series of three to four (or more) notes, but it also gives a single-note *chip*. ▶ Large. Color varies by region. Coastal form is dark, with reduced contrast on back stripes, and can be identified by range in a limited area (see maps). Inland form is fairly bright, tinged orange and with strong contrast on back stripes; easily confused with Long-eared Chipmunk (p. 62).

SISKIYOU CHIPMUNK *Tamias siskiyou*

Another large drab chipmunk found locally on the coast and inland, living mainly in humid forests. Callnote is a unique, loud, one-syllabled *chyip* that starts and ends at a low pitch, rising in the middle. ▶ The only chipmunk in its limited range on the coast. Inland, overlaps with Yellow-pine Chipmunk (p. 54), which is smaller with redder sides and whiter back stripes.

YELLOW-CHEEKED CHIPMUNK *Tamias ochrogenys* (not illustrated)

Also called "Redwood Chipmunk," historically limited to humid redwood forests, now also found in second-growth forests. Callnotes are a unique low-pitched *chi-chip* and a high whistling *chipper*. ▶ Large, dark above, with relatively thin and long tail. Best identified by range (within 25 miles of coast, from Van Duzen River to Bodega).

TOWNSEND'S TYPE CHIPMUNKS

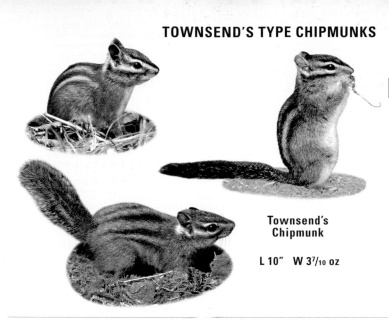

Townsend's Chipmunk

L 10" W 3^{7}/$_{10}$ oz

Shadow Chipmunk

L 9^{3}/$_{4}$" W 3^{3}/$_{4}$ oz

Siskiyou Chipmunk

L 10^{1}/$_{4}$" W 2^{3}/$_{5}$ oz

Many of the chipmunks shown on previous pages are also found in California. In fact, more than half the North American species of chipmunks, 13 out of 22, occur somewhere in California. Checking the range maps is an essential first step in identifying any of these.

MERRIAM'S CHIPMUNK   *Tamias merriami*

Widespread on the coast and in the mountains of central and southern California, Merriam's Chipmunk lives in a variety of wooded habitats, from the upper limits of chaparral and other scrub to pinyon-juniper woods and redwood forests. ▶ Large and dull-colored, with a very long and bushy tail almost three-quarters the length of its head and body. Overlaps with several similar chipmunks in mountains (see maps). Long-eared Chipmunk (p. 62) has brighter stripes, Lodgepole Chipmunk (p. 62) is smaller and has bright white stripes rather than gray, and Shadow Chipmunk (previous page) has cheeks *brown* rather than gray. California Chipmunk is nearly identical, not safely identified where their ranges overlap.

CALIFORNIA CHIPMUNK   *Tamias obscurus*

Localized in southern California, mainly in the San Jacinto and San Bernardino Mountains, as well as in mountains of Baja. Mostly in arid, rocky places with pinyon pines, junipers, and oaks, but also gets up into Jeffrey pine forest in the San Bernardinos, where it overlaps with the nearly identical Merriam's Chipmunk. ▶ Large, bushy-tailed, dull in color, back stripes gray rather than white. Range and habitat are among best clues. Very similar to Merriam's Chipmunk, but averages slightly smaller and tends to be in drier, more open places.

SONOMA CHIPMUNK   *Tamias sonomae*

A shy denizen of northwestern California, living mostly in brushy country, chaparral, and thickets within forest of redwoods or pines. Its callnote is a low, slow chirp that drops in pitch and then rises. ▶ Medium-sized to large, brightly marked. The tail is long and bushy and has a pale outer edge (more obvious on the inland forms). In its limited range on the coast (see maps), this is the only chipmunk. Inland it overlaps with Shadow Chipmunk (previous page), which averages slightly larger and shorter-tailed, and with Yellow-pine Chipmunk (p. 54), which averages smaller and more yellowish and is often in more open habitats.

Merriam's Chipmunk

L 9³/₄″   W 2²/₃ oz

California Chipmunk

L 9″   W 2¹/₂ oz

Sonoma Chipmunk

L 9¹/₂″   W 2¹/₂″

belong to the squirrel family **(Sciuridae)**. All of them are active strictly by day, not at night, and all nest in underground burrows, which they usually dig themselves. In open country, they replace the tree squirrels and chipmunks (preceding section) as the most conspicuous of rodents.

Four very distinctive groups are included in this section.

Antelope squirrels (genus *Ammospermophilus*): p. 70. Although they look superficially like washed-out chipmunks, and they act somewhat like hyperactive versions of the typical ground squirrels, these animals are really quite distinct from either. They are dry-country creatures, and the ranges of our four species are neatly divided by different desert types: we have one

each in the Sonoran, Chihuahuan, and Great Basin Deserts, plus one in the central valleys of California. Unlike the typical ground squirrels, they do not hibernate, remaining active all year. Although they occasionally climb in shrubs or cactus, they spend the vast majority of their time on (or under) the ground. When running about, they often hold their tails curled up above their backs, and this may give them some shade from the hot midday sun.

Typical **ground squirrels** (genus *Spermophilus*): pp. 72–84. A diverse group, with 21 species in North America, mostly in the central and western regions. A few have contrasting patterns (like the golden-mantled species of western mountains, which look almost like big chipmunks), but most are rather plain brownish or grayish. To identify them, start by studying the range maps to see which species are possible where you are, and think about habitat, subtle color variations, and the shape of the ground squirrel's tail.

Ground squirrels are talented diggers, constructing burrow systems that may be quite elaborate with multiple entrances. They vary in how social they are, with some species living in colonies with much interaction and others leading more solitary lives. All are somewhat omnivorous. They feed on a wide variety of plant materials, including seeds, leaves, roots, and berries and nuts if available, but they will also eat insects and sometimes birds' eggs, small animals, and carrion.

Unlike tree squirrels, most ground squirrels hibernate in winter, especially those living in colder climates. In addition to hibernation, some also practice *estivation,* entering a dormant state similar to hibernation but during the warmer months of summer. The timing of these dormant periods often varies by sex and age. In many species, adult males emerge from hibernation first in early spring, followed by adult females and yearlings within a week or two. In many cases, the males enter estivation by midsummer and will remain dormant through the winter (thus merging estivation into hibernation) until time for their emergence the following spring. Females often enter estivation or hibernation later than males, and the young born that year may remain active on the surface for several weeks thereafter, so that in many populations the only ground squirrels that we see in fall are young ones. In preparing for hibernation, ground squirrels eat constantly to build up the fat reserves that will sustain them for their long dormant period; they may double their body weight in the space of a few weeks.

Prairie dogs (genus *Cynomys*): pp. 86–88. These are squirrels, not dogs, but they make a "barking" note in alarm. Highly social, prairie dogs live in colonies, called *towns,* with many burrows in a concentrated area. At one time, huge prairie dog towns (with millions of individuals) were prominent features of the Great Plains and of grasslands of the intermountain west, supporting a diverse community of creatures in addition to the prairie dogs themselves. Today only scattered colonies remain. Our four species of prairie dogs are most easily identified by range (since there is little or no overlap in their distributions) and by the color of their tails.

Marmots (genus *Marmota*): pp. 90–94. These are the largest of the ground squirrels and the most powerful diggers in the family. Their muscular forelegs and strong front claws give them the ability to dig lengthy tunnels even in hard rocky soils. Marmots put on heavy layers of fat during late summer to sustain them while they hibernate through the winter. Their emergence from hibernation in early spring is responsible for the most famous folklore about the family. According to the story, the only marmot in eastern North America, known as the Woodchuck or "groundhog," comes out on February 2 each year (with a bit of human coaxing at times) to predict how much longer the winter will last.

These frenetically active little ground squirrels are often mistaken for chipmunks (pp. 52–66) but live mostly in desert regions, and lack the head stripes of chipmunks. They often carry their tails arched over their backs, perhaps as a sunshade. Active all year and even in the hottest midday temperatures. Calls are long high-pitched trills.

WHITE-TAILED ANTELOPE SQUIRREL   *Ammospermophilus leucurus*

Most widespread of the antelope squirrels, found in open shrubby habitats with poor soil from the Great Basin region south through the Mojave Desert to Baja California. Feeds on a variety of green vegetation, seeds, insects, and even small rodents. ▶ Gray or buff above with white stripe from shoulder to hip on sides, reddish on forelegs and anterior hindlegs, white below. Tail is blackish above, bright white below with narrow dark border.

NELSON'S ANTELOPE SQUIRREL   *Ammospermophilus nelsoni*

Found mainly in the southern San Joaquin Valley, from southwest Merced County through western Kern County, California, in open shrubby and grassy habitats. Like other antelope squirrels, they may carry large numbers of seeds in their cheek pouches. ▶ Very similar to White-tailed Antelope Squirrel, but tends to look more buff overall, with underside of tail buffy white. Best identified by range.

HARRIS'S ANTELOPE SQUIRREL   *Ammospermophilus harrisii*

Common in Sonoran Desert of the southwest. An omnivore like its relatives, but especially favors cactus fruits, climbing into the prickliest of cacti without injury. Like other antelope squirrels, may tolerate high temperatures by resting briefly in shade or in a shallow scrape in the soil, flattening belly-down to lose heat to the ground. ▶ Same basic pattern as others on this page, but tail peppered black and white below, not plain white. Best identified by range.

TEXAS ANTELOPE SQUIRREL   *Ammospermophilus interpres*

Found in rocky terrain of the Chihuahuan Desert from central New Mexico south through west Texas and Mexico. Like its relatives, will drink when water is available but can survive without it, drawing moisture from its food. Lower-pitched trill than other antelope squirrels. ▶ Similar to White-tailed Antelope Squirrel, but two black bands may be visible on underside of tail. Best identified by range.

**White–tailed
Antelope Squirrel**

L 8¹/₂″
W 3³/₄ oz

**Nelson's
Antelope Squirrel**

L 9³/₄″
W 5²/₃ oz

**Texas
Antelope Squirrel**

L 9″   W 4 oz

**Harris's
Antelope Squirrel**

L 9¹/₂″   W 4¹/₂ oz

Most ground squirrels live in very open country, but these two are typically found in forest clearings.

GOLDEN-MANTLED GROUND SQUIRREL   *Spermophilus lateralis*

hind track up to 1″ long

Very common and widespread in mountains of the west, in woodland edges, meadows, sagebrush flats, and rocky slopes. Familiar to vacationers for its cheeky begging behavior around campgrounds and picnic areas, this species is often mistaken for a chipmunk, and it often behaves more like a chipmunk than like the other ground squirrels of open country discussed on the following pages. Its omnivorous diet includes not only a wide variety of junk food garnered from well-intentioned humans but also seeds, nuts, berries, fungi, bird eggs, insects, and carrion. Given a sufficiently healthy diet, it will put on much body fat in fall, spending the winter in a deep hibernation in an underground burrow (although those in warmer climates, such as lower elevations, may sometimes come out in midwinter). Females produce one litter of two to eight young per year, usually in July. ▶ Suggests the color patterns of chipmunks (pp. 52–66) and often found with them, but larger, and lacks the obvious pale facial stripes shown by all chipmunks. Also note the orange-red color on the head and nape, forming the distinct "golden mantle." Antelope squirrels (previous page) are smaller and less colorful and live in lowland desert areas, not in mountain clearings.

CASCADE GOLDEN-MANTLED GROUND SQUIRREL   *S. saturatus*

Closely related to the Golden-mantled Ground Squirrel (and sometimes considered just a subspecies of it), replacing it locally in the Pacific Northwest. Lives only in the Cascade Mountains of Washington and British Columbia, mostly on the eastern slopes. Like the previous species, it favors open areas in wooded country, such as forest clearings, meadows, and the edges of sagebrush flats or talus slopes. It feeds heavily on seeds, berries, and leaves in summer and underground fungi in fall, increasing its body weight by as much as 50 percent so that it can hibernate through the winter on stored body fat. Hibernates at least three feet underground, lowering body temperature to a few degrees above freezing. ▶ Similar to Golden-mantled Ground Squirrel. Most easily separated by range, as the two do not overlap. Differs from all chipmunks in its range by its lack of facial stripes.

**Golden-mantled
Ground Squirrel**

L 9–12"
W 4–14 oz

babies
playing

**Cascade Golden-mantled
Ground Squirrel**

L 12"
W 9–12 oz

These occur in very open areas with short grass. Like all our ground squirrels, they are active only by day.

THIRTEEN-LINED GROUND SQUIRREL   *Spermophilus tridecemlineatus*

tracks less than 1″ long

Originally a resident of short-grass prairies, this distinctive and adaptable ground squirrel is now abundant in many places where people mow grass: golf courses, cemeteries, parks, yards, and along roadsides throughout much of central North America. Frequently seen standing upright on hind legs; when alarmed it gives a birdlike trilled whistle and dives into its burrow. Has a varied diet, mostly seeds, other plant material, and large insects, but also sometimes such items as birds' eggs, mice, or lizards. Stores food in burrows to feed on during bad weather, but survives on its own stored fat during its hibernation from fall to spring. ▶ Strong pattern above, with *distinct alternation* between pale stripes and rows of pale spots against a dark field. At southern edge of range, compare to next species.

MEXICAN GROUND SQUIRREL   *Spermophilus mexicanus*

Native to grasslands of the southern Great Plains and Chihuahuan Desert, this ground squirrel has adapted well to mowed areas such as roadsides, parks, and golf courses. Often social, building complex burrow systems in sandy soils. Feeds on seeds, other plant materials, and insects. In northern part of range, hibernates from fall to spring. Voice includes a short alarm trill. ▶ Similar to the related Thirteen-lined Ground Squirrel, but averages larger with slightly bushier tail. Back pattern somewhat less distinct: has regular rows of square pale spots, but *lacks* the strongly contrasting pale stripes between these rows.

SPOTTED GROUND SQUIRREL   *Spermophilus spilosoma*

Fairly common in dry grassland and desert scrub, especially on sandy soils with sparse plant life. Feeds mainly on green plants and seeds, also some insects and occasionally other small animals. Northern populations have a long hibernation, from early fall to midspring; southernmost populations may be active all year. ▶ Noticeably *small*. Variable in color, from brownish to grayish; paler square spots sprinkled on back, sometimes very indistinct. More irregularly spotted, and paler below, than the two preceding species. Plainer individuals might be confused with Round-tailed Ground Squirrel (p. 84), which lacks any trace of spots and usually looks paler, especially on cheeks.

**Thirteen-lined
Ground Squirrel
L 10″   W 4–9 oz**

with cheek
pouches full

young

**Mexican
Ground Squirrel
L 12¹/₂″
W 4–11 oz**

**Spotted Ground Squirrel
L 8¹/₂″   W 3–6 oz**

ROCK SQUIRREL   *Spermophilus variegatus*

hind track to more than 1½″ long

Widespread and common in canyons, rocky desert, and cliffs of the southwest. Its thick bushy tail gives it some resemblance to the tree squirrels, and it sometimes behaves like them as well, clambering up into trees to feed on such items as juniper berries and mesquite seeds; however, it is more at home on the ground. Most of its diet consists of plant material, such as seeds, buds, and cactus fruits, but it will also eat insects, and it occasionally catches and eats smaller animals. Rock Squirrels tend to live in colonies, digging burrows in the ground in rocky places; the same burrows may be used for several years or may be adopted by other animals after they are abandoned by Rock Squirrels. Females produce one or two litters per year of three to nine young. Voice: a piercing, short whistle, repeated at intervals, suggesting the tooting call of a Northern Pygmy-Owl; also an alarm bark followed by a trill. ▶ Mostly grayish but with a variegated or mottled look, often with a variable amount of black on shoulders, head, or back. Distinguished from other ground squirrels in its range by large size and very bushy tail, but compare to tree squirrels on pp. 40–48.

CALIFORNIA GROUND SQUIRREL   *Spermophilus beecheyi*

Very common in the far west, in open country such as rocky slopes, forest edges, roadsides, pastures, and farmland. Also found in parks, where they can become numerous and fat from living on handouts. Often forms loose colonies, in which individuals may share burrows but usually have their own entrances. Feeds mostly on plant material, including seeds, leaves, buds, and fruits, but also eats insects and sometimes other items such as birds' eggs or young, the eggs of grunion (a beach-spawning fish), or carrion. Females produce one litter per year, usually of five to nine young, with larger litters in the southern part of the range. Adults may remain underground from midsummer to early spring, so California Squirrels seen above ground in late fall are likely to be young of the year. ▶ Similar to Rock Squirrel, but ranges do not overlap. Generally grayish with mottled appearance, and usually with paler gray wash across shoulders and neck. Larger and with bushier tail than other ground squirrels in its range.

Rock Squirrel

L 18–20"
W 16–31 oz

California Ground Squirrel

L 14–20"
W 12–31 oz

juvenile

PLAIN GROUND SQUIRRELS WITH BUSHY TAILS

These three are all seen above ground from midspring to early fall, hibernating the rest of the year. All are rather vocal, giving a variety of sharp whistles, chips, and trills.

UINTA GROUND SQUIRREL *Spermophilus armatus*

Named for the Uinta Mountains east of Salt Lake City, its name sounds like a question: You inta ground squirrels? Fairly common in sagebrush flats, meadows, pastures, and sometimes large lawns. Seen above ground from March to September, but a given individual will be active for only about three months of that time. Eats green vegetation in spring, then switches to seeds in summer, storing large amounts of body fat for hibernation. ▶ Large and plain, with faint mottling on brownish to grayish back; head always *grayish,* underside of tail gray. Wyoming Ground Squirrel has underside of tail buff. Barely overlaps in range with other plain ground squirrels; see Piute (p. 82) and Belding's (p. 84), also White-tailed Prairie Dog (p. 88).

WYOMING GROUND SQUIRREL *Spermophilus elegans*

This drab ground squirrel has a limited range, occurring locally in mountain meadows in some areas, sagebrush flats and grassy valleys elsewhere. May be seen above ground from March to September. Lives in colonies, but each squirrel has its own burrow and stores food there. ▶ Similar to other plain ground squirrels; note *tail* shape and pattern, gray and buff above, *buff to light brown below.* Uinta Ground Squirrel is grayer overall, with gray underside of tail. Townsend's and Piute Ground Squirrels (p. 82) are smaller and paler. Belding's Ground Squirrel (p. 84) has shorter tail that is reddish tipped with black.

FRANKLIN'S GROUND SQUIRREL *Spermophilus franklinii*

Can be harder to see than other ground squirrels, because it often inhabits relatively dense cover: areas of tall grass, shrubby meadows, woodland edges. May be detected first by voice, including whistled alarm note and musical trill. Although most of its diet consists of plant material, Franklin's is often more of a carnivore than other ground squirrels, eating many insects as well as small animals like mice, baby birds, and eggs of birds as large as ducks. ▶ Larger and darker gray than other ground squirrels in its range, such as Richardson's (next page). Where it occurs in woodland edges, might be confused with Eastern Gray Squirrel (p. 40), which has a *longer tail and larger ears.*

**Uinta
Ground Squirrel**

**L 11"
W 9–21 oz**

**Wyoming
Ground Squirrel**

**L 10–12"
W 10–15 oz**

**Franklin's
Ground Squirrel**

**L 15"
W 12–34 oz**

RICHARDSON'S GROUND SQUIRREL   *Spermophilus richardsonii*

Historically lived in short-grass prairie, but has adapted as most of its former habitat has been converted to agricultural fields, shifting its diet from native grasses to cultivated crops. Has two different alarm calls: when it sights a predator on the ground, it gives a shrill whistle, causing its neighbors to stand upright and scan for danger. When it sees a hawk or owl in the air, it gives a sharp chip, and other squirrels dash for their burrows. ▶ Pale gray-brown with mottling above; underside of tail buff. Very similar to some other species, such as Wyoming Ground Squirrel (p. 78), but separated from most by range. Franklin's Ground Squirrel (p. 78) larger and grayer above.

COLUMBIAN GROUND SQUIRREL   *Spermophilus columbianus*

Common in the interior of the northwest, in mountain meadows, prairies, and farmland, sometimes becoming so numerous as to be a pest in agricultural fields. Very social, with much interaction between individuals in a colony, but both females and males defend individual territories within the colony. Like the preceding species, uses different alarm calls when it spots aerial predators than for those on the ground. May store food in its burrow in summer to feed on when it emerges from hibernation the next spring. ▶ Large, dark gray above, quite *reddish below* and on the face, forelegs, and tail. Larger, darker, and more colorful than other ground squirrels in its range.

ARCTIC GROUND SQUIRREL   *Spermophilus parryii*

Abundant in the Arctic and subarctic, north of the range of other ground squirrels. Lives in meadows, forest clearings, gravel ridges, and areas of tundra where the permafrost is at least a meter below the surface, to allow room for digging extensive tunnels. Constructs many different types of burrows, including hibernating dens (used for at least seven months of the year) that are lined with dry grasses and sedges. The Arctic Ground Squirrel's common call, *tseek-tsik*, is reflected in its Inuit name of "sik-sik." ▶ Large and brown, with whitish mottling on back and *cinnamon wash on head.* Tends to be more reddish in spring and summer, grayish in fall and winter. Easily separated from other ground squirrels by range, but compare to various marmots (pp. 90–94), which are much larger.

**Richardson's
Ground Squirrel**

L 11"
W 6–26 oz

**Columbian
Ground Squirrel**

L 13–15"
W 12–20 oz

**Arctic
Ground Squirrel**

L 13–20"
W 19–29 oz

WASHINGTON GROUND SQUIRREL *Spermophilus washingtoni*

Formerly common in the native grassland and open sagebrush areas of the Columbia Basin of Washington and Oregon. Now localized and rare, listed as threatened, as much of its habitat has been converted to farmland. Active above ground from late January or February to June or July. Callnotes are relatively squeaky and faint. ▶ Small, with small ears. Brownish gray above with fairly distinct whitish spots on back. Other ground squirrels in its range *lack* spotted effect above; also, Columbian (p. 80) and Belding's Ground Squirrels (p. 84) are larger and redder.

IDAHO GROUND SQUIRREL *Spermophilus brunneus*

The rarest ground squirrel, with very limited range in western Idaho. Divided into two subspecies (which actually may be full species), each matching the color of soil where they live. *S. b. brunneus* occupies meadows surrounded by pine forest in Adams and Valley Counties; it is reddish gray with a buff eye-ring. *S. b. endemicus* lives in foothills areas of grassland and sagebrush in Payette, Washington, and Gem Counties; it is brownish gray with a whitish eye-ring.

TOWNSEND'S GROUND SQUIRREL *Spermophilus townsendii*

Limited to cold sagebrush desert of south-central Washington. Active above ground from late January through June. ▶ Townsend's, Piute, and Merriam's Ground Squirrels are identical, differing only in number of chromosomes, but apparently they do not interbreed. All are separated from other ground squirrels in their ranges by small size, small ears, plain grayish buff appearance without mottling or spots, and rather thin tail.

PIUTE GROUND SQUIRREL *Spermophilus mollis*

Fairly common and widespread in the Great Basin region, in arid country of sagebrush, saltbush, and greasewood, with an isolated population in Washington just north of the range of Townsend's. Not particularly social but can form dense colonies. Active above ground mainly from February through June; may double its body weight to store fat for survival during long dormant period. ▶ Visually identical to Townsend's and Merriam's Ground Squirrels, differing only in chromosome number.

MERRIAM'S GROUND SQUIRREL *Spermophilus canus*

Fairly common in natural habitats of big sagebrush, juniper, and greasewood, as well as some areas of pasture and farmland, in the northern Great Basin. Active above ground mainly from March through July. Feeds mainly on grasses and weeds. ▶ Visually identical to Townsend's and Piute Ground Squirrels, differing only in chromosome number.

GROUND SQUIRRELS

Washington Ground Squirrel

L 8½" W ¼ oz

Idaho Ground Squirrel

L 9⅕" W 7¼ oz

Townsend's Ground Squirrel
Piute Ground Squirrel
Merriam's Ground Squirrel
(virtually identical)

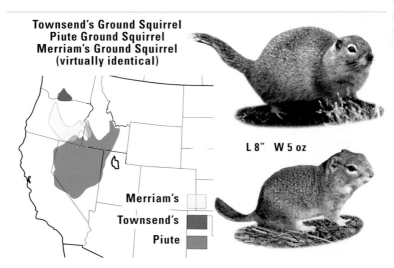

L 8" W 5 oz

Merriam's

Townsend's

Piute

ROUND-TAILED GROUND SQUIRREL   *Spermophilus tereticaudus*

A desert squirrel, tolerant of extreme heat, living mostly in flat, open areas of the Sonoran and Mojave Deserts. Feeds mainly on plant material, especially the seeds, leaves, and buds of creosotebush and mesquite, and is quite adept at climbing about in these plants. Active most of the year in some parts of its range, mainly spring and summer elsewhere. The number of young per litter varies; more young may be born in wet years. The common callnote is a high-pitched peep. ▶ Small, *thin-tailed,* and very *plain* all over. Color tone of upperparts may be grayish tan or warmer cinnamon. Most ground squirrels in its range are not so plain above. In the Mojave Desert, compare to the next species. Sometimes mistaken for prairie dogs (next page), which are much larger.

MOHAVE GROUND SQUIRREL   *Spermophilus mohavensis*

In the Mojave Desert (pronounced Moe-HAH-vee), this squirrel inhabits open areas with creosotebush, saltbush, or Joshua trees. It is active above ground only in spring and early summer, during the short time that green growing plants are available in its environment. Its limited and patchy range is being reduced further by the expansion of urban areas. ▶ The only plain-backed ground squirrel in most of its range. At its eastern limits it overlaps with Round-tailed Ground Squirrel, which has paler whitish or grayish cheeks and a longer tail that is buff or cinnamon below (Mohave Ground Squirrel's tail is white below).

BELDING'S GROUND SQUIRREL   *Spermophilus beldingi*

Often heard before it is seen by hikers, this squirrel is common in alpine meadows of the Sierra Nevada and Cascades Ranges; it also ranges to lower elevations eastward, along roadsides and farmland. It lives in colonies, sometimes quite large. Active above ground mainly from late spring to midsummer, with most individuals hibernating eight or nine months of the year. Males battle fiercely for females, often resulting in injury to themselves. Adult females sound a warning call of five to eight short whistles to alert their offspring to danger. ▶ Plain above, lacking spots or mottling, but with a broad orange-brown stripe down center of back. Separated from other plain-backed ground squirrels in its range by reddish tail tipped with black.

PLAIN GROUND SQUIRRELS

**Round-tailed
Ground
Squirrel**

**L 8–11″
W 4–6 oz**

female

male

young

**Mohave
Ground Squirrel**

**L 8¹/₄–9″
W 3–11 oz**

young

**Belding's
Ground Squirrel**

**L 10¹/₂–12¹/₂″
W 8–16 oz**

young

PRAIRIE DOGS

are large social ground squirrels that live in colonies called *towns*. They sit upright near their burrows and sound alarms by giving a shrill bark — hence the "dog" name. Four species occur in the United States, another in Mexico. Once abundant, these fascinating animals have been almost exterminated by farmers and ranchers concerned about competition for food with their livestock and injuries to livestock from burrows.

BLACK-TAILED PRAIRIE DOG *Cynomys ludovicianus*

pale orange indicates former range

each track to 1¼″ long

Historically abundant throughout the short-grass prairies. The continental population may have been as high as five billion. These animals lived in "towns" that stretched on for miles; one huge dogtown in Texas was estimated to have held 400 million residents. Within the colonies, the Black-tailed Prairie Dogs kept the vegetation cropped close to the ground, and from the tops of the bare mounds of earth surrounding their burrow entrances they would have a clear view in all directions. Prairie dog towns were centers of activity for other creatures as well. Burrowing Owls lived in abandoned burrows, and Mountain Plovers favored the open short-grass areas for nesting. Other animals came here as predators; the Black-footed Ferret (p. 118) was a specialized predator on prairie dogs, and coyotes, badgers, rattlesnakes, hawks, and eagles preyed on them as well. The biggest dogtowns were almost completely wiped out by poisoning and shooting under the guise of "pest control" and by destruction of their habitat. Today the species exists mostly in small and scattered colonies.

Intensely social, Black-tailed Prairie Dogs even excavate their burrow systems cooperatively. They have a variety of vocalizations, including a long *weeyyoo* in greeting relatives and neighbors, and a two-syllabled alarm bark given from the tops of bare mounds surrounding their burrows. There is some evidence that these prairie dogs use recognizably different alarm calls for different kinds of predators. Active only by day, they feed on grasses and weeds. Black-tailed Prairie Dogs do not hibernate, even in the northern parts of their range, but put on fat and store food in their burrows to get through the winter. They do not breed until they are at least two years old, producing one litter of three or four young in early spring.

▶ Prairie dogs are much larger than most other ground squirrels and have shorter, less bushy tails than Rock Squirrel (p. 76). This is the only prairie dog with a black tail tip. See other species on next page.

defense
barking

**Black-tailed
Prairie Dog**

L 13–17"
W 21–53 oz

young

mouth-to-mouth
greeting

eating

at entrance
to burrows

PRAIRIE DOGS

These three have more limited ranges than the Black-tailed Prairie Dog (previous page) and lack the black tail tip shown by that species.

WHITE-TAILED PRAIRIE DOG *Cynomys leucurus*

Less social than their Black-tailed relatives, these prairie dogs live at higher elevations on sagebrush plains and in mountain meadows. Unlike the Black-tailed Prairie Dog (but like most other ground squirrels), they hibernate during the winter. Although some may begin hibernating as early as August, some may be active around a colony any time from late February to early November. When threatened, they give alarm barks similar to those of the Black-tailed, but their greeting call has a distinctive laughing sound. ▶ Prairie dogs are mostly separated by range (see maps). Where this species overlaps others, note the dark smudges above and below its eyes, and its white tail tip.

GUNNISON'S PRAIRIE DOG *Cynomys gunnisoni*

Forms smaller, more loosely organized colonies than those of the Black-tailed Prairie Dog and does not cut the vegetation down near its mounds as that species does. Lives in mountain valleys and high plateaus and hibernates during the colder months. Raises one litter per year, usually of three to five young, born in spring. Vocal, like other prairie dogs; alarm call is one or two barks, with the second bark deeper. Greeting call between family members is a harsh chatter. Its numbers have been decimated by plague, hunting, and so-called "pest" management. ▶ Resembles White-tailed Prairie Dog but averages smaller and has tail tip gray, bordered with white.

UTAH PRAIRIE DOG *Cynomys parvidens*

Limited to southwestern Utah, where it was once locally abundant until "pest control" programs wiped out most colonies. Now absent from 90 percent of former range and listed as endangered. Feeds on herbs and grasses in short-grass prairies. Hibernates in deep burrows during the winter. ▶ Closely related to White-tailed Prairie Dog (and has white tail tip like that species), but averages smaller and redder. Generally best identified by range.

**White-tailed
Prairie Dog**

L 13–15"
W 25–59 oz

**Gunnison's
Prairie Dog**

L 12–15"
W 16–46 oz

**Utah
Prairie Dog**

L 11–15"
W 14–44 oz

are our largest squirrels, some weighing up to 15 pounds, with massive heads, short bushy tails, and strong claws on the front feet for digging.

WOODCHUCK *Marmota monax*

each track
2½" – 3" long

Affectionately referred to as our "groundhog" and consulted (according to folklore) for its opinion on when spring will arrive, this is the only marmot in the eastern U.S. and across most of Canada. Over much of its range it is a common sight in pastures, roadsides, and overgrown fields. Not very social, Woodchucks live singly in burrows up to 30 feet long, excavated under stumps, rocks, or edges of buildings. The main entrances to their burrows are obvious: eight to twelve inches across, with big mounds of dirt nearby. Digging Woodchucks turn over great gobs of earth, fertilizing and aerating millions of tons of soil every year. They use their burrows for shelter, for raising young, and for deep hibernation. Woodchucks put on heavy layers of fat in order to survive cold winters and enter hibernation in late autumn. During hibernation, their body temperature drops to just above freezing, heartbeat slows to about four times per minute, and breathing slows to once every few minutes. According to tradition, these "groundhogs" emerge from hibernation around February 2 (Groundhog Day), although of course emergence is later in the far north. Feeds on grasses, weeds, and garden crops, even raiding picnic areas for food. Also will eat buds and twigs in early spring before green vegetation appears. Forages during daylight hours, but is most active in early morning and late afternoon. For mating, males join females briefly in their burrows just after emerging from hibernation in early spring. Four weeks after mating, in April or May, females give birth to four or five blind, naked young in grass-lined nests in their dens. Young are crawling by one month and have dispersed to live on their own by two months of age. Calls include hisses, grinding teeth, and squeals, but the "whistle-pig" is known mostly for its shrill whistles as it runs for cover to its den.

▶ Stout and short-legged, with short bushy tail, overall brown color with darker feet. No other animal in eastern part of range is really similar. Hoary Marmot (p. 92), which overlaps in far northwest, is larger, with silvery gray body and head marked with black and buff. Yellow-bellied Marmot (p. 92), which barely overlaps in range, usually has contrasting yellow on belly and neck, whitish band across top of nose.

**Woodchuck
(Groundhog)**

**L 16–26"
W 6–9 lbs**

juveniles

YELLOW-BELLIED MARMOT *Marmota flaviventris*

These "rockchucks" live mostly on mountains wherever there are rocks and boulders to den in and enough green herbs to eat, preferring these to grasses. Forms small colonies (consisting of one adult male, one or more adult females, and their young), which both the male and females defend from other marmots. Puts on heavy layers of fat before entering hibernation sometime between August and October, emerging from its den in early spring, with the exact timing of hibernation depending on local climate. Usually dens alone, but the young of the year may hibernate their first winter with their mother. Females raise one litter of three to eight young per year. ▶ Typical stout marmot build, brown overall, usually with white patches between the eyes and with *yellowish belly and neck*. The only marmot in most of its range. Woodchuck (previous page) has darker feet and lacks the yellow belly and whitish head patches. Compare to Hoary Marmot.

HOARY MARMOT *Marmota caligata*

Commonly called the "whistler" for its loud human-like alarm whistle, this large marmot lives in mountainous rocky areas above treeline throughout most of its range, although in northern Alaska it occurs down to sea level. Hibernates from September through May in dens under boulders, where it is safe from any predators except the most determined bear. More social than most marmots, with unrelated individuals sometimes foraging together in groups. Lives in family colonies consisting of one adult male, one or more adult females, and young of various ages up to two years old. Family members groom and offer each other nose-to-cheek greetings. Individuals often engage in "wrestling" matches, on hind feet pushing at each other with the forefeet. Feeds on sedges, grasses, and other meadow plants, putting on more than 20 percent of its total weight in body fat before hibernation. ▶ Large and bushy-tailed, with front half of body mostly gray to whitish; has white patch on forehead, blackish markings around ears, eyes, and muzzle. Feet have dark brown or black "boots." Larger, longer-haired, and lighter in color than Yellow-bellied Marmot, and lives at higher elevations where their ranges overlap. Woodchuck (previous page) is darker and lacks whitish forehead patch. Also see rare marmots on next page.

**each track
2½″ – 3″ long**

marmot family
in rocky den

juveniles

**Yellow-bellied
Marmot**

**L 23"
W 4–12 lbs**

**Hoary
Marmot**

**L 24–33"
W 11–13 lbs**

ALASKA MARMOT   *Marmota broweri*

Our northernmost marmot, found only in the Brooks Range of northern Alaska. Dens are located among large boulders on frozen tundra, always close to enough vegetation to support the colony. Hibernates approximately from September to June; colony residents may hibernate all together, thus sharing body heat throughout the long cold winters. ▶ Large and dark, with body grayer toward the front and more reddish toward the rear, and with a solid blackish cap from nose to neck. Guard hairs have black tips, not pale tips like those of most marmots. Hoary Marmot (previous page), once considered to belong to same species, lacks the solid black-capped appearance.

OLYMPIC MARMOT   *Marmota olympus*

Confined to the Olympic Peninsula of western Washington, this large marmot is mostly found at elevations of 5,000 to 6,000 feet in the mountains, in areas with moist meadows and rocky talus slopes. Very social, living in extended family groups that may include an adult male, more than one adult female, one-year-old and two-year-old young, and a litter of new pups. Young do not leave home until their second year, and females produce a litter every other year. Family members engage in grooming and nose-to-cheek greetings. Hibernates from about September to May. ▶ Most easily identified by range, as it is the only marmot on the Olympic Peninsula. Resembles Hoary Marmot but is more brown and yellowish in color, not so gray.

VANCOUVER ISLAND MARMOT   *Marmota vancouverensis*

Now limited to a small area in the mountains of southeastern Vancouver Island, British Columbia, mostly at elevations between 3,000 and 5,000 feet, in areas with open meadows and large rocks. Vancouver Island lies in a wet climate where winter snowfalls in the mountains are often heavy, and this marmot favors south-facing slopes where the snow melts earlier in spring. Hibernates from September or October through April. Listed as endangered, with total population recently down to only about 100 individuals. ▶ Distinctively patterned, dark brown or black with white patches on forehead, nose, chin, and underparts. When seen in early to midsummer, may look mottled and motley, with patches of new fur growing in. Most easily recognized by range, as it is the only marmot on Vancouver Island.

MARMOTS WITH LIMITED RANGES

**Alaska
Marmot**

L 23"
W 7½ lbs

**Olympic
Marmot**

L 29" W 13 lbs

molting

**Vancouver Island
Marmot**

L 26" W 10 lbs

This is a catch-all section in which we have included a number of unrelated animals, representing different families and even different orders. Many of these animals are either familiar or famous, including raccoons, opossums, skunks, porcupines, armadillos, and badgers. Most can be described as "medium-sized," meaning larger than rats but smaller than deer, but beyond that they have little in common, aside from the fact that they would not fit neatly into any of the other categories in this book.

Here are the groups represented in this section:

Raccoons and relatives (family **Procyonidae**): pp. 98–100. These are active omnivores, foraging on the ground or in trees, mostly in wooded or brushy country and often near water. We have three species: one widespread raccoon, one ringtail, and one coati found mainly in the southwest. All three have long ringed tails, and all have a varied diet, with the blunt cheek teeth to match.

Opossums (family **Didelphidae**): p. 102. These are marsupials, members of an ancient group of mammals in which the young are born tiny and embryonic, finishing their development in a pouch on the mother's body. Australia is famous for its marsupials, from kangaroos to koalas, but there are also dozens of species of opossums in the American tropics and one that extends into North America.

Skunks (family **Mephitidae**): pp. 104–106. Famed for their odiferous defenses, skunks have scent glands below the tail that can shoot an intensely foul-smelling spray for several feet, deterring most predators. Bold patterns of black and white serve as warnings. Skunks are omnivores, almost always on the ground. Five species live in North America, a few more in the tropics.

New World Porcupines (family **Erethizontidae**): p. 108. These are large slow-moving rodents, protected from most predators by their covering of sharp spines or quills. They feed on bark and other plant material, high in trees and on the ground. At least ten species live in the American tropics, one in North America. Porcupines in the Old World belong to a different family.

Armadillos (family **Dasypodidae**): p. 108. These armor-plated mammals belong to the same order as the sloths and anteaters of the American tropics. The skin of armadillos develops hard, bony plates, with small areas of flexible skin in between. These animals are excellent diggers, rooting out insects and other food from the soil and digging burrows for themselves.

Beavers (family **Castoridae**): p. 110. Big aquatic rodents with wide, flat tails, famed for their ability to cut down trees and use them to build elaborate dams and lodges. They feed entirely on bark and other plant material. One species lives in North America, the other in Europe and Asia.

Nutria (family **Myocastoridae**): p. 110. A unique aquatic rodent from South America. Introduced into the southern United States and now very abundant in some areas there, especially in brackish marshes in the Gulf Coast region.

Muskrats (part of family **Muridae**): p. 112. These are true rats, closely related to voles, as well as other rats and mice. However, they have a totally aquatic lifestyle, living mainly in marshes and rivers. They feed mostly on plants growing in the water and build nests for themselves out of marsh plants.

Weasels and their relatives (family **Mustelidae**): pp. 114–122. This is the most diverse group included in this category. They stretch our definition of "medium-sized," as they range from the tiny Least Weasel, only about seven inches long, to the Sea Otter, which can be almost five feet long. Members of the weasel family are found worldwide; representatives in North America include otters, minks, badgers, ferrets, weasels, wolverines, fishers, and martens. All are predators, and some are capable of taking prey larger than themselves. All have glands near the tail that exude a musky oil that can be used to mark their territories.

NORTHERN RACCOON   *Procyon lotor*

**hind track
about 3" long**

This is our familiar "masked bandit" — sometimes a little too familiar, with its nighttime raids of garbage cans and garden plots. However, this adaptable behavior reflects one reason for its widespread abundance. Raccoons are omnivores: their diet on land includes nuts, fruits, insects, small rodents, and birds' eggs and nestlings, while near water they will take frogs, fish, mollusks, crayfish, insects, and practically anything else they can catch. They use their front feet like hands to manipulate food items and are famed for appearing to "wash" their food before eating it (they may be just examining the items more closely by touch while holding them underwater). Raccoons live in a variety of habitats, from forests to prairies to city parks, but they always favor the vicinity of water and trees and are most abundant in wooded swamps.

The mating season for raccoons is any time in winter and spring, with a peak of activity in late winter. About 63 days after mating, typically in April or May, the female gives birth to a litter of young (usually three or four, but sometimes as many as eight). The young are born fully furred in a woolly coat, but with their eyes closed. They are raised in a den in a hollow tree or log, rock crevice, cave, or abandoned building. The mother sometimes carries the babies about in her mouth, in the manner of a domestic cat. Males do not take part in caring for the young. The grown young may leave home in fall or may den up with the mother for the winter. Raccoons sleep a lot during bad weather in winter, living on their stored fat; this is not a true hibernation, as they do not lower their heart rate, breathing rate, or metabolism.

Raccoon tracks are commonly seen in soft mud near ponds and streams. They walk on the bare soles of their feet, like bears or humans, and the five long toes on both the front and back feet are usually visible in the tracks. Their voices are varied, including whines, hisses, growls, and purrs. ▶ Size varies with climate: very small in the Florida Keys, much larger and stouter in cold northern zones. When walking, appears hunchbacked in profile. Usually grizzled gray-brown, but sometimes much darker or paler overall. Tail is long (but shorter than body length, bushy, banded with black and white, and tipped with black; black face mask is surrounded with white fur. Compare to White-nosed Coati and Ringtail (next page).

RACCOON

tree
den

color variations

mother
carrying baby

eating frog

**Northern
Raccoon**

**L 23–37″
W 9–34 lbs**

WHITE-NOSED COATI *Nasua narica*

**front track
about 2¾" long**

This tropical relative of raccoons is widespread in Mexico and Central America, entering the southwestern U.S. in mountain forests and brushy canyons near streams. Often seen in groups, as adult females and their young travel together in tight-knit bands of up to 40 individuals. Adult males are solitary except for a few weeks during the breeding season. Coatis (pronounced co-WAH-teez) forage mostly by day, rooting around in leaf litter and climbing trees, seeking fruit as well as large insects, spiders, lizards, and other small animals. In spring, females leave the band to give birth to a litter of up to six young, caring for them in sheltered dens for about five weeks; they rejoin the band when the young are able to keep up. More vocal than raccoons (probably because they are more social), coatis growl, screech, snuffle, whimper, chatter, and chirp. ▶ Note the long flexible snout, white muzzle and white spots around the eyes, and long thin tail that is held erect in the shape of a question mark. Slimmer than Northern Raccoon (previous page), and with a longer, plainer tail and less distinct mask. Ringtail (below) is smaller, with larger ears and bushier tail. Isolated populations in Florida and southern California may actually be the South American coati *(N. nasua),* with a dark brown or black muzzle and more distinct bands on the tail.

RINGTAIL *Bassariscus astutus*

**front track
a little over
1"long**

Sometimes called "Ring-tailed Cat" for its catlike appearance and climbing ability, this is our smallest raccoon relative. Widespread and often common in wooded and rocky areas of the southwest, but not often seen because it is active only at night. However, some Ringtails will inhabit buildings and attics and can become accustomed to humans. By day and when caring for their young, ringtails use dens in rock crevices, tree hollows, or burrows dug by other animals. Both males and females are usually solitary and territorial. Their diet includes insects, spiders, small animals, birds, eggs, acorns, and fruits. Females have one litter per year of up to four young, born in spring. Calls: barks, screeches, and snarls. ▶ Note the large ears and long, very bushy tail with distinct black and pale bands. The claws are retractable, and the pawprints resemble those of a housecat. Compare to Northern Raccoon (previous page) and White-nosed Coati (above).

White-nosed Coati

L 41″   W 10 lbs

Ringtail

L 31″   W 2½ lbs

101

is our only species of marsupial, a group of mammals in which the young are born very early in the embryo's development, finishing their growth in the mother's external fur-lined pouch with nipples. Australia is famous for hosting the greatest variety of marsupials, but many also live in Central and South America.

VIRGINIA OPOSSUM   *Didelphis virginiana*

hind track can be more than 2″ wide

Our sole marsupial (pouched mammal) is widespread in the east and has been introduced into various parts of the west. Commonly lives in deciduous woodlands near water, but also along wooded streams in prairie regions and in suburbs and city parks. Best known for its defensive behavior of curling into a limp ball and feigning death, "playing possum." When attacked, will also hiss and snarl, salivating with mouth open showing numerous teeth. Opossums feed on insects, small animals, various fruits, and even snakes. They also eat carrion, including road kills, and as a result they are often killed on roads themselves. Although they fatten in the autumn, 'possums do not hibernate and are sensitive to cold weather: their hairless ears and tail are susceptible to frostbite. During inclement weather and for daytime sleeping, they use leaf-lined dens in any sheltered area: Woodchuck burrows, hollow trees or logs, and abandoned buildings. Mating takes place any time between January and August, and a female may have two to three litters per year. Each litter contains eight to a dozen or more young, born after less than two weeks' gestation. The babies are born in an embryonic state: naked, undeveloped, and the size of a bumblebee. They make their own way through their mother's fur into her pouch and attach to a nipple, which swells in their mouth, attaching them securely for the next two months. If the litter size exceeds the number of nipples (13), unattached young die. During their third month, the young ride around on the mother's back, returning to the pouch only to nurse. Voice: hisses, screams, and clicks.

▶ Size of a small dog, but with a ratlike appearance. Can be blackish, cinnamon-colored, or albino, but usually appears grayish with dark feet, white head and throat, and hairless ears. Unlike any other North American mammal, opossums have naked tails that can curl and grasp a tree limb, allowing the animal to hang upside down. Their hind feet have an opposable and clawless thumb that is used for grasping. Not easily confused with any other mammal in its range.

OPOSSUM

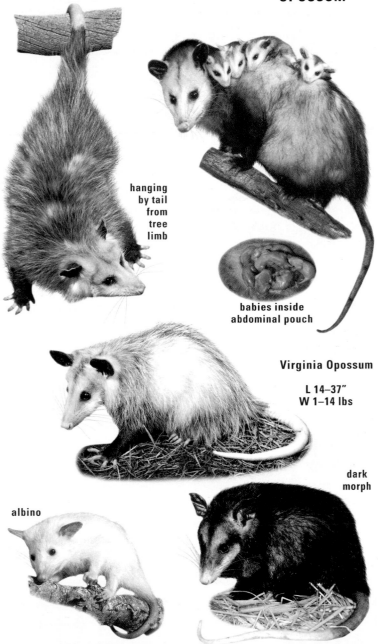

hanging
by tail
from
tree
limb

babies inside
abdominal pouch

Virginia Opossum

L 14–37"
W 1–14 lbs

dark
morph

albino

103

are familiar to many by their odor. They have glands near the tail that can spray a noxious sticky substance up to 15 feet. They are not cryptically colored, but sport bold black and white warning patterns. A frightened skunk may precede spraying by stamping its front feet, erecting its tail in a handstand, and snapping its teeth together. Skunks behaving oddly may have rabies and should be avoided.

STRIPED SKUNK · *Mephitis mephitis*

**front track
about 1½" long**

Our most common skunk, widespread in many habitats, but most abundant along forest and field edges. A carrion feeder often seen dead on highways, it also feeds on insects, mice, frogs, crayfish, eggs, and fruit. A skunk competing against other species for food may simply raise its tail and back into the other animal, then turn around and collect the desired tidbit after its adversary beats a hasty retreat. Sleeps during the day in any sheltered spot, but will den underground in burrows when raising young or during winter. Striped Skunks do not hibernate, but may go dormant during bad weather. Usually not social, may den in winter with other skunks to conserve body heat. Not bothered by most predators, but owls and other raptors apparently are not repelled by the stink. ▶ Variable in pattern, but easily recognized over most of its range. Hog-nosed Skunk (next page) has bare snout and lacks white stripe down center of forehead and nose. In the southwest, compare to Hooded Skunk.

HOODED SKUNK · *Mephitis macroura*

A skunk of the desert southwest, found in rocky canyons, desert scrub, and along wooded streams. Feeds on insects, small animals, and cactus fruits. Active mostly at night. Commonly dens in hollow logs, rock crevices, underground burrows, or under buildings. ▶ Pattern varies: black with two narrow white stripes on sides or one wide white stripe and white tail with sprinkling of black hairs, or a combination. Thin white stripe down center of forehead. The white-backed form can be difficult to separate from Striped Skunk (which is mostly white-backed in the southwest). However, Hooded Skunk is much smaller but with longer tail (longer than head and body combined — Striped Skunk has tail equal to or shorter than head and body) and has a hood of longer hair on back of head and neck. Its white back lacks a black patch on the rump but is peppered with black, giving it a grayish wash.

Striped Skunk

L 23–31"
W 3–11 lbs

young

typical pattern

threatening to spray

various patterns

Arizona form

other common patterns

Hooded Skunk

L 22–31"
W 1½–3½ lbs

most common pattern

WESTERN SPOTTED SKUNK *Spilogale gracilis*

Widespread in the west, in habitats ranging from farmland to brushy country to open forests, but uncommon and may be declining in numbers. Active mostly at night, and not often seen. Feeds on carrion, mice, small reptiles, birds, and insects, as well as occasional fruits and berries. ▶ Glossy black with a *striking pattern of white spots and stripes,* including a triangular white patch on the forehead and much white in the tail. When the animal is running at a rapid scamper, its pattern looks amazingly flashy. Eastern Spotted Skunk is almost identical, but other skunks are much larger with less complicated patterns.

EASTERN SPOTTED SKUNK *Spilogale putorius*

An eastern replacement for the Western Spotted Skunk. Similar in habits, including its carnivorous nature, feeding on mice, birds, eggs, and insects, with some plant material in summer and fall. Dens in a variety of places, including hollow trees, Woodchuck burrows, and under buildings. ▶ Almost identical to Western Spotted Skunk, but white markings may average smaller (especially white forehead patch) and tail is *mostly black,* not white below. Usually identified by range, although the two occur together on the western Great Plains, apparently without interbreeding.

COMMON HOG-NOSED SKUNK *Conepatus leuconotus*

The digger of the skunk family, with powerful forelegs, long curved claws, and a naked piglike snout, is well adapted to rooting in the soil and under rocks for the insect grubs that form a major part of its diet. Also feeds on mice, other small animals, and fruits. Lives in canyons and other rocky areas in deserts, mesquite grasslands, and oak-pine woodlands. Still fairly common in parts of the southwest, but has disappeared altogether from some regions, including most of eastern Texas, northern New Mexico, and southern Colorado. ▶ Sharply bicolored, black below and white above. Separated from Striped and Hooded Skunks (preceding page) by *hairless snout,* very long front claws, and *lack* of white stripe on forehead. The Eastern Hog-nosed Skunk (southern Texas and eastern Mexico) was formerly considered a separate species from Western Hog-nosed Skunk (remainder of range); it differs in having the white back stripe a bit narrower and some black on the underside of the tail.

**Western
Spotted
Skunk**

L 13–23″
W 7–32 oz

**Eastern
Spotted
Skunk**

L 11–24″
W 7–31 oz

handstand
in preparation for spraying

**Common Hog-nosed
Skunk**

L 16–33″
W 3–6 lbs

nose muddy from
rooting in soil

NORTH AMERICAN PORCUPINE   *Erethizon dorsatum*

The slow-moving "porky-pine" is our second-largest rodent. Its sharp quills (actually modified hairs) are solid at the base and and at the barbed tip, with a hollow shaft. They are fastened loosely to muscles just under the skin on the rump and tail; this allows a quill embedded in an attacker to come loose easily from the porcupine. Few predators (aside from the agile Fisher) attempt to bypass its formidable defenses, but when a porcupine is threatened it will try to retreat up a tree rather than attack. If further threatened, it chatters its teeth and emits a strong musk, finally erecting its quills and lashing about with its tail. Feeds mainly on the inner bark and twigs of trees in winter. Has a more varied diet in summer, feeding on sedges, grasses, acorns, and other plant material. Fond of salt, and will chew on wooden handles of tools soaked with human sweat. Sign: trees with bark stripped in irregular patches, and nipped twigs littering the ground. ▶ Large and stout with short legs, a humped back, long guard hairs on the front half of the body, and quills on the rump and tail. Black or dark brown with grizzling of gray in the west, yellowish in the east. Not easily confused with any other mammal.

**hind track
about 3″ long**

NINE-BANDED ARMADILLO   *Dasypus novemcinctus*

The only North American mammal protected by bony skin plates. Escapes predators by running away or by curling into a ball to protect its soft belly. A tropical animal, first reported in south Texas in the mid 1800s, it has spread well northward from there. Does not hibernate and cannot survive long periods of freezing weather. Requires soft sandy soils for constructing burrows and for digging for its food (mostly insects). Crosses streams either by walking across the bottom or by swallowing air so it can float and swim across. ▶ The size of a small dog and usually the color of the soil it has been digging in most recently. Scaly-looking, broad, bony plates cover the head, shoulders, rump, and long pointed tail. The midsection of the body is crossed by a series of narrow bands of armor (usually nine, sometimes eight to eleven). These moveable bands give the armadillo some flexibility, allowing it to move normally and to curl into a ball.

ARMORED MAMMALS

gnawing on wood

North American Porcupine

L 24–50"
W 8–40 lbs

mother and baby

Nine-banded Armadillo

L 24–32"
W 8–17 lbs

covered in Texas mud

juvenile

AMERICAN BEAVER   *Castor canadensis*

**hind track
about 6″ long**

North America's largest rodent is famous for its engineering feats, building dams of sticks and mud across streams to create ponds. Once almost exterminated by trappers seeking the valuable dense fur, the beaver has been restored to much of its former range. Active mainly at night, often seen or heard at dusk swimming with just its head showing above water or slapping its tail on the surface of the water in alarm. An oil, castoreum, spread through the fur from a gland near the base of the tail, improves the fur's ability to shed water. A clear membrane over the eyes, and valves sealing the ears and nostrils, allow adult beavers to stay underwater for up to 15 minutes. Beavers along rivers live in burrows in banks, but those in quieter waters build elaborate lodges with underwater entrances, dry living quarters, floors lined with wood chips, and vents for fresh air. Eats the inner bark of willow, aspen, and other trees, using the stripped logs for construction. Sometimes carries mud or its young (kits) in its forepaws, walking upright on hind legs, using its tail for balance. Kits are born fully furred, eyes open, and are able to swim within the lodge an hour after birth. Sign: gnawed trees, dams of sticks and mud, and domed lodges. ▶ Large, bulky, and dark brown. Hind feet are webbed between all five toes, and two claws are split for use in grooming. The hairless, scaly tail is broad and flat. Muskrats and Nutria are smaller and have slender tails.

NUTRIA   *Myocastor coypus* (Coypu)

Native to South America, the Nutria was introduced into the U.S. in the 1940s. It has become so abundant as to be a nuisance in some areas, damaging habitat for waterfowl and displacing the native muskrats. Comfortable in salt as well as fresh water, eating aquatic vegetation such as sedges and cattails, but also shellfish and agricultural crops. Nutria build nests in burrows in banks or in muskrat or beaver lodges. ▶ Large (but not as bulky as a beaver), with long coarse guard hair colored red-brown. Hind feet are longer than the front feet and webbed between four of the five toes. Ears and eyes are small, muzzle is squared off and tipped with white. Ratlike tail is rounded, sparsely haired, and scaly. Compare to muskrats (next page).

BIG AQUATIC RODENTS

American Beaver

L 43"   W 50 lbs

dams on stream

lodge

gnawing down tree

family swimming

adult with young

Nutria

L 38"   W 17 lbs

eating plant

might seem like smaller cousins of the beaver, but they are actually classified in the same family as typical rats, mice, and lemmings, and they are thought to be closely related to the voles (pp. 218–226).

COMMON MUSKRAT   *Ondatra zibethicus*

hind track about 2″ long

A familiar animal of freshwater and brackish marshes, abundant in such habitats over most of Canada and the U.S., except for parts of the southeast where it is replaced by the next species (or where it has been edged out by the introduced Nutria). Feeds on cattails, bulrushes, sedges, and other aquatic plants, as well as opportunistically taking frogs, fish, and various invertebrates such as clams and crustaceans. Usually most active from dusk to dawn but sometimes abroad by day. The most frequent sign that muskrats are present is their musky smell (the source of the name). Especially during the breeding season, male muskrats will actively mark their territorial boundaries with scent from musk glands near the tail. These animals may also be detected by their domed houses built of cattails — resembling a beaver lodge, but smaller. Within these houses, or in burrows in streambanks, muskrats may raise up to six litters per year. The young are born naked and with their eyes shut, but are independent from their mothers within a month. ▶ Larger in northern latitudes than in the south, but always smaller than the Beaver and Nutria (preceding page). Brown above, lighter on the sides, and whitish underneath (especially on the throat and face). Hind feet are larger than the forefeet and partially webbed. Tail is tapered, hairless, scaley and flattened vertically (higher than wide). American Beaver is much larger and has a broad tail that is flattened horizontally. Nutria is larger and its tail is rounded.

ROUND-TAILED MUSKRAT   *Neofiber alleni*

This smaller species replaces the Common Muskrat in shallow freshwater marshes of Florida and southern Georgia. It feeds on aquatic plants and builds globular houses of grasses and other marsh plants at the level of the water's surface. ▶ Gray brown or dark brown with glossy dark brown guard hairs. Hind feet longer than forefeet and only slightly webbed. Much smaller than Common Muskrat, with tail rounded, not flattened laterally; ranges do not overlap. Compare to other rodents such as rice rats and cotton rats.

lodge
(in winter)

Common Muskrat

L 20″ W 44 oz

swimming

**Round-tailed
Muskrat**

L 14″ W 12 oz

In behavior, this fascinating animal could be classified as a marine mammal, but it belongs to the same family as the weasels and badgers.

SEA OTTER   *Enhydra lutris*

Almost driven to extinction by fur trappers in the 18th and 19th centuries, the Sea Otter has gradually recovered in numbers in many areas. It is now common in much of south coastal Alaska and in isolated populations along our Pacific Coast as far south as central California. This smallest seagoing mammal spends most of its life floating on its back in shallow waters within a mile of the coastline, seldom coming to land. Its dense fur, effective at trapping small air bubbles for insulation, protects the otter against the cold water.

A playful and athletic swimmer, the otter can dive to depths of 300 feet or swim underwater for up to four minutes. Wresting shellfish from the ocean floor with its powerful forearms, it feeds on sea urchins, clams, mussels, crabs, abalone, and other aquatic creatures. It opens shellfish by bashing the hard shells against a rock held on the otter's chest, a rare example of tool-using in a nonprimate mammal.

A Sea Otter sleeps floating on its back, wrapped in kelp that is anchored to the ocean floor. In this secure position, it won't be swept away by currents, and it is hidden from killer whales, white sharks, and other predators. When alarmed, it turns over on its stomach and swims rapidly away, using webbed feet and short powerful tail as both rudder and propellers.

Adults tend to forage alone but often rest in groups, called "rafts." Breeding males are territorial, defending large areas from other males, while females move freely among male territories. The single pup is born at sea in California, but in Alaska the female bears her young on land. Pups are born fully furred and able to swim. Nursed from six months to a year, the weanling may then stay with its mother for another year, even when she has another pup. Pups play, nurse, and sleep on their mother's chest as she floats on her back.

▶ Adult males up to almost five feet in length, females smaller. Blackish when wet, dark brown when dry. Head and neck gray or buffy, or white in old males. Tail is short, thick, and tapered to a point. Feet are webbed. Told from seals and sea lions by its armlike forelegs. Compare to River Otter (next page).

SEA OTTER

raft of otters

old male

breaking clam
on stone

eating crab

Sea Otter

L 50"   W 62 lbs

females with
young on chest

115

NORTHERN RIVER OTTER   *Lontra canadensis*

**front track
about 3″ long**

This playful mammal was once common along rivers, lakes, and coastal wetlands over much of North America, but it has disappeared from many areas because of habitat loss and water pollution. Where it still occurs, snowslides or mudslides on riverbanks are a telltale sign of its presence. During the day, families of otters frolic in the water and toboggan on their slides in play. An astonishing swimmer, can dive to more than 50 feet and swim underwater for several minutes. Feeds on slow-moving fish, shellfish, turtles, and frogs as well as mice, birds, and eggs. In early spring, up to six young are born (fully furred, but with eyes closed) in a nest of sticks in a burrow in the riverbank, in natural cavities, or in homes made by other mammals. Young are weaned at four months and disperse in fall. Voice: whistles, chatters, grunts, and growls. ▶ One of our largest weasels, with broad flattened head and webbed feet. Blackish when wet, dark brown with silvery gray on throat and sides of face when dry. Sea Otters are larger, with gray or buffy head and flipperlike hindlegs. Other weasels are smaller.

AMERICAN MINK   *Mustela vison*

**front track
about 1⅔″ long**

Often fairly common around marshes, rivers, and lakes, this large weasel builds its own dens in banks or appropriates the use of a muskrat lodge — often after killing and eating the previous owners. Muskrats may be a favorite item on the menu, but minks are opportunistic carnivores, feeding on any meat they can catch and hunting mostly at night. Males have large home territories overlapping those of several females. Females line their dens with soft materials and raise one litter of three to six young per year. Formerly the mink was one of the most important wild fur-bearers, as mink coats were considered ultimate status symbols. Most pelts now come from commercial mink ranches. ▶ Lithe and slender, dark chocolate brown with a slightly paler face and with white spots on chin or throat. Larger and more uniformly colored than Ermine and Least and Long-tailed Weasels (p. 120). Compare to Fisher and American Marten (p. 122).

otter playing
on snow slide

**Northern
River Otter**

**L 35–44"
W 10–26 lbs**

juveniles in
hollow trunk

**American
Mink**

juvenile

**L 19–27"
W 19–44 oz**

with wet fur

AMERICAN BADGER   *Taxidea taxus*

front track
about 1¾″ long

Widespread in open country, from mountain meadows to grasslands and deserts, this big digger is usually uncommon (and is becoming more so) and is often underground, so any sighting should be considered a treat. Its diggings are often easy to find, however: large round or oval burrow openings, with dirt kicked out toward the sides. Badgers have powerful forelegs with long claws, and they are adept at digging up various mice, pocket gophers, ground squirrels, snakes, insects, and other creatures on which they feed. Badgers do not hibernate, but may reduce their body temperature and heart rate while sleeping through periods of cold weather in their winter dens. One to five young are born in spring and stay in their mother's den until six weeks of age. They leave home when about two-thirds grown in late summer. ▶ Short-legged, short-tailed, stocky, and with bold gray and white pattern on face and head, the badger is unlikely to be mistaken for any other animal. Southwestern populations have white head stripe continuing down the center of the back.

BLACK-FOOTED FERRET   *Mustela nigripes*

orange area is
former range;
green spots show
sites of
reintroduction
attempts

One of the most endangered mammals in North America. It once ranged from Mexico to Canada across the Great Plains and western grasslands, wherever there were big prairie dog towns. This ferret feeds on prairie dogs and lives in their abandoned burrows; although it will feed on other small prey, it never thrives away from the dogtowns. With the near-total extermination of prairie dogs by misguided humans, the ferret was also wiped out in the wild. Captive breeding programs saved it from total extinction; since 1991, it has been reintroduced into dogtowns in Montana, South Dakota, Wyoming, and Arizona. Seldom seen even in these few areas where it lives, it comes aboveground mainly at night. Diggings at prairie dog burrows that are not tamped down may signal the presence of ferrets. Females have their first litter at one year of age, averaging three or four young. Young are born in late spring, come aboveground when around six weeks old, and are independent and disperse by fall. ▶ Long, slender body. Very active, darting about quickly and constantly. Light buffy color, black feet, and black mask around the eyes distinguish it from the weasels on the next page.

badger family at den

American Badger

L 24–31″
W up to 26 lbs

juveniles

Black-footed Ferret

L 19–24″
W 23–37 oz

119

LONG-TAILED WEASEL   *Mustela frenata*

**hind track
almost 1½" long**

Widespread (from Canada to South America) but usually uncommon, this weasel lives in a wide variety of habitats but often favors areas near water. May be active day or night. Favorite prey includes rodents and small rabbits, but will take any prey up to and exceeding its own size. Weasels will go on killing sprees when the opportunity presents itself, caching extra meat for leaner times. Dens are often in rodent burrows, and nests are lined with hair. Females have one litter per year, averaging four or five young. Voice: squeals, trills, and purrs. ▶ Slender, with a black-tipped tail more than half as long as its head and body. In summer, and all year in the south, brown above with yellow neck, throat, and underparts. Feet are yellow-brown. Northern animals turn white (with black-tipped tail) in winter. Many in the southwest and Florida have white markings on face and head. Compare to next two species. American Mink (p. 116) is much larger and more uniformly dark.

ERMINE   *Mustela erminea*   (Short-tailed Weasel)

Common in the more northern parts of its range, in habitats ranging from forest to tundra, but seldom seen. Active by night and day, preying on mice, voles, and other small creatures. Dens in old rodent burrows or in hollow logs, building a nest of fur, feathers, and grass. ▶ Dark brown with white underparts and white feet in summer, all white in winter. The tail is just over one-third the length of the head and body and black-tipped year-round. Long-tailed Weasel is larger with a longer tail, and its underparts are usually not white. Least Weasel is smaller and lacks the black tail tip.

LEAST WEASEL   *Mustela nivalis*

This tiny carnivore lives in open areas such as meadows and marshes. Active day and night at all seasons, it is seldom seen even where common. With its small size and rapid metabolism, it must eat about half its body weight each day or starve. Feeds mostly on mice and voles, but also on birds, eggs, and insects. ▶ Very small, brown with white underparts in summer. In the north, turns all white in winter. The tail is much shorter (about one-fifth the length of the head and body) than those of Ermine and Long-tailed Weasel, and it lacks the black tip.

SMALL WEASELS

southwestern form

summer

winter

Long-tailed Weasel

male L 15"   W 11 oz
female L 12"   W 6 oz

summer

fall

winter

Ermine

male L 11"   W 3 oz
female L 9"   W 2 oz

summer

winter

young compared to matchstick

summer

with cicada

Least Weasel

L 7"   W 1½ oz

121

WOLVERINE *Gulo gulo*

**front track
4″ to 7½″ long**

A powerful and aggressive carnivore, found primarily in the far north, with isolated populations south of the Canadian border in mountains of the west. Always occurring in very low numbers, and usually nocturnal, the Wolverine is seldom seen. Males range over huge territories, up to hundreds of square miles, that encompass several smaller home ranges of females. A carrion eater, but also a hunter of ptarmigan, hares, porcupines, beavers, marmots and other ground squirrels, and has been known to take down animals as large as caribou. Ferociously defends its food from other predators, even bears and mountain lions. Also sprays the area around the food with a pungent musk. ▶ Stocky build, resembling a large dog or small bear with a bushy tail. Dark brown with a lighter yellowish stripe from neck down side of body and across base of tail. Head also has lighter-colored band above eyes, light patches on throat.

FISHER *Martes pennanti*

This furry weasel is misnamed: its main prey is not fish but rodents, hares, birds, and other small animals. It is one of the few predators able to take porcupines, flipping them upside down to get at their unprotected belly flesh. Solitary, active by day or night, the Fisher lives in wilderness forests and is not often seen. Dens in ground burrows or tree hollows during winter but does not hibernate. ▶ Built like a bulky weasel, with long dark brown fur and (especially in winter) darker legs and feet. Head and shoulders often washed with yellow or silver. Has different body shape and lacks the gold body stripe of the Wolverine.

AMERICAN MARTEN *Martes americana*

Agile and fast-moving, the marten is as adept in the trees of its forest habitat as on the ground. It lives mostly in mature, dense, coniferous forests and is more often seen than other large weasels. Preys on many small animals, including voles, squirrels, chipmunks, and birds, but also eats berries, seeds, insects, and carrion. Dens in squirrel nests, tree hollows, or even woodpecker cavities. Voice: huffs, screeches, growls, and whines. ▶ Fur color ranges from dark brown to blond, but the legs are always darker than the body, and the throat and chest are a shade of orange. Smaller than the Fisher. American Mink (p. 116) is darker, with smaller ears.

Wolverine

L 26–41"
W 18–31 lbs

Fisher

L 30–47"
W 4–12 lbs

American Marten

L 20–27"
W 10–14 oz

DOGS, CATS, AND BEARS

These are the best-known members of the order **Carnivora** but not the only ones, as this order also includes the weasels, skunks, raccoons (in the preceding section), and, surprisingly, the seals (beginning on p. 286). Despite the name, these animals are not all strictly carnivorous: some foxes and bears, for example, eat much plant material in addition to meat.

Among the characteristics that unite the Carnivora are details of the teeth. Behind the large canine teeth at the front of the mouth, most members of this order have a set of teeth called *carnassials:* an upper premolar and a lower molar that are pointed and that fit together in a way that makes them ideal for slicing through flesh. These carnassials are well developed in dogs and cats, less so in bears.

When animals are released in areas where they were not native, if they survive at all they usually spell trouble, and there are several examples among this group. Red Foxes on the loose in the San Francisco Bay area have had a serious impact on some small creatures that had never adapted to the presence of these predators. Arctic Foxes, released on remote northern islands (by people who hoped to start new colonies and harvest their valuable furs), have had a devastating effect on populations of some seabirds. Even domestic dogs that have gone feral have caused much damage, killing animals as large as deer and cattle. And housecats that are allowed to run loose kill many millions of songbirds every year.

On the other hand, there is much to be said for reintroducing an animal to a place where it occurred historically. Gray Wolves have been brought back to areas of the northern Rockies where they had been exterminated, Canadian Lynxes are being reintroduced to parts of Colorado, and Swift Foxes are being returned to the prairie provinces of southern Canada, helping to restore a little of the ecological balance of those regions.

Dogs (family **Canidae**), pp. 126–134. The domestic dog, descended from the Gray Wolf, is familiar the world over. Wild dogs are a diverse group with very different habits. Wolves live in packs, with a complex social hierarchy, each pack under the leadership of a dominant (alpha) male and female. Coyotes may live in small packs, in pairs, or as solitary individuals, adapting to local situations. Foxes are solitary in their hunting, but may have complex social interactions with others of their own kind when they are not hunting.

Although wolves tend to be strictly predators, foxes and Coyotes are omnivores, feeding on much plant matter and scavenging carrion as well as hunting for themselves.

Cats (family **Felidae**), pp. 136–140. These are graceful predators, more strictly carnivorous than dogs or bears, seldom eating much plant material. Much of their hunting involves careful stalking of prey followed by a quick attack at close range. Most species of cats are built for short bursts of speed, with large hindquarters, long legs, and broad chests. Their heads are blunt, with the eyes facing forward for good depth perception in their vision, and with large canine teeth. Their front feet have five toes (only four touching the ground), and the hind feet have four, all with retractable claws.

Increasing human populations have been hard on members of the cat family. Most wild cats around the world, particularly the larger ones and the forest species, are now threatened or endangered in some parts of their original ranges.

Bears (family **Ursidae**), pp. 142–146. This group includes some of the largest land animals in North America. As predators they do not have the stealth of cats or the speed of dogs, and two of our three bears are omnivores, living on plant matter for much of the year (the Polar Bear, living in the harsh climate of the Arctic, is more strictly carnivorous). However, the awesome strength of all bears makes them capable of taking down very large prey on occasion.

All bears are potentially dangerous to humans, but the widespread Black Bear is generally timid and rarely attacks. The Grizzly, or Brown Bear, is more aggressive, and when we venture into its realm we are forced to pay more attention to our surroundings and to what we are doing. In hiking through country where bears are numerous, it is a good idea to make some noise regularly so as to avoid taking a bear by surprise. Brown Bears should be viewed from upwind (so they will know of our presence) and from a substantial distance. Feeding wild bears is always a bad idea and greatly increases the risk of attack.

GRAY WOLF

GRAY WOLF *Canis lupus*

**front track
about
4½" long;
hind track
about
3¾" long**

Once found almost throughout North America, these magnificent animals were virtually wiped out in the lower 48 states, through deliberate programs of extermination, before finally gaining some legal protection in the 1970s. Even today, they are still maligned by some who believe the fairy-tale image of wolves as bloodthirsty killers. In fact, these are intelligent creatures with a complex social system. They play an essential role in natural habitats, maintaining healthy populations of deer and other hoofed mammals by weeding out the weak and infirm. In recent decades, wolves have been reintroduced into central Idaho, northwestern Montana, and Yellowstone National Park. An attempt to reintroduce the Mexican subspecies into Arizona has had limited success thus far.

Gray Wolves live in packs, usually of five to ten individuals, consisting of a breeding pair, their young of recent years, and sometimes unrelated wolves. All pack members cooperate in hunting and sharing kills. They travel great distances over home ranges that may encompass 1,000 square miles. When hunting, they can put on bursts of speed up to 45 miles per hour. In addition to preying on hoofed animals (as large as moose or bison), they take hares, beavers, and many smaller creatures. Wolves communicate — and maintain distance from other packs — by howling. At closer range, they also communicate with each other through body language, scent marking, barks, whines, and growls.

The breeding adult female of a pack will bear a litter, averaging five or six young, in an underground den. The young are cared for by the female for about three weeks, while other pack members bring food to her, before the young venture out of the den. Later, after the pups are weaned at about two months, they are moved to a "rendezvous" site where they are "baby-sat" by another pack member while the others hunt. Offspring usually leave the pack at one to three years of age.

▶ Often grizzled gray-brown, but varies to black, white, or reddish. Long bushy tail has a dark tip. Looks much like a German Shepherd but has a narrower chest, longer legs, and bigger feet. Has a broader snout and proportionately larger feet than the Coyote (next page). When running, wolves usually carry their tails straight out behind them, while Coyotes usually hold their tails curled down, and domestic dogs usually hold their tails up.

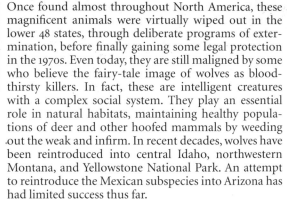

wolf
howling

wolf pack

Gray Wolf

L 35–75"
W 50–150 lbs

running

color variations

Mexican
subspecies

female
and pups

COYOTE   *Canis latrans*

**front track
about
2³/₄″ long**

This adaptable canine is more successful than any of its relatives in living near humans. Historically it was probably kept in check by larger carnivores, but since humans have wiped out most large predators, Coyotes have greatly expanded their range and increased in numbers. They are now common in most North American habitats, from deserts to forests to suburbs. Coyotes are great opportunists, either hunting or scavenging and feeding on many kinds of animals and plant material. Their social behavior varies as well: they may live singly, in pairs, or in packs. Packs consist of a mated pair, their puppies, and sometimes young of previous years that have not yet left home. Pack members assist in raising the puppies and defending the home range. Puppies are born in a den dug in the ground. Coyotes communicate with each other by howling, yipping, and barking. ▶ Grizzled gray and reddish brown. Smaller than a wolf, with narrower and more pointed snout, smaller feet, and shorter legs. Larger, with longer, sturdier legs and broader snout than all foxes. Coyotes are known to have interbred with wolves and with domestic dogs; hybrid "coydogs" are sometimes seen, especially near cities.

RED WOLF   *Canis rufus*

Historically found throughout the southeast, Red Wolves were largely exterminated by early settlers, and then the remaining populations were further compromised by interbreeding with the Coyote, which was spreading eastward. By 1967, when efforts began to save the Red Wolf from extinction, only one relatively "pure" population could be found, on the Texas-Louisiana border. Animals from this population were captured for a captive breeding program, and wolves raised in captivity have been released in eastern North Carolina and in Great Smoky Mountains National Park. Even in these areas, there is still the threat that Red Wolves may be swamped out genetically by interbreeding with Coyotes. ▶ Larger than the Coyote, with broader muzzle, broader nose pad, larger feet, longer legs, and broader chest and body. White area around lips may extend up onto face, whereas it is thin and well defined on a Coyote's face.

FERAL DOG   *Canis familiaris* (not illustrated)

Descended from the Gray Wolf, domesticated dogs differ in being able to breed year-round. This fecundity has contributed to an alarming rise in numbers of feral dogs, which run in packs, feeding on refuse and attacking wildlife and domestic livestock. ▶ Variable. Some breeds resemble Coyotes or wolves, but they usually run with tails up, not straight out or lowered.

WILD DOGS

coyote
howling

Coyote
L 30–49"
W 15–45 lbs

with pups

Red Wolf
L 51–67"
W 40–85 lbs

129

RED FOX   *Vulpes vulpes*

**front track
about
2½″ long**

Common and widespread in most regions where there is a mix of open fields and wooded or brushy country, this wily fox survives even in some cities. Its original range in North America is uncertain: Red Foxes from Europe were brought to the eastern U.S. around 1790, and the native population probably expanded its range also after settlers wiped out wolves and other large competitors. An adaptable hunter and scavenger, it has a varied diet that includes rodents, rabbits, birds, insects, fruits, earthworms, reptiles, and carrion, and it frequently stores extra food in caches. A litter, averaging five pups, is cared for by the female until autumn, when the pups disperse. The male brings food to the maternity den. ▶ Color of the coat is usually a variation on reddish brown but can be silver, black, or reddish brown with a black cross on the back (called "cross fox"), or intermediate variations (all of which can occur in the same litter). The lower legs and feet are black, and the tail has a white tip. Compare to other foxes.

GRAY FOX   *Urocyon cinereoargenteus*

The only North American wild dog that regularly climbs trees. Common in mixed hardwoods and old fields in the east, and in desert scrub, oak or juniper woodlands, and even pine-fir forests in the west. Generally avoids the farmlands favored by the Red Fox. Of all wild dogs, Gray Fox has the most varied diet, including rabbits, rodents, birds, fruits, insects, and grasses. One litter of up to seven pups is tended by both parents. Nocturnal, the Gray Fox dens each day in a hollow tree, rock crevice, or underground burrow. ▶ Grizzled gray with reddish accents; black stripe extends down top of tail to tip. Red Fox lacks black tail stripe, has black on lower legs and feet, and has white tail tip. Kit and Swift Foxes (next page) are smaller, with proportionately larger ears.

ISLAND GRAY FOX   *Urocyon littoralis*

Occurs only on six Channel Islands off the coast of southern California. Active day and night and not as shy as the Gray Fox of the mainland. Feeds largely on fruits, berries, deermice, and insects. Mated pairs raise only two pups per year. Seriously endangered; its population was about 1,200 in 1995 but has since dropped to only about 300. ▶ The only fox on the Channel Islands. One-half to two-thirds the size of its mainland relative.

FOXES

color variations

Red Fox
L 33–43"
W 7–15 lbs

pups

Gray Fox
L 32–45"
W 7–15 lbs

Island Gray Fox
L 23–31" W 3–6 lbs

pups

131

SMALL FOXES

Kit Fox and Swift Fox often have been treated as belonging to the same species. Both are very fast runners over short distances, hunting rabbits, kangaroo rats, and other small animals. They also feed on fruit, grasses, birds, lizards, and insects. Frequently preyed upon by Coyotes, these small foxes have numerous underground dens with many entrances for beating a hasty retreat. The entrances to their dens often have a keyhole shape, rounded at the top with a narrower space below. Not very wary of humans, small foxes often fall victim to poison bait put out for Coyotes.

KIT FOX *Vulpes macrotis*

Widespread in the southwest, in desert scrub and farmland, and still locally common in some areas. Usually spends the day in one of its extensive underground burrows, coming out only at night. The Kit Fox is able to survive without drinking water, obtaining moisture from its food. Mated pairs, sometimes helped by another adult female, raise two to six pups each year. Usually rather quiet but does have a variety of shrill yaps, squeaks, purrs, whines, and growls. The San Joaquin Kit Fox, a subspecies found only in the western and southern portions of the San Joaquin Valley of California, is listed as endangered. ▶ Kit and Swift Foxes are our smallest wild dogs, about the size of a housecat. They are slim, with proportionately very large ears and long legs; buff, tan, or yellowish gray, depending on season and region, always with a black-tipped tail. Gray Fox (previous page) is larger and darker, with smaller ears and with a dark line along the top of the tail as well as at the tip. Red Fox has a white-tipped tail. On the prairies, see Swift Fox.

SWIFT FOX *Vulpes velox*

area mapped in
pale orange
is former range

A ghost of the short-grass prairies, active mainly at night and not often seen. Now quite rare over much of its former range, it is classified as endangered in Canada, and there are efforts under way to reintroduce it to the prairie provinces. Like the Kit Fox, it is an accomplished burrower, digging numerous dens and long tunnels with many entrances. Swift Foxes usually live in pairs. One litter per year, of three to six pups, is born in early spring. ▶ Very similar to Kit Fox but with shorter tail, broader muzzle, and slightly smaller ears. Best identified by range and habitat.

SMALL FOXES

mother and
pups
in den

Kit Fox
L 29–33"
W 4–7 lbs

**San Joaquin
Kit Fox**

Swift Fox
L 28–35"   W 4–7 lbs

ARCTIC FOX *Alopex lagopus*

A tough little wild dog of the far north. Arctic Foxes range widely over Alaska and northern Canada, reaching the northernmost of the Canadian islands and even beyond: wandering over the pack ice of the Arctic Ocean, they have been spotted not far from the North Pole. They have several adaptations for dealing with extreme cold, including the small size of the ears, muzzle, and legs to reduce the amount of surface area from which heat might be lost. The soles of their feet are densely furred, and their body fur is several inches thick. The quality of their fur has not gone unnoticed by humans, and they are often trapped for their pelts.

Variable in color, the Arctic Fox has two distinct color morphs, and both of them change the colors of their coats seasonally. The more common morph is pure white in winter and molts to brownish gray in summer. The "blue morph" is blue-gray in winter, molting to darker gray or deep brown in summer. The blue morph is scarce in most mainland areas but is common in some coastal and island situations, especially where there is little snow cover in winter, presumably because a white winter coat would be poor camouflage indeed without snow.

Arctic Foxes are solitary most of the year, but members of a mated pair both care for the young, sometimes helped by another young adult. They raise young in an underground den with many entrances. Litters average 6 to 10 young but may be much larger (up to 25 young!) in summers when lemmings or voles are at population peaks, providing a superabundant food source. Arctic Foxes also feed on birds and their eggs, ground squirrels, hares, and other prey in summer. During the winter, they depend on cached food that they have buried deep in the ground, but they also follow Gray Wolves on land and Polar Bears across the ice, eating leftovers from their kills or feasting on carcasses of whales that have died after being trapped in the ice.

▶ Small and compact, with small ears, short muzzle, and short legs. White or blue-gray in winter, slaty to brownish in summer. Gray Wolf (p. 126) and Red Fox (p. 130) are the only other wild canines occurring in its range; both are much larger, with longer legs, longer muzzles, and usually different colors.

white morph

winter

Arctic Fox
L 28–43"
W 3–21 lbs

summer

pups

blue morph

summer

winter

summer
blue morphs

PUMA   *Puma concolor*

**track about
3½″ long**

Also known as cougar, mountain lion, panther, and catamount, its variety of names reflecting its hold on the public imagination, even though this secretive cat is seldom seen by most people. The most widespread land mammal in the western hemisphere, living in habitats from forests to swamps to dry brushlands. It is now extinct in eastern North America, except for the endangered subspecies (Florida Panther) in the Everglades.

The home range of a male Puma may be well over 100 square miles in extent, and although a male's range will overlap with those of several females, he will not tolerate another male in his territory. Pumas are solitary for most of the year, forming pairs only briefly in the mating season. Females care for the young alone, usually giving birth to three young in a den among rocks or in dense thickets. Young are born spotted and have blue eyes until about three months of age. They are taught to hunt by their mothers until they leave home at one and a half to two years of age.

Pumas hunt mostly at night and feed mainly on hoofed mammals such as deer, although they will also take practically any animal their own size or smaller. Pumas are generally good for the health of deer populations, as they tend to focus on the easiest prey, thus thinning the herd of its weakest members. Until the 1960s, government bounties were still paid for dead Pumas, but fortunately public attitudes toward these superb cats are improving.

▶ Large, long-tailed, and uniformly tan to gray-brown or reddish brown, with dark markings on the face and tail tip. The head appears proportionately small for the body, and the tail is held low when walking. Eyes are brown or golden in adults. Usually quiet but hisses, growls, purrs, whistles, and screams, especially in mating season.

JAGUAR   *Panthera onca*

The largest cat in the Americas, now threatened or endangered over much of its range. Populations still exist just south of the border in Sonora, Mexico, and individuals sometimes wander north into Arizona. Feeds on turtles, coatis, and javelinas as well as the largest animals available in its habitat; the Jaguar runs into trouble with ranchers over who gets to eat their cows. ▶ Massive, powerful, with a big head and stout legs. Yellowish with black rosettes from head to tail; rarely all blackish with faint rosettes. Ocelot (p. 140) is *much* smaller, often has stripes (not rosettes) on neck.

Puma
L 35–60"
W 65–265 lbs

Florida Panther

cubs

Jaguar
L 45–75"
W 70–350 lbs

BOBCAT *Lynx rufus*

**track about
2″ long**

A good survivor, the Bobcat thrives in a wide variety of habitats across North America, from forests to deserts to swamps, and it has managed to persist even in many areas heavily settled by humans. It is mostly active at night and may have several alternate dens where it rests by day, among rocks, in hollow logs, or in dense thickets. An opportunistic hunter, it takes many rabbits but also feeds on squirrels, mice, birds, reptiles, insects, and sometimes animals as large as deer. Bobcats are solitary, with females doing all the care of the young. Litters average three young, born with eyes shut, well-furred, and spotted like adults. Weaned at four months, the young disperse by one year of age. ▶ As large as a medium-sized dog, with males usually bigger than females, brown with numerous indistinct darker spots, and with a short tail that is tipped black on top and white below. Backs of ears are black with a large white spot. Thin black stripes in ruff of fur around face. Black stripes on legs and tail. Canadian Lynx (below) has an even shorter tail, entirely tipped black. Puma cubs (previous page) have longer tails.

CANADIAN LYNX *Lynx canadensis* (Canada Lynx)

A cat adapted to the far north. Its thick, soft fur insulates it from winter cold. Its large, heavily furred feet act as snowshoes, to help it run across the surface of snow — often in pursuit of the Snowshoe Hare (p. 32), its main prey. Snowshoe Hares go through population cycles, with peaks every few years, and Canadian Lynx populations also rise and fall with changes in the availability of food. They also prey on squirrels, voles, birds, deer, and carrion, especially when hares are scarce. Lynxes are solitary except for a brief period in the breeding season. Females normally have three young, in a den in a hollow log, dense thicket, or other hidden site. Recent efforts to reintroduce lynxes to southwestern Colorado have had some success. ▶ Similar to the Bobcat, but with a shorter tail that is entirely black at the tip, not white underneath. The lynx also has proportionately longer legs and larger feet, longer black tufts on the ears, and usually less distinct spotting. Its facial ruff often forms a two-pointed beard below its chin.

WILDCATS

kittens playing

Bobcat
L 30–34"
W 20–26 lbs

with
rabbit

kittens

Canadian Lynx
L 35"
W 24 lbs

OCELOT   *Leopardus pardalis*

Widespread in the American tropics, this spotted cat survives in many habitats, from rain forest to savannah to dry scrub. North of the Mexican border probably no more than 100 Ocelots remain, in dense brushlands and oak woods of south Texas. In addition, a few from Mexico may still wander into Arizona. Mostly nocturnal, Ocelots hunt by walking their territories in search of small mammals, reptiles, and birds. The territories of females do not overlap, but a male may overlap the home ranges of several females. In Texas, Ocelots mate in summer and give birth to usually one or two young (up to four) in fall. ▶ Grayish to tawny yellow with variable dark stripes and spots all over. About the size of a Bobcat (previous page) but slimmer and more spotted with a longer tail. Jaguars (p. 136) are *much* larger.

MARGAY   *Leopardus wiedii*

An agile and acrobatic climber living in the canopy of tropical forests. Its ankle joints can rotate 180 degrees, enabling it to go down tree trunks headfirst and to hang by its hind feet from a limb. The Margay's place on our list is based on one old record from Eagle Pass, Texas, in 1852 or earlier; the northernmost populations today are at least 300 miles farther south, in Mexico. ▶ About the size of a housecat. Gray, buff, or dark brown, with variable darker patches, rosettes, and streaks. Very similar to the Ocelot, the Margay differs in having a shorter body, smaller head, proportionately larger eyes, and *longer,* thicker tail.

JAGUARUNDI   *Puma yagouaroundi*   *(Herpailurus yagouaroundi)*

An elusive cat of tropical thickets, most active at dawn and dusk, moving about mainly on the ground. There are currently no known populations north of the Mexican border, but occasional sightings are reported in Arizona, and possible tracks were found in Texas in 1999. There are also reports that Jaguarundis escaped from captivity may be roaming in Florida or elsewhere in the southeast. ▶ Plain dark gray all over, or reddish brown with paler belly, throat, and muzzle; the two color morphs can occur in the same litter. Best recognized by distinctive shape, with long tail and distinctly flattened, elongated head. The hindlegs appear longer than the forelegs, giving an odd profile to the back, with the hindquarters the highest part of the back when the animal is walking. Some reported sightings of Jaguarundis probably pertain to feral housecats.

TROPICAL CATS

kitten

Ocelot
L 36–54″
W 15–32 lbs

Margay

L 32–51″
W 7–15 lbs

kittens

Jaguarundi

L 35–54″
W 10–20 lbs

two color morphs

141

BLACK BEAR · *Ursus americanus* (American Black Bear)

**front track
about 6″ long;
hind track
about 7″ long**

While some other big predators have disappeared from large areas of North America, this adaptable bear has managed to thrive. It roams forests, swamps, tundra, and even the edges of suburbia in the crowded northeast. Although there are sometimes tense encounters between bears and humans, the timid Black Bear is rarely aggressive in these situations: it tends to run rather than fight, unless it has been habituated by people feeding it.

Black Bears are omnivores, able to eat practically anything. Much of their food consists of plant matter: fruits and berries of all kinds, acorns and other nuts, newly sprouted plants, roots, grass, bark, and seeds. They turn over logs and rocks with their powerful front legs to find grubs, break open beehives to feed on the honey and the larval bees, raid the nests of birds and ground squirrels, catch fish, and feed on carrion.

In the north, Black Bears den up throughout the winter, sleeping without eating, drinking, or excreting wastes for up to seven months — living on the fat accumulated during the spring and fall by lowering their heart and metabolic rates. However, a dormant bear can be roused within a few minutes, unlike most true hibernating animals. In the warmest climates of the south, only pregnant females den up in winter.

Black Bears mate in spring, but the embryo does not implant itself in the womb of the female and start to grow until November. Normally two or three tiny cubs are born in January or February, eyes shut, hairless, and helpless. Only 1/250 the size of their mother, bear cubs are almost as undeveloped at birth as marsupials. The cubs do little but nurse and sleep until the family emerges from the den in spring. Cubs stay with their mother until they are about 18 months old, and then they disperse.

▶ Variable in color, despite its name: in the east usually all black with brown muzzle, in the west normally either black, brown, cinnamon, or blond. Localized color morphs in coastal British Columbia and Alaska include the blue-gray "glacier bear" and the whitish "Kermode bear." The snout is convex or straight in profile. The long claws on the front paws are black. Grizzly Bears are usually larger and have a humpbacked look, longer pale yellow or brown claws, proportionately shorter ears, and a muzzle that is concave in profile.

BLACK BEAR

female and cubs

typical eastern morph

fall

spring

"cinnamon bear"

Black Bear
L 4¼–7'
W 100–900 lbs

"Kermode bear"

"glacier bear"

GRIZZLY BEAR

front track about 10" long; hind track about 12" long

size: length (from nose to tail) 4' to 9'; weights average 200 to 800 lbs., rarely to 1,200 lbs.; males average larger than females, and individuals on coast average heavier than those inland

Ursus arctos **(Brown Bear)**

One of our largest carnivores, the magnificent Grizzly was once common over much of western North America, ranging well out onto the Great Plains and south to Mexico. Still common in parts of Canada and Alaska, it is considered endangered in the lower 48 states. Flexible in its choice of habitats, living in forests, plains, and tundra. The Grizzly is an omnivore, feeding on a wide range of plant food, from nuts and berries to roots, leaves, grass, and mosses. It also uses its long front claws to dig up burrowers such as ground squirrels and marmots. Will kill young (or sick or injured adults) of large animals such as deer, Caribou, Moose, Bison, and sometimes domestic livestock; also feeds on carrion. Mostly solitary, but will gather in large numbers to gorge on fish at rivers where salmon are spawning.

Like other bears, does not truly hibernate, but becomes dormant in winter, denning up for three to seven months, during which time it does not eat or drink. Upon emerging in spring, the now-thin Grizzly may not eat for up to two weeks. During this long period of starvation (it may lose up to 40 percent of its body weight), it lives on fat gained by gorging on food the previous summer and fall. The bear is able to become obese each fall without risking heart disease because cholesterol does not stick to the walls of its blood vessels (causing arteriosclerosis) as it does in humans.

Grizzlies are potentially quite dangerous. Larger than Black Bears, they are often more aggressive toward humans (especially mother bears with cubs). They have highly developed senses of hearing and smell. When hiking in Grizzly country, use caution, and make noise regularly so as to avoid taking them by surprise.

Grizzlies mate in early summer; young are born while the female is denned up for winter. Cubs stay with their mother until their second or third year. ▶ Always shades of brown, from pale yellowish tan to dark brown. Inland populations often have longer hairs tipped white, creating grizzled appearance, hence the name. Populations of coastal Alaska (often called Brown Bears), including those on Kodiak Island, average larger. Compared to brown individuals of Black Bear (previous page), this species is usually larger with a big shoulder hump and more massive head; its front claws are much longer and are pale yellow to brown, not blackish. Grizzly has different facial profile, with more convex muzzle than Black Bear.

mother and cubs

Coastal or Kodiak

Grizzly Bear
L 4–9' W 200–800 lbs

size
compared
to
6' man

Toklat
(inland
Alaska)

POLAR BEAR *Ursus maritimus*

A huge carnivore of the north. Polar Bears may not appear that large from a distance, but visitors to Hudson Bay, Canada, get a truer idea of their size when a bear stands on its hind legs and looks hungrily in the window of a tundra buggy, 15 feet off the ground!

Polar Bears range over northern coastlines and islands within the reach of winter ice, with their southern limits dependent on how far south the pack ice drifts. They spend much of their time roaming over the pack ice, far from land, even in the darkness and extreme cold of the Arctic winter. Thick fur and thick deposits of body fat insulate them against the cold of the air and water, and the hair on the soles of their feet provides both insulation and traction on the ice. Their fur is actually clear and hollow, allowing sun to pass through and be absorbed by their black skin, while insulating effectively against heat radiating outward.

On the pack ice in winter, Polar Bears hunt Ringed and Bearded Seals. Incredibly powerful, a bear will plunge through the ice to drag seals through their breathing holes when they surface for air, crushing them instantly. They also hunt other seals, walruses, fish, Beluga, and Narwhals. In summer, Polar Bears have an amazing capacity to fast while still active. As the pack ice melts, leaving them stranded on land (as in Hudson Bay), the bears fast for up to four months while waiting for the fall freeze-up. During fasting, the bears neither drink nor urinate, living on the water formed by the metabolism of fat.

Only pregnant female Polar Bears den up for the winter; their two cubs are born around November. The cubs don't leave the den until late March when they weigh 20 to 30 pounds, having grown to this size on the milk of their fasting mother. Cubs go out on the pack ice with their mothers to learn how to hunt until they are two to two and a half years old.

Polar Bears have no natural predators except humans. The greatest threat to their survival may involve global warming and the melting of the pack ice where they spend much of their lives.

▶ Very large, white in winter, Polar Bears may appear yellow or grayish in summer owing to oxidation of their coats by the sun. Proportionately longer neck and smaller head than other bears, and no prominent shoulder hump.

bears with seal carcass (and lurking Arctic Fox) on ice floe

males

older cub

Polar Bear

L 6–9'
W 400–1,750 lbs

female with young cub

juveniles play fighting

HOOFED MAMMALS

Also known as ungulates, these are mammals in which the foot is simplified into a lengthened design with fewer bones, and the claws are modified into hooves. This streamlined design is good for speed, and many hoofed mammals are very fast runners. The animals in this group are all vegetarians, grazing on grasses and other ground plants or browsing on the leaves and twigs of shrubs and trees, usually in open habitat where speed is their best defense against large predators.

Most hoofed mammals are sociable, living in herds at least part of the time. In several of these families, the males (or sometimes both sexes) have either horns or antlers. Such headgear may be useful for defense against predators, but males often use it in fighting for dominance, in anything from mild sparring and posturing to all-out battles. In many species, dominant males wind up fathering most of the offspring, so the stakes are high.

**male
Bighorn Sheep
sparring
for dominance**

A high percentage of the important domesticated animals come from this group, including such familiar farm animals as cattle, sheep, goats, pigs, horses, and donkeys (and others that are very important in other parts of the world, such as camels, llamas, and yaks).

Most hoofed mammals in North America (including all of the native species) belong to the order Artiodactyla, or even-toed ungulates. They are divided among several families, as follows.

Deer (family **Cervidae**): pp. 150–158, plus introduced species on p. 166. Native species include deer, elk, caribou, and moose. Males grow antlers anew every year. Bony outgrowths of the skull, the antlers grow from late winter or early spring to late summer. During their growth phase, the antlers are covered by a layer of skin, called "velvet," filled with nourishing blood vessels. In late summer or fall, this velvet sloughs off, leaving the antlers bare. Members of the deer family are browsers and grazers, feeding on a wide variety of plants.

Cattle, Antelopes, Sheep, and Goats (family **Bovidae**): pp. 160–164, plus introduced species on p. 168. Native species include bison, muskox, wild sheep, and mountain goat. Among our native species, both males and females have horns, although those of the males are often larger. Unlike antlers, horns are not shed yearly, but may continue growing gradually throughout the animal's life. Our species in this family are mostly grazers, found in open country.

Pronghorn (family **Antilocapridae**): p. 164. The only member of its family, the fleet-footed Pronghorn (also called Pronghorn Antelope) is native to the North American prairies. It grazes in small herds in very open terrain, relying on its extremely keen eyesight to spot predators at a distance, and relying on its great running speed to evade them.

Peccaries (family **Tayassuidae**): p. 170. These animals of the American tropics are similar to pigs but have short straight canine teeth rather than curving ones. One species of peccary reaches our southwestern states, where it is commonly referred to by the Spanish name of *javelina*. Small herds of peccaries live in deserts and brushlands, feeding on cacti and other tough plant material.

Pigs (family **Suidae**): p. 170. This family is native to the Old World, but domestic pigs (descended from the Eurasian Wild Boar) have escaped from captivity in many parts of North America and have established feral populations.

The other major order of hoofed mammals is the Perissodactyla, or odd-toed ungulates, which includes the horses, zebras, tapirs, and rhinoceroses. We have no surviving native members of this order in North America, but members of one family have established feral populations.

Horses (family **Equidae**): p. 172. Feral horses and donkeys now live in wild country of several states, especially in the west. They are grazers, favoring open terrain. Horses are herd animals, but donkeys are often more solitary.

149

WHITE-TAILED DEER *Odocoileus virginianus*

**track about
2½″ long**

Common and widespread in a variety of habitats, the White-tail is undoubtedly the most familiar large mammal in North America today. Given its current abundance, it seems hard to believe that its population in the U.S. was probably down to fewer than 500,000 in the late 1800s. Careful management and changes in habitat brought their numbers back up to an estimated 15 million in the U.S. alone, with more in Canada, Mexico, and Central America.

White-tailed Deer prefer open forests bordering old fields or natural meadows. They are browsers and grazers, feeding on a wide variety of plant materials, from twigs and leaves to grasses, berries, acorns, and fungi — and, at times, row crops and garden plants. When alarmed, this deer bounds away in leaps (its hind feet hitting the ground before its front feet), flagging with its tail (the tail erected and spread, showing the bright white underside).

Males grow new antlers each year. These grow from early spring through late summer; in fall, the softer velvet covering sloughs off, leaving the antlers bare during the season when the males are using them to spar for dominance. The females mate with dominant males in autumn or winter, and give birth to one to three fawns the following spring or summer. Fawns are able to stand and nurse within minutes of birth. They lie still instinctively, hidden on the ground, when not attended by their mother. In recent decades this strategy has become a hindrance to survival wherever the South American fire ant has invaded the U.S.: the ants may bite the young fawn to death if it does not move out of their path. Fawns are weaned at about two and a half months of age but follow their mother until they are one or two years old.

▶ Variable in size, with the smallest in North America being the endangered subspecies in southern Florida, the Key Deer. (The subspecies in coastal Oregon and Washington is also listed as endangered.) Grayish in winter, reddish brown in summer. Antlers have *one* beam from which the branches rise vertically. Tail is *brown* above, *white below* and *fringed with white on the sides.* Fawns are reddish brown with white spots until three months of age. Over much of its range, this is the only deer. From the Great Plains westward, compare to Mule Deer (next page). Elk (p. 156) has a contrastingly darker neck and pale rump patch.

White-tailed Deer
L 3–8′
W 50–300 lbs

mature buck
with
fall antlers

doe
and fawns

"Key Deer"

151

MULE DEER   *Odocoileus hemionus* (Black-tailed Deer)

**track about
2³/₄″ long**

Common throughout the west, from desert to forest, wherever it finds both cover and open areas in which to feed. Especially in mountain regions, it often migrates between habitats with the seasons. The Mule Deer usually forms very small herds of just a few individuals. Females tend to band together only with their fawns and yearling offspring, although they may form larger groups in winter. Mule Deer browse and graze on a wide variety of plants, including new growth of grasses, bushes, and trees, and consume many acorns in fall. As befits frequent prey animals, they have excellent vision, hearing, and smell, enabling them to detect approaching predators. When running away, Mule Deer often "stot," bouncing with all four feet hitting the ground at the same time, unlike the leaps of White-tailed Deer.

Only males have antlers, and their size and number of tines are related to the age of the animal and its nutritional status. Males spar with their antlers, establishing dominance, and dominant males get to mate with most females. The breeding period for Mule Deer usually peaks in November and December. Females bear one or two fawns, usually in June or July. The fawns follow their mother until one or two years of age. Most bucks disperse at about 16 months of age, while does stay with their mother longer.

▶ Dark gray or pale brown in winter, reddish brown in summer, often with a darker stripe down the back. Coastal individuals are smaller, with a large tail that is *mostly black above;* those of the interior are larger and have the tail only *black-tipped above.* Mule and White-tailed Deer overlap widely in range, but the White-tail occupies moister habitats. In the northern Rockies, White-tails are mostly along rivers, Mule Deer in drier and higher places; in the southwest Mule Deer are mostly in deserts and grasslands, White-tails mostly in mountain forests. The antlers of males differ: those of the Mule Deer branch into *two main forks* before branching into smaller forks, while those of the White-tail have one main antler beam from which the tines rise vertically. Mule Deer have larger ears, about two-thirds the length of the head; those of the White-tail are about half the length of the head. Mule Deer (especially males) often show a distinct dark patch on the forehead. Tail patterns also differ between the species, and White-tails are more likely to bound away with their tail raised.

MULE DEER

mature buck

doe

winter deer

Mule Deer
L 4–6 ft
W 65–265 lbs

young buck

summer buck in velvet

does and fawns

153

MOOSE   *Alces alces*

**track about
5″ long**

This magnificent member of the deer family, about the size of a horse, is common in forests, meadows, and tundra of the north. With its massive body, long legs, and fur that is hollow for insulation, the Moose is well adapted for living in cold regions with lots of snow. It is not so well adapted to heat: unable to perspire, it cools off in summer by spending a lot of time standing in water or mud or in the shade. Thus the moose does not occur where the temperatures rise above 80°F for much of the summer, or where deep shade and cool rivers and ponds are lacking.

With an appetite to match its size, the Moose consumes up to 45 pounds of forage per day, or about eight tons per year. Favored foods include willow and aspen leaves and many aquatic plants in summer, twigs and woody stems of various plants in winter. The Moose is usually solitary, which is probably just as well — where numbers congregate in winter at good browse, they can make quite a dent in the forest.

As with other deer, the males shed their antlers annually in late winter, regrowing the whole thing again between March and August, shedding the nurturing velvet of skin before the fall rut. During the fall rut, aggressive males compete for females by posturing, having mock battles with the nearby vegetation, and actually jousting with their antlers. The breeding season occurs in September and October, and calves are born in May and June. Normally a female will have a single calf, but she may have twins (or rarely triplets) in years when food is abundant.

Despite their formidable size, adult Moose are sometimes taken by predators, such as wolves, especially in deep snow. Wolves and bears take many calves, but the mother Moose can often defend the calf successfully against large predators, striking out powerfully with her hooves. As a matter of common sense, humans should avoid females with calves, as well as cranked-up males in fall.

▶ Large, with shoulder hump and very short tail, pendulous flap of skin hanging under the lower jaw, long upper lip, and elongated head. Males are much larger than females and have large, broadly flattened antlers. Gray undercoat of woolly fur covered with light brown to black long guard hairs. All other deer are smaller and lack the exceptionally broad flattening of the antlers.

MOOSE

bulls fighting

bulls

antlers
in velvet

Moose
L 8–10'
W 600–1,320 lbs

cows
with calves

ELK *Cervus elaphus* (Wapiti)

**track about
4″ long**

This large regal deer was once common over most of North America, from the mountain west across the Great Plains and the eastern forests, but hunting pressure wiped out the eastern and prairie populations by the middle of the 1800s. Recently Elk have been reintroduced into several eastern states, and they are doing well in areas such as central Michigan and central Pennsylvania. In the west, Elk are a major attraction at some parks and preserves, such as the refuge at Jackson Hole, Wyoming, and Jasper and Banff National Parks in western Canada.

Elk are most common in country with a mix of forest and open grassland. They are most active from dusk to dawn, grazing on grasses and weeds and browsing on trees and shrubs. In spite of their size and large antlers, they can move through even dense woods rapidly and quietly. Gregarious, they form herds of up to 400 animals in open habitat. Elk are our most vocal deer, and bulls rutting in fall are often heard bugling — a bellow followed by a loud whistle and ending in grunts. A bull warns off other bulls in this way, but also uses antlers to joust with other bulls for his harem of cows (as many as 60). A single calf is born to each female around the beginning of June. Calves may nurse for their first nine months. In summer, calves and females gather together and the bulls stay on the outside of these herds. Adolescent males leave the maternity herd when they mature.

A population in the valleys of central and eastern California, the Tule Elk *(C. e. nannodes),* was once reduced to only a few hundred individuals, but intensive conservation efforts have brought its numbers back up into the low thousands.

▶ Very large, with a thick neck and long thin legs. Overall color varies from red-brown in summer to tan in winter, contrasting with a yellow-brown rump patch and tail and dark brown head, neck, chest, and legs. Mature males are larger than females and have antlers that consist of a main beam (up to five feet long) and branching tines. Young are spotted until three months of age. White-tailed Deer and Mule Deer (pp. 150–152) are smaller and lack the yellowish rump patch. Moose (p. 154) averages larger, is darker overall, and has a longer muzzle and palmate antlers. Caribou (next page) has the neck contrastingly pale, not dark, and mostly occurs farther north.

bellowing bull
with cows

bulls
sparring

Elk
L 6–9′
W 370–1,050 lbs

antlers
in velvet

bulls

cow
and calf

CARIBOU

CARIBOU   *Rangifer tarandus*

track about 4″ long

The toughest North American deer, able to survive year-round in the harsh climates of the tundra far north of the Arctic Circle, although some populations live farther south in boreal forest and bogs. Gregarious at all seasons, Caribou are usually seen in herds. Most of the year, smaller herds of bulls segregate from those larger herds consisting of cows and calves. In late fall, bulls will join the cows and calves until the cows become receptive to their advances. Breeding occurs in October and November, and the single calf is born around the first of June. The calf is precocious, able to stand within half an hour, and able to keep up with the herd within a day.

The northernmost populations (known as Barren Ground Caribou) are among the most migratory of land mammals: in late winter, migrating herds of up to 100,000 animals of both sexes move to traditional calving grounds on tundra, such as on the Arctic National Wildlife Refuge in Alaska. In summer, Caribou feed on a wide variety of plant material, including grasses, shrubs, sedges, twigs, and mushrooms. In winter, remarkably, they feed mostly on lichens (especially the abundant reindeer lichen or "reindeer moss").

Unlike other deer, both males and females have antlers. These are shed annually, bulls losing theirs shortly after the fall rut, females retaining theirs until calving in spring. Caribou compete with rodents to consume the fallen antlers, recycling their calcium.

In Eurasia this species is called the reindeer. In some areas it is domesticated for its meat and hide.

▶ Larger and bulkier than most deer. Dark face and muzzle with light cream neck, blackish legs. Caribou bulls have large semi-flattened antlers that project forward over the muzzle as well as backward over the shoulders, and pendulous flaps of skin (dewlaps) hanging from the throat. Cows have spindly small antlers. Old antlers are whitish, and new velvety ones are black. Size and color vary with geography. The southern Woodland Caribou is largest and darkest, Peary's Caribou of the high Arctic islands is smallest and palest. Color also varies with season, the animals appearing darker and browner in summer, paler and grayer in winter. Smaller and paler than the Moose (p. 154), with a shorter snout. Elk (previous page) has yellow-brown rump patches and a much darker neck.

bull

Barren Ground Caribou
(tundra regions)

Peary's Caribou
(Arctic Islands)

cow

calf

Caribou
L 4–7'
W 140–335 lbs

antlers
in velvet

Woodland
Caribou
(forested
regions)

159

AMERICAN BISON   *Bison bison* (Buffalo)

**track about
4″ long**

Our largest land mammal, males weighing up to a ton. An estimated 30 million bison once roamed the central prairies in massive herds. Native Americans had lived with the bison for ages, regarding them as sacred and relying on them for many of their material needs. European settlers had a more sinister impact. During the 1870s and 1880s, bison were nearly driven to extinction by massive commercial slaughter for their meat, bones, tongues, and hides. By the time they received any kind of protection, only about 1,600 bison remained in captivity, plus a few small herds in the wild. Conservation measures restored the bison to its current population of several hundred thousand, in scattered herds in the central and western U.S. and Canada. In a natural setting, herds are migratory, making them difficult to contain in fenced areas. At the midsummer breeding season, mature bulls mingle with cows and become aggressive, sparring with other bulls and bellowing hoarsely. Cows have a single calf each year, usually in late spring. Grazers who thrive on mixed and short grasses, bison are so large that they are often mistakenly judged to be slow-moving. Some unwary tourists have discovered the hard way that bison can run 30 miles per hour and turn faster than a horse. Natural predators include grizzlies and wolves. ▶ Unlikely to be confused with other animals. Males are larger than females, they have longer hair on the front quarters, and their horns are stouter and more widely spaced.

MUSKOX   *Ovibos moschatus*

Named for the musky odor that the males exude, the Muskox lives only on high arctic tundra where winters are long and cold and summers are short. In summer, grazes on grasses, sedges, and herbs. In winter, finds shrubs such as willows and birches in windswept areas where the snow is not too deep. Muskoxen live in herds at all seasons. When threatened by wolves, the herd defends their calves by forming a circle, horns pointed outward. This is not a good defense against humans with guns, and the Muskox was almost driven to extinction in the late 1800s. With conservation efforts, they have recovered to more than 85,000. ▶ Stocky with dark brown hair hanging nearly to the ground. Prominent shoulder hump and permanent odd-shaped horns in both sexes. Males are larger and have bigger, thicker horns than females.

BISON AND MUSKOX

cows
and calves

"Woods
Bison"

bull

**American
Bison**
L 7–12'
W 800–2,000 lbs

young
bulls
sparring

bull

Muskox
L 6–9'
W 350–900 lbs

cow
and calf

defensive
circle

BIGHORN SHEEP   *Ovis canadensis* (Mountain Sheep)

track
about 3″ long;
about 15″
between tracks

These sure-footed animals are found from high alpine meadows to low deserts, wherever grassy areas for feeding are close to the steep rocky terrain where they find safety from predators. Bighorns often occur as local populations, isolated from other populations by stretches of unsuitable habitat. Still common in the northern Rockies, but has become rare in some desert regions and has disappeared from much of its former range. Populations have been reintroduced in some areas. Bighorns usually live in herds, ranging from five to eighty or more; rams (males) older than three years tend to live separately from the females and young, except during mating season. Rams battle for dominance with head-on bashing of horns, sometimes continuing for hours. Their brains are cushioned from the shock by the bony cores of their horns and by the large sinuses in the skull, but the rams are sometimes injured, even fatally, by these clashes. Dominant males get to father most of the lambs. Females normally have one lamb (rarely two); lambs are able to stand, run, and climb shortly after they are born. Bighorn Sheep eat many grasses, also shrubs and even cacti. ▶ Males are larger than females, and northern populations larger than those in southern or desert regions. Always shades of brown (from chocolate to tan) with white on muzzle, rump, belly, and backs of legs. Older rams have large thick horns that eventually curve so far as to form almost a complete circle. Females are smaller, with thinner, shorter, cream-colored horns. In British Columbia, compare to Dall's Sheep (below). Also see Mountain Goat (next page) and exotic Aoudad or Barbary Sheep (p. 168).

DALL'S SHEEP   *Ovis dalli* (Thinhorn Sheep)

purple area
is range of
"Stone Sheep"

Found in rugged mountainous terrain of the far north. Similar in habits to Bighorn Sheep, including the behavior of rams (males) fighting for dominance in noisy head-on clashes. ▶ In most of range, white overall, sometimes with yellow or brown wash. Rams have large curling horns, females have shorter spikes. Some individuals have black tails. Mountain Goat (next page) is also white but looks shorter-legged and has darker horns. A darker subspecies, sometimes called "Stone Sheep" (see map), might suggest Bighorn Sheep, but is shades of *gray,* not brown; males have slightly thinner horns that flare more widely at the tips.

WILD SHEEP

males
L 5–6'
W 165–300 lbs

Bighorn Sheep

"Desert Bighorn"

females and lambs
L 4'1"–5'
W 100–200 lbs

Dall's Sheep

males
L 4'3"–5'11"
W 161–243 lbs

females and lambs
L 4'3"–5'3"
W 101–110 lbs

"Stone Sheep"

male

163

PRONGHORN   *Antilocapra americana*

track about 2³/₄″ long

The fastest mammal in North America, able to run more than 40 miles per hour and to jump 20 feet in a single leap. Does not usually jump fences, however, but crawls through or under, so certain kinds of fences can severely limit its movements. Pronghorns live in very open terrain, with no attempt at camouflage or concealment; their safety depends on their incredibly keen eyesight and on their ability to outrun most predators that they spot. Pronghorns feed on a great variety of shrubs, weeds, and sometimes grasses, including some plants poisonous to domestic cattle. Males sometimes defend territories with a harem of females during the breeding season in September. Females usually produce twins, which hide in a hollow or in dense grass until they can run. Fawns can outrun a human when they are a few days old. ► Patterned in tan and white. The white rump patch, erected and flared when the animal is alarmed, can be seen for miles. Male has a black line under the lower jaw. Horns of males have a short prong aiming forward, while females have shorter horns lacking the prong (or sometimes no horns). The horn sheaths are shed and regrown annually.

MOUNTAIN GOAT   *Oreamnos americanus*

introduced into several states south of historic range

track about 2³/₄″ long

An agile climber, famously sure-footed, found at or above timberline in country with rocky cliffs, talus slopes, and meadows in which to graze. It often lives on mountain slopes that rise more steeply than a 45-degree angle. Its hooves have rough pads on the bottom, and the cloven shape of the hooves allows them to move with a pincerlike action, helping the Mountain Goat to gain traction on slippery rocks and ice and to find footholds on narrow ledges. On the steep cliffs where it spends much of its time, it is safe from most predators except Golden Eagles (which prey on young goats) and Mountain Lions. In summer and autumn, forages alone or in small groups. Will travel many miles to gather in large groups at salt licks; also gathers on winter bedding grounds. One or sometimes two kids are born in late May, and the newborn is able to follow its mother within hours. The young stay with their mother until the next kid is born. ► Stout and compact with strong forelegs. Very shaggy coat in winter. White overall with short black horns. Female Dall's Sheep (previous page) has horns dull yellow, not black.

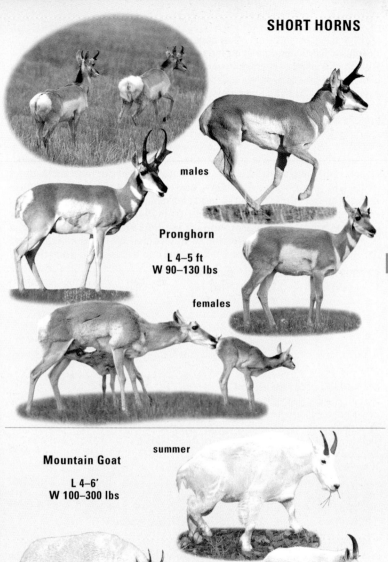

males

Pronghorn

L 4–5 ft
W 90–130 lbs

females

Mountain Goat

L 4–6′
W 100–300 lbs

summer

female
and kid

winter

165

Many grazing animals from other continents have been introduced onto ranches in North America to be farmed for their meat or to provide sport hunting. A number of species have established feral populations in Texas, and a few in other states; we illustrate some of those most likely to be seen (deer on this page and antelopes, sheep, and goats on the following page). Exotic deer sometimes interbreed in captivity, producing hybrids that are impossible to identify in the field.

CHITAL   *Axis axis* (Axis Deer or Spotted Deer)

The most common native deer in India and Sri Lanka. Thousands now occur on some ranches in Florida and Texas. Chital live in large herds of females and young with a few stags; most males live in bachelor herds. A nervous animal, the chital has a loud alarm bark when frightened, and the males give loud mating bellows. These tropical deer can breed at any time of year. ▶ Bright reddish coat with white spots, a prominent white throat patch and belly, with a black stripe running down the spine. Males' antlers are almost as long as the deer is tall, curved and with three points.

COMMON FALLOW DEER   *Dama dama*

Imported from the Mediterranean region, the fallow deer has been farmed for venison for thousands of years. In North America, feral populations occur in at least eight states and provinces. They do much of their feeding in open grassy areas but need forests for shelter and winter browse. ▶ Variable. Most commonly chestnut with white spots; sometimes creamy tan with white spots, all whitish, or gray-brown. Best recognized by its broad palmate antlers.

SIKA DEER   *Cervus nippon*

"Sika" is the Japanese word for deer, and this deer is native to Japan and other areas of east Asia. Feral populations have been established in Texas, Wisconsin, Maryland, and Virginia. Originally forest dwellers, Sikas adapt well to captivity and will eat a variety of vegetation. Sikas are quite vocal: females whistle in alarm, and males serenade females with a sound like a rusty hinge. ▶ Size varies from tiny (in Japan) to larger in the northern regions. Color varies with range and changes with the season. Light ash brown to black in winter without much spotting. In summer, red or dark ash brown with distinct spots. Males have a thick neck mane when in rut. The hairs of the white rump patch are erected in alarm.

SAMBAR   *Cervus unicolor*

Native to much of Asia, Sambar are found in the U.S. mostly on game ranches in Texas and California but are free-ranging in St. Vincent Wildlife Refuge, Florida. Females form small groups, while males are solitary at most seasons. Apparently needs dense woods for mating and raising young. ▶ Very large, mostly dark brown with a whitish rump patch. Adult males have mane of long hair on neck in breeding season and large antlers with three tines.

EXOTIC DEER

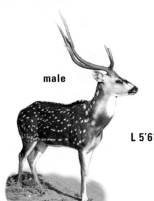

male

female

Chital

L 5′6″ W 110 lbs

Common Fallow Deer

L 5′3″ W 130 lbs

males— color variations

female

Sika Deer

L 4′6″ W 200 lbs

male

Sambar

L 6′7″ W 550 lbs

NILGAI   *Boselaphus tragocamelus*

The largest Indian antelope, introduced into Texas by the King Ranch in the 1930s. Now so abundant that their numbers are of concern to wildlife managers. Males and females segregate into separate groups except during the breeding season, when a dominant bull will defend a harem of several cows. ▶ Males are blue-gray with black legs and have short black horns. Cows and calves are light brown.

GEMSBOK   *Oryx gazella*   (Oryx)

Native to Africa and Saudi Arabia, this antelope can survive on very little water. Introduced into New Mexico as a game animal in the 1970s, it rapidly became a nuisance in and near the White Sands National Monument. It cost over a million and a half dollars to erect a fence and relocate most of the animals into the White Sands Missile Range, where they continue to multiply despite continued hunting. ▶ Light brown with distinctive black and white face markings, long thin horns.

BLACKBUCK   *Antilope cervicapra*

Native to open grasslands of India, now free-ranging over much of Texas, especially the Edwards Plateau. Blackbucks are flexible in their feeding and can switch from the preferred grasses to any other kind of browse when necessary. ▶ Dominant males are black with white patterning, while non-dominant males, females, and young have the black replaced by brown. Mature males have long, spiraling horns.

HIMALAYAN TAHR   *Hemitragus jemlahicus*

Introduced from the Himalayas onto game ranches in several areas of North America, this agile relative of the goats now has herds roaming wild at least in New Mexico, California, and Ontario. ▶ Dense woolly winter coat of dark reddish brown, with short legs and a small head. The male has a long mane. Both sexes have horns, but the bull's are longer and heavier.

DOMESTIC GOAT   *Capra hircus*   (not illustrated)

Domesticated in Iran 10,000 years ago and now found worldwide, both as a domestic animal and as a feral pest. Herds of feral goats eat practically any plant matter, destroying native habitats and competing with native animals for food. Goats eat undergrowth down to the ground and up to seven or eight feet high, eliminating not only food for other browsers but the cover required by many small mammals and birds. They have played a part in erosion and the spread of deserts in many regions. ▶ This familiar animal occurs in a multitude of forms and colors, horned and hornless.

AOUDAD   *Ammotragus lervia*   (Barbary Sheep)

Originally from the Barbary Coast of North Africa. Large feral populations now exist in California and New Mexico and in Palo Duro Canyon in the Texas panhandle. They live in social groups of females with young led by a dominant female most of the year. ▶ Both males and females have horns, and sometimes those of females are larger. Aoudads have manes on their necks and long hair on their legs.

EXOTIC UNGULATES

Gemsbok

L 6'2"   W 460 lbs

Nilgai

L 6'3"   W 450 lbs

female

Himalayan Tahr

L 3'10"   W 135 lbs

female

male

Blackbuck

L 4'2"   W 65 lbs

Aoudad

L 5'
W 190 lbs

male

female
and kid

169

COLLARED PECCARY *Pecari tajacu*

**track about
1²/₃" long**

Widespread in the American tropics, this piglike creature extends north into our southwestern states, where it is commonly known as "javelina" (pronounced HAHV-eh-LEE-nah). Peccaries are intensely social, living in herds of up to 50 animals and lying close together to share body heat on cold winter nights. Mature adults defend their territory against other herds. The dominant males father most of the young in a herd, usually breeding from November to January. One to three young (but typically twins) are born usually during July or August, but occasionally at other times of year. The young are defended by the entire herd, often sleeping on top of the adults for warmth and security. Peccaries feed on a wide variety of plant material, including prickly pear cactus, mesquite pods, acorns, and agave leaves. At the edges of southwestern cities, they raid gardens at times. Shy and elusive in wild habitats, they may become unnervingly tame around the fringes of suburbia. These animals can deliver nasty bites when provoked; observers should use common sense and not approach them too closely. ▶ Long muzzle with piglike bare snout, small ears, very short tail. Grizzled gray-black coarse hair all over, with a paler collar. Feral pig has larger ears and longer tail and lacks the pale collar. A mane of black bristles on neck is erected when the peccary is alarmed. Young are reddish brown with a black stripe down the back.

FERAL PIG *Sus scrofa*

The domestic pig is descended from the Eurasian Wild Boar. Populations of feral pigs, reverting to the wild from domestic stock, now roam at will in almost half the states of the U.S., mainly in the south. However, there are also some pure wild boars that have been imported as exotic game animals and released on game ranches in several states. The second-most-popular game mammals in North America (after the White-tailed Deer), feral hogs are wary, fast, and tough. They will eat just about anything, including rattlesnakes. As they don't sweat, they love water and will wallow in mud to prevent sunburn and deter flies. A common sign of their presence is plowed-up ground where they have been rooting with their snouts. ▶ There are hundreds of variations on domestic pigs, but the wild boar type usually differs in having a longer snout, smaller ears, and higher broad shoulders that taper to narrow and lower hindquarters. It is usually blackish, with coarse bristles down the center of the back, hence the common name "razorback." Both males and females have tusks, canine teeth that never stop growing. Piglets are often striped lengthwise.

PIGLIKE ANIMALS

young

Collared Peccary

L 3'   W 35–55 lbs

female with piglets

European Wild Boar

Feral Pig

L 5'   W 75–400+ lbs

in mud wallow

male with tusks

171

FERAL HORSE *Equus caballus*

The fossil record indicates that horses evolved in North America and migrated to Siberia via the Bering Land Bridge — and then spread into Europe and Asia. The horse disappeared from North America about 10,000 years ago, possibly extirpated by the hunting activities of early man. Horses were returned to North America in the late 15th century when European settlers reintroduced them. Native Americans loved horses and their speed, finding them useful for hunting and transportation in their nomadic lives, and helped the horse spread throughout the Great Plains and the West. By the early 1800s, two to three million horses roamed the Great Plains and western states. Ranchers and commercial hunters killed many horses, displacing them with grazing cattle. About 39,000 feral horses are now protected on public rangelands in ten western states. The Bureau of Land Management manages the herds, culling them frequently and adopting horses out to qualified owners for taming. Horses are herd animals, forming bands of mares and foals guarded by a stallion, who battles other stallions for the privilege. A common sign of a herd's presence is piles of stallion dung, which they use to mark their territories. A dominant mare leads the family band and decides where to go to graze and drink. Young males ousted from the band of their birth form bachelor herds, until they are ready to challenge a stallion for a mare to start their own band. ▶ One of the most beautiful and well-known animals in the world, the horse needs no description.

FERAL DONKEY *Equus asinus*

The wild donkey originated in arid areas of North Africa, but all "burros" in the U.S. are feral, descendants of domestic livestock introduced by the Spaniards in the 1500s. Feral animals now occur in deserts of California, Arizona, Nevada, Oregon, and Utah. Unlike the horse, the burro is not a herd animal. Females generally raise their young alone, or in the company of another female. Grazers, burros also eat herbs and woody plants. They can live on low-quality forage but need access to drinking water. According to some studies, they can tolerate losing up to 30 percent of their body weight from dehydration and can then replenish it in one drink. Donkeys compete with native animals such as Bighorn Sheep (p. 162) for food and water. ▶ Typically mouse gray, but comes in varied colors and patterns. Often has a dark stripe running from the mane to the tail and across the shoulders. Smaller than the horse, with a larger head, erect black mane, longer ears, and black-tipped tail.

horse herd running

stallions fighting

mare and colt

Feral Horse

burro in creosote bush flat

Feral Donkey

colt

adult

The next four chapters are devoted to the small rodents. What these animals lack in size, they make up for in diversity: 120 species are included here, well over one-fourth of all the mammal species in North America.

Mankind has had varied associations with these small rodents. Cults of mouse worship existed in the Mediterranean region more than 3,000 years ago, and ancient China and Japan had more than a casual interest in mice as well. In modern times, laboratory rats and mice have been of major value in research of many kinds. On the negative side of the ledger, mice and rats consume vast amounts of grain and other crops, estimated in the millions of tons annually. They are also involved in spreading disease: the plague, murine typhus, and hantavirus are just a few examples of rodent-borne diseases that can be fatal to humans.

Much of the damage caused by rodents can be traced to just three species: Brown Rat, House Rat, and House Mouse. These three are native to the Old World and came to this continent with European colonists. Our native North American mice and rats are sometimes pests in farmland also, but in natural habitats they play important roles — including the unglamorous role of being at the bottom of the food chain. Predators of many kinds rely on these rodents as staple food items.

Not all small rodents are prolific — some woodrats, for example, have only one litter per year, of two or three young. But many of the mice, rats, and voles can sustain heavy predation pressure because they are able to reproduce at a remarkable rate. For example, the Meadow Vole, famed as the most prolific mammal on earth, can start breeding about a month after it is born, and a female can give birth to another litter of up to ten young every three weeks! Not surprisingly, some rodents have population explosions at times. Some have regular population cycles over a period of three or four years, their numbers building to a peak and then crashing. These boom-and-bust cycles affect the populations of predators and of other animals as well. On the arctic tundra, various small birds are likely to raise more young in a peak lemming year: when lemmings are abundant, predators tend to focus on them and leave the nesting birds alone.

The majority of these species are active only at night; many are such creatures of darkness that they even become less active when the moon is bright. Therefore, most of the animals in the next four sections are hard to observe. They are even harder to identify. Even for expert mammalogists, many small rodents can be identified only by examining details of their teeth or their skulls. When you observe one of these rodents in the wild, you should not expect to name it to species by the way it looks. However, you may be able to name it to group — for example, as a deermouse, cotton rat, vole, etc. — and then, by studying the range maps and habitat descriptions in this book, you can make an educated guess about which rodent you have seen.

We divide the animals in this group into four rather artificial sections for convenience, rather than following the technical classifications of families.

"Typical" mice and rats: pp. 176–196. Here we include such widespread groups as the deermice, harvest mice, grasshopper mice, cotton rats, and woodrats. All of the species in this section belong to the family **Muridae;** all but three belong to the subfamily Sigmodontinae, or New World rats and mice. (The three exceptions are House Mouse, House Rat, and Brown Rat, introduced from the Old World, which belong to the subfamily Murinae.) The animals in this section are diverse in appearance, but most have fairly long tails, most are not excessively furry (the cotton rats are exceptions to these first two generalizations), and they do not have enlarged hind feet adapted for powerful hopping.

Kangaroo rats and kangaroo mice: pp. 198–206. These belong to the family **Heteromyidae,** subfamily Dipodomyinae. Like real kangaroos, they get around by hopping on their very large hind feet, using their long tails for balance. They feed mainly on seeds, and they have external cheek pouches, lined with fur, that they use to carry large numbers of seeds at a time. Adult kangaroo rats are usually solitary, defending territories, and they may drum on the ground with their big hind feet to communicate with others of their own kind. Most kangaroo rats (and their small cousins, kangaroo mice) live in very dry country, and several species are able to survive without ever drinking water, obtaining all the moisture they need from their food.

Pocket mice and jumping mice: pp. 208–216. Pocket mice belong to the family **Heteromyidae,** subfamilies Perognathinae and Heteromyinae. Like the related kangaroo rats, they have external cheek pouches, lined with fur, which they use for carrying the seeds that make up the majority of their diet. Small and long-tailed, they look superficially like deermice, but they have smaller ears and larger hind feet and are more likely to escape by hopping instead of running. The jumping mice (p. 215) belong to a different group from all other North American rodents, the family Dipodidae, subfamily Zapodinae. They have large hind feet and very long tails, and some can reportedly jump more than 10 feet when alarmed.

Voles and lemmings: pp. 218–230. These belong to the family **Muridae** (like our "typical" mice) but are placed in a separate subfamily, Arvicolinae. Voles and lemmings are generally short-tailed and fuzzy, and most live in cool, damp climates. Many species live in dense grass and follow regular narrow paths or runways through the ground cover. They tend to eat more green vegetation and fewer seeds than most small rodents. Even when the voles themselves are out of sight, their presence may be detected by their runways, by small piles of clippings of green grass, and by their droppings, which are usually in the form of small green pellets.

HOUSE MOUSE   *Mus musculus*

Native to the Old World, this resourceful rodent has been associating closely with humans for more than 3,000 years, probably starting with civilizations in the Middle East. Today it is found almost worldwide except in the coldest regions. In North America it lives mostly around human habitations, from city buildings to farmhouses and barns, but it also occurs in disturbed habitats such as vacant lots, farmland, and old fields. ▶ Habitat is often a clue — if it's in your house, it's likely a House Mouse — but not infallible, as it may overlap with various deermice (below and subsequent pages). Best known by overall dusty brownish gray look, without contrast anywhere. Deermice and other native mice are generally white below and often have bicolored tails. Compare to harvest mice (p. 186). Escaped pet mice or laboratory mice, descended from the House Mouse, may show a wide variety of colors.

NORTH AMERICAN DEERMOUSE   *Peromyscus maniculatus*

The most widespread native mouse in North America, and the most variable. Common in a wide variety of habitats, from deep forest to open fields. This deermouse is an adaptable little omnivore, feeding mainly on seeds and berries but also taking insects, mushrooms, roots, and other items. It often gathers food and stores it away, leaving caches of dry seeds in such places as underground burrows, tree cavities, or crevices among rocks. These food caches may help to sustain the deermouse during bad weather, because it remains active all year even in cold climates. Generally abroad only at night, running about on the ground and also climbing ably in trees or vines. During the day it mostly hides in its nest, which may be in any concealed spot such as a hollow log, old bird's nest, or empty container in a shed or barn. ▶ A medium-sized mouse with whitish feet and usually with sharply bicolored tail. Extremely variable, divided into 57 or more subspecies; in some places, 2 subspecies live side by side without interbreeding. Two general forms are widespread: a large-eared, long-tailed forest type, and a small-eared, short-tailed form of open country. Those in humid areas tend to be darker, those in dry country tend to be paler. Some populations have two color morphs (buff and gray). Juveniles are grayer than adults. Usually has more obviously bicolored tail than White-footed Deermouse (next page); compare to other deermice (pp. 178–184).

front track
about ¼″ long;
hind track
about ⅓″ long

babies in nest

House Mouse
L 6½"
W ¾ oz

open-country type

forest type

North American Deermouse
L 5–8"   W ½–1 oz

color variations

DEERMICE

(genus *Peromyscus*, pp. 176–184) have rather long tails, large eyes, and large ears. Our 15 species are hard to tell apart, but range and habitat offer clues. The group name "deermouse" was adopted only recently, and older books simply use the group name "mouse."

WHITE-FOOTED DEERMOUSE *Peromyscus leucopus*

Often the most abundant rodent in eastern forests, but also lives in farm country and dry southwestern brushlands. Active at night, it feeds on seeds, berries, leaves, and insects. By day it remains in its nest in a sheltered spot, such as inside a hollow tree or log, or in a building. May take over an abandoned bird's nest and build a dome over the top of the open cup. ▶ Reddish brown to gray-brown above, white below. North American Deermouse (previous page) is very similar but usually has tail more heavily furred and more sharply bicolored. In the southeast (p. 184), Cotton Deermouse is larger, Oldfield Deermouse is smaller and paler. Most deermice in the southwest have longer tails.

NORTHWESTERN DEERMOUSE *Peromyscus keeni*

Common in Pacific Northwest from the mountains westward, including the coast and many islands. Seems to prefer forest edge and clearings rather than unbroken forest. Often enters houses and other buildings, especially in winter. ▶ A large, dark deermouse with dense fur. Similar to North American Deermouse (previous page) but larger and longer-tailed where they overlap. No other deermice in its range.

TEXAS DEERMOUSE *Peromyscus attwateri* (Texas Mouse)

Although it ranges over parts of five states, this mouse has a fragmented distribution, being closely tied to rocky places. Habitats include open woodlands of juniper or oak as well as forested ravines. ▶ Medium-sized, dark above. Tail is about as long as head and body combined, with a tuft of hair at the tip, and hind feet are relatively large. Difficult to separate from Brush Deermouse (next page) and White-ankled Deermouse.

WHITE-ANKLED DEERMOUSE *Peromyscus pectoralis*

Another mouse of rocky places, living around rock outcrops, ledges, ravines, and canyons with brushy cover, usually in very dry situations. ▶ Medium-sized, with tail at least as long as head and body combined. Ankles are usually white (as opposed to usually dark in Texas Deermouse), but this is rarely noticeable. Overlaps the ranges of several other deermice; very difficult to identify in the field.

DEERMICE

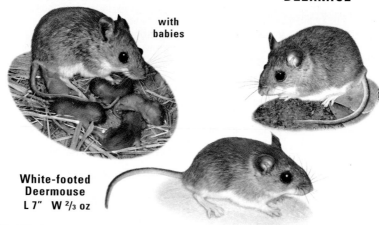

with
babies

**White-footed
Deermouse
L 7" W 2/3 oz**

**Northwestern Deermouse
L 8" W 3/4 oz**

**Texas Deermouse
L 8" W 1 oz**

**White-ankled Deermouse
L 8" W 1 oz**

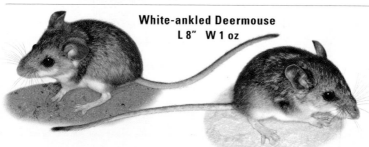

179

BRUSH DEERMOUSE   *Peromyscus boylii* (Brush Mouse)

Widespread in mountainous regions of the west, mostly at middle elevations. It occurs in habitats that range from coniferous forest to desert scrub, but always where there is dense ground cover of brushpiles, fallen trees, or boulders; it usually places its nest under a rock or dead tree or in a crevice among rocks. ▶ Medium-sized, with tail longer than head and body combined, tufted at the tip. Gray-brown above and whitish below, with a *broad orange stripe* along the side of the body, more obvious than on other deermice in its range.

PINYON DEERMOUSE   *Peromyscus truei* (Pinyon Mouse)

Most often found in association with pinyon pine and juniper in arid foothills, but also lives in other kinds of coniferous and oak woodlands and in chaparral. The subspecies in the Palo Duro Canyon area of the Texas panhandle is regarded as endangered. ▶ Variable in color, from yellowish buff to darker gray-brown. The ears are proportionately *larger* than on most deermice; the tail, usually shorter than the head and body combined, is relatively hairy, with a tuft of hair at the tip.

CANYON DEERMOUSE   *Peromyscus crinitus* (Canyon Mouse)

Lives in slickrock canyons and mesas, often in places with very little plant life and few other mammals. Active only at night, it runs about with great agility in its spartan habitat, through crevices and up and down vertical cliff faces. It can survive without drinking water, obtaining moisture from its food, which consists of insects, green plants, fruits, and seeds. ▶ Medium-small, brown to yellowish buff, with relatively large ears. Its tail is as long as the head and body combined, thinly haired but with a tuft of hair at the tip.

CACTUS DEERMOUSE   *Peromyscus eremicus* (Cactus Mouse)

A deermouse of desert lowlands and foothills, living mainly in rocky places with scattered shrubs and cacti. Its nest is usually in an underground burrow, but it may use any sheltered spot such as a rock crevice or old woodrat nest. ▶ Gray-brown above, white below, with a broad pale buff stripe along the sides, less pronounced than that of Brush Deermouse. Tail is longer than head and body combined, but lacks the tuft of hair at the tip shown by the other species on this page. California Deermouse (next page) is much larger, and Merriam's Deermouse (next page) is usually larger and darker.

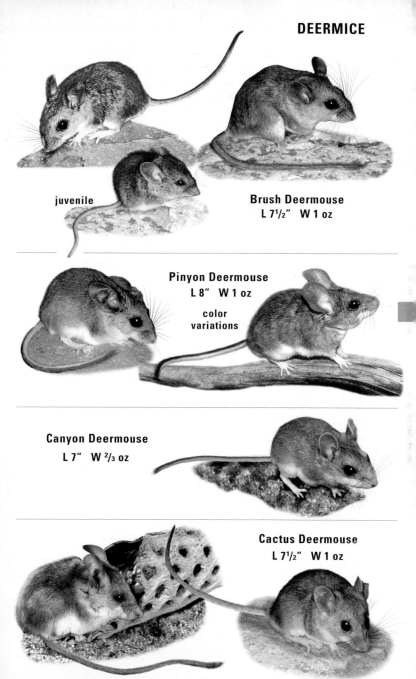

DEERMICE

juvenile

Brush Deermouse
L 7¹/₂″ W 1 oz

Pinyon Deermouse
L 8″ W 1 oz
color variations

Canyon Deermouse
L 7″ W ²/₃ oz

Cactus Deermouse
L 7¹/₂″ W 1 oz

181

CALIFORNIA DEERMOUSE   *Peromyscus californicus*

Common in southern California and Baja, in varied habitats including chaparral, coastal sage scrub, oak woods, and coniferous forest. Has a more stable family life than most rodents; males and females stay together in long-term pairs, and males help to care for the young. California Deermice build nests on the ground or in trees. ▶ The *largest* of the deermice, with a very long tail, longer than the head and body combined, and only vaguely bicolored. Overall color varies from buff to grayish above.

MERRIAM'S DEERMOUSE   *Peromyscus merriami* (Mesquite Mouse)

Quite localized north of the Mexican border. Has a limited habitat in southern Arizona, along desert washes, where stands of mesquite trees have a good understory of grasses, shrubs, and cacti. ▶ A medium-sized deermouse with a tail longer than its head and body combined. The only deermice likely to overlap its range and habitat are two on the preceding page. Merriam's is usually larger and darker than Cactus Deermouse and lacks the orange-buff side stripe of Brush Deermouse.

SAXICOLOUS DEERMOUSE   *Peromyscus gratus* (Osgood's Mouse)

The fancy name merely means that it lives around rocks, and it does, making its nest in rock crevices or under boulders. The surrounding habitat may be open or wooded, from foothills to mountains. ▶ Usually grayish to gray-brown above. May be darker where it lives among blackish lava rocks. Tail is often longer than head and body combined, with a tuft of hair at the tip. Difficult to distinguish from other deermice in its limited U.S. range; averages larger than next species, longer-tailed and slightly smaller-eared than Pinyon Deermouse (previous page).

NORTHERN ROCK DEERMOUSE   *Peromyscus nasutus*

Generally uncommon at middle elevations in the southwest, around rocky places within woods of pinyon pine, juniper, or oak. A good climber in trees and on rocks. ▶ Gray-brown above; may be darker where it lives among the blackish rocks of old lava flows. Tail is longer than head and body combined and often has more fur than the tails of most deermice. Difficult to distinguish from Pinyon Deermouse (previous page) and from Saxicolous Deermouse (above), although both have somewhat larger ears.

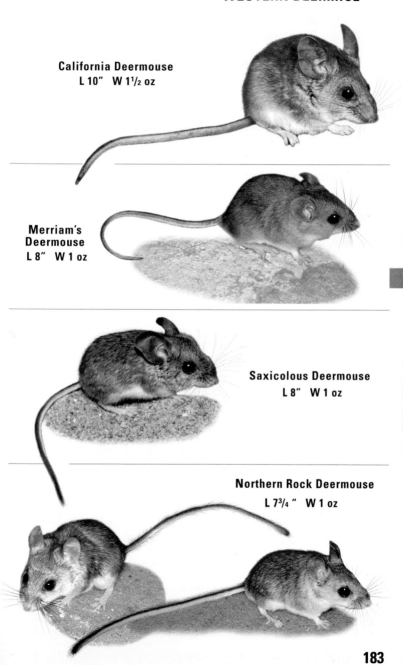

WESTERN DEERMICE

California Deermouse
L 10″ W 1½ oz

Merriam's Deermouse
L 8″ W 1 oz

Saxicolous Deermouse
L 8″ W 1 oz

Northern Rock Deermouse
L 7¾ ″ W 1 oz

COTTON DEERMOUSE   *Peromyscus gossypinus* (Cotton Mouse)

Common in a variety of habitats in the southeast, especially in swamps and bottomland forests, but also in overgrown fields and upland woods (and occasionally the edges of cotton fields, hence the name). Like other deermice, it is omnivorous, although it may eat more insects than plant material. ▶ Medium-sized, warm brown above, with tail shorter than head and body combined. North American Deermouse (p. 176) has longer tail, but White-footed Deermouse (p. 178) can be very similar. Compare to next species.

OLDFIELD DEERMOUSE   *Peromyscus polionotus* (Oldfield Mouse)

Common in open habitats, especially in recently disturbed or cleared areas with a good growth of grass and weeds; also in beach grass areas along the coast. Usually nests underground, digging burrows to three feet or more below the surface. ▶ Overall color varies: inland forms are medium brown above, beach forms are often quite pale buff. Smaller (and often paler) than other deermice in its range. Compare to Eastern Harvest Mouse (next page).

GOLDEN MOUSE   *Ochrotomys nuttalli*

A beautiful mouse of southeastern forests. Most numerous in floodplain forest with dense understory and many vines, it climbs about with great agility, building its globular nest usually 5 to 15 feet up in a shrub, vine, or tree, or sometimes on the ground. It feeds mostly on seeds and other plant material, often carrying food to a feeding platform that it has built well above the ground. ▶ Similar to the deermice but can be recognized by its *rich golden color;* its soft, dense fur; and its arboreal habits in lowland forests.

FLORIDA MOUSE   *Podomys floridanus*

Restricted to native scrub on dry sandy soils in Florida. Closely associated with the gopher tortoise and with the long, deep burrows that it digs, this mouse enters these burrows and digs its own small side tunnels to make its nest. It comes to the surface mostly at night to feed on acorns, seeds, fruits, and insects. Although it resembles the deermice, studies suggest that its closest relatives are mice in southern Mexico. Like other residents of the Florida scrublands, it is probably threatened or endangered. ▶ Larger than most mice in its range, with *big ears* and *big feet.* Tricolored pattern with white belly, orange sides, and dark brown back.

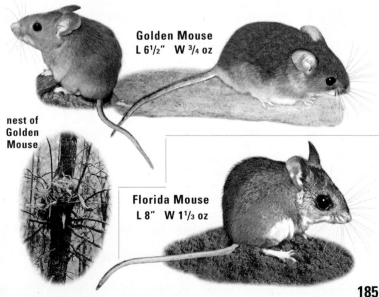

Cotton Deermouse
L 6³/₄" W 1 oz

Key Largo race (endangered)

Oldfield Deermouse
L 5" W ¹/₂ oz

Golden Mouse
L 6¹/₂" W ³/₄ oz

nest of Golden Mouse

Florida Mouse
L 8" W 1¹/₃ oz

185

look like miniature deermice (pp. 176–184) but are classified in a separate genus because they have a groove on their upper incisors.

WESTERN HARVEST MOUSE   *Reithrodontomys megalotis*

The most widespread harvest mouse and the most adaptable, found from low deserts and marshes to mountaintops. It favors open habitats with dense low growth; it also adapts well to farmland. ▶ Tail is distinctly bicolored (dark above, light below) and about the same length as the head and body combined. Ears are cinnamon to buff and relatively small. Juveniles are grayer than adults.

PLAINS HARVEST MOUSE   *Reithrodontomys montanus*

Most numerous in short-grass prairies but also lives on farmland such as hayfields or wheatfields. Typical of harvest mice, it builds a nest of grasses shaped into a ball, usually lodged just above the ground in dense grass. ▶ Rather pale and dull, with a bicolored tail usually shorter than the length of the head and body combined. Western and Fulvous Harvest Mice have longer tails, and Eastern Harvest Mouse is darker.

FULVOUS HARVEST MOUSE   *Reithrodontomys fulvescens*

Common in brushland, mesquite grassland, and other open habitats. Like other harvest mice, it has a varied diet, eating many insects when available and concentrating on seeds at other seasons. ▶ Tail is at least as long as head and body and is vaguely bicolored. Coarse fur often shows a grizzled effect. Eastern and Plains Harvest Mice are duller and shorter-tailed; Western Harvest Mouse has a more distinctly bicolored tail.

EASTERN HARVEST MOUSE   *Reithrodontomys humulis*

Inhabits weedy fields, broom-sedge meadows, marsh edges, and other damp open areas, avoiding dense forest. Although some other rodents accumulate large caches of food, harvest mice do very little "harvesting" and storing of food. ▶ Small and relatively dark brown. Tail is shorter than head and body combined. In much of its range, this is the only harvest mouse; at its western limits, compare to the three species above.

SALTMARSH HARVEST MOUSE   *Reithrodontomys raviventris*

Limited to salt marshes in San Francisco Bay, where it favors dense stands of pickleweed. Classified as endangered because so much of its habitat has been destroyed. ▶ Reddish brown (darker in the southern part of the bay). Western Harvest Mouse (above), which lives in adjacent grasslands, is much more active and has a more blunt-tipped, more distinctly bicolored tail.

HARVEST MICE

Western Harvest Mouse
L 5¹/₂″ W ²/₅ oz

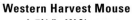

juvenile

Plains Harvest Mouse
L 4¹/₂″ W ¹/₃ oz

with young

Fulvous Harvest Mouse
L 6¹/₃″ W ³/₅ oz

Eastern Harvest Mouse
L 4¹/₂″ W ¹/₂ oz

Saltmarsh Harvest Mouse
L 5¹/₂″ W ²/₅ oz

Grasshopper mice are more predatory than most rodents, pursuing large insects and other invertebrates and even other small mammals. They communicate with others of their own kind with a "howl" or "song," a clear note about one second long, audible to human ears.

NORTHERN GRASSHOPPER MOUSE   *Onychomys leucogaster*

Widespread in the west, mostly in dry grassland and shrubland. Active all year, it breeds mostly in spring and summer; males and females have complex courtship behavior. Males take part in raising the young, unlike most rodents, perhaps because the young need more help learning to be hunters. ▶ A bulky mouse with a rather *short, thick tail*. Occurs in two color morphs, either gray or rusty cinnamon above, clean white below. Separated from most rodents in its range by shape and color.

SOUTHERN GRASSHOPPER MOUSE   *Onychomys torridus*

This little predator is common in scrubby habitats of the southwest, including Sonoran desert, Great Basin desert, and California chaparral. Like other grasshopper mice, it actively pursues large invertebrates and sometimes other small animals. It regularly preys on scorpions, deftly avoiding the venomous sting in their tails. ▶ Similar to Northern Grasshopper Mouse (with the same variations in color) but averages smaller, with a proportionately longer tail.

CHIHUAHUAN GRASSHOPPER MOUSE   *Onychomys arenicola*

Also known as Mearns's Grasshopper Mouse, this species was separated from the Southern Grasshopper Mouse (above) on the basis of genetic studies as recently as 1979. It inhabits dry scrub in the lowlands of the Chihuahuan (pronounced chee-WAH-wahn) Desert region of Mexico's central plateau, extending north into New Mexico and western Texas. ▶ Visually identical to Southern Grasshopper Mouse, identified only by range, since there is little or no overlap between them (see maps).

NORTHERN PYGMY MOUSE   *Baiomys taylori*

This tiny mouse, our smallest rodent, occurs locally in Texas and the southwest. Although it lives in a variety of habitats from grasslands to open woods, it requires dense ground cover and is most numerous in areas of prickly pear cactus on short-grass prairies. ▶ *Very small* and usually rather dark, with tail shorter than head and body combined. Overall color varies from brownish to gray, with the underparts usually paler.

GRASSHOPPER AND PYGMY MICE

Northern Grasshopper Mouse
L 6″   W 1⅓ oz

eating
grasshopper

**Southern
Grasshopper Mouse
and
Chihuahuan
Grasshopper
Mouse**

L 5½″   W 1 oz

singing

Northern Pygmy Mouse
L 4″   W ⅓ oz

BROWN RAT　　*Rattus norvegicus*　(Norway Rat)

Despite its alternate name, this rodent probably was not native to Norway originally but may have come from central Asia. Regardless of its origins, it developed the winning strategy of associating with humans, and it has followed us and hitched rides on ships to become established worldwide. An omnivore and a prolific breeder, it can become superabundant at times; a female may have as many as 12 litters of young in a year. This rat probably reached North America around 1775, and it now lives almost throughout the lower 48 states and southern Canada, extending north on the Pacific Coast to southern Alaska. Its favored habitat on this continent is around manmade structures, from cities to farm buildings, but in warm weather it is often widespread in farmland. ▶ Variable in color, from dusky brown to dark gray, only a little paler below. Its tail is scaly, mostly hairless, and only a little shorter than the length of the head and body combined. House Rat has a longer tail and often has darker body fur. Woodrats (pp. 194–196) have white bellies, and their tails are usually hairy, not scaly.

HOUSE RAT　　*Rattus rattus*　(Black Rat or Roof Rat)

Probably native to Asia, this rat spread across Europe centuries ago and reached North America with colonists in the early 1500s. Not as widespread as the Brown Rat (above), it favors warmer climates. It is found mostly in the south, and in coastal areas north to Maine and southern British Columbia. More of a climber than Brown Rat, it often moves about in the rafters of buildings, climbs trees, or runs along high wires. ▶ Usually quite dark overall, sooty black to dusky gray above, paler gray below. Its tail is scaly, mostly hairless, and longer than the head and body combined. Brown Rat has shorter tail. Woodrats (pp. 194–196) have white bellies and have tails that are usually hairy, not scaly, and typically shorter.

MARSH RICE RAT　　*Oryzomys palustris*

An excellent swimmer and diver, this clean little native rat is common in southeastern marshes. Its varied diet includes insects, crabs, fish, baby turtles, and eggs and nestlings of birds, as well as much plant material and sometimes carrion. It builds a globular nest, often well above the water in marsh plants or shrubs. ▶ A small rat, near the size of a deermouse, with tail nearly as long as head and body combined. Strongly washed with gray. Smaller than the two introduced rats above, slimmer and more graceful, with smaller feet.

COUES'S RICE RAT　　*Oryzomys couesi*

Widespread in Mexico and Central America, this rodent reaches the U.S. only in the two southernmost counties of Texas. There it appears to be limited to cattail and bulrush marshes around *resacas* (oxbow lakes). ▶ Larger than Marsh Rice Rat (above) and much browner overall. Range and habitat are among the best clues for separating this species from other rodents.

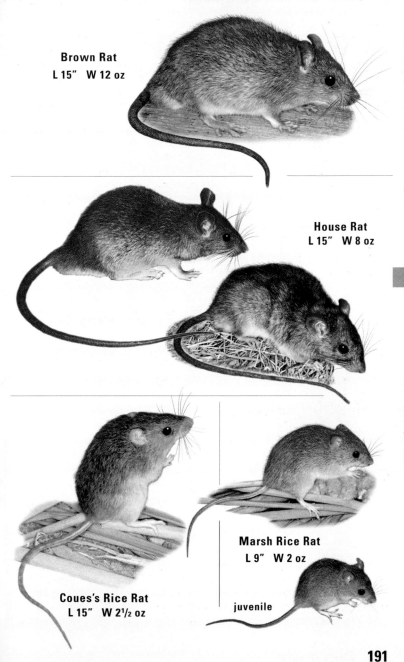

ALIEN RATS AND RICE RATS

Brown Rat
L 15″ W 12 oz

House Rat
L 15″ W 8 oz

Coues's Rice Rat
L 15″ W 2½ oz

Marsh Rice Rat
L 9″ W 2 oz

juvenile

(genus *Sigmodon*) have short rounded snouts and coarse fur, suggesting the appearance of voles (pp. 218–226), but they are larger. Cotton rats are also somewhat like voles in behavior: they live in grassy habitats, feeding mostly on grass and other green matter and making runways through dense low vegetation.

HISPID COTTON RAT   *Sigmodon hispidus*

Widespread and common in the southeast (and locally in the southwest) in prairies, overgrown pastures, and farmland. Human-caused changes in the landscape may have favored an expansion of its range in recent decades. In the northern parts of its range, it builds a nest woven of grass for shelter. ▶ Shape and size are distinctive in most of range; voles (beginning on p. 218) are similar but much smaller. In the southwest, compare to the next three species.

ARIZONA COTTON RAT   *Sigmodon arizonae*

Formerly considered to belong to same species as Hispid Cotton Rat (above), but they differ in chromosome number. Limited to areas with a good growth of grass, it may have been impacted by overgrazing in the past; two subspecies from central Arizona are now probably extinct. ▶ Very similar to Hispid Cotton Rat, mostly separated by range. Not reliably identified by sight where they overlap.

TAWNY-BELLIED COTTON RAT   *Sigmodon fulviventer*

Fairly common in its limited range in the southwest, in grassland areas. Like other cotton rats, it may weave nests for itself out of grass and may use these nests for raising litters of four to six young. ▶ May average a bit larger than other cotton rats but mainly recognized by color, with grizzled gray and white hairs on back and *tawny to buff underparts*.

YELLOW-NOSED COTTON RAT   *Sigmodon ochrognathus*

A resident of isolated mountain ranges in the southwest, where it lives in grassy patches at all elevations, from the foothills to the mountaintops. Young cotton rats tend to develop rapidly, and young of this species may be running around like small versions of the adults within a few hours after birth. ▶ Smaller than other cotton rats, dull brownish gray above and pale below, with an *orange-yellow patch* at each side of nose.

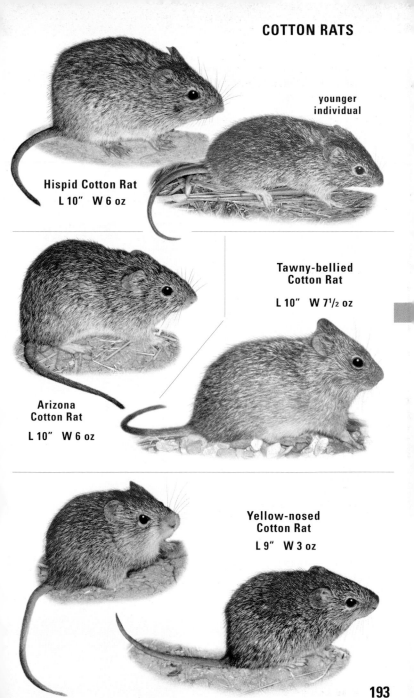

COTTON RATS

Hispid Cotton Rat
L 10" W 6 oz

younger individual

Tawny-bellied Cotton Rat

L 10" W 7¹/₂ oz

Arizona Cotton Rat

L 10" W 6 oz

Yellow-nosed Cotton Rat
L 9" W 3 oz

193

WHITE-THROATED WOODRAT   *Neotoma albigula*

Woodrats are also known as packrats or trade rats for their habit of collecting objects and sometimes appearing to "trade" one found item for another. This species is widespread in the southwest, mainly in deserts and foothills. It builds a bulky nest of sticks and cactus pads on the ground. ▶ Brown above, white on throat, belly, and feet. Bicolored tail is well furred but not bushy.

DESERT WOODRAT   *Neotoma lepida*

Common in open habitats from desert to coastal sage scrub. It feeds on succulent plants, including stems and pads of cholla and prickly pear cactus, and leaves of yucca. ▶ Mostly gray-brown. Generally larger on the coast than inland. White-throated Woodrat has whiter throat, Arizona Woodrat is usually paler, Dusky-footed Woodrat (next page) is larger, with darker hind feet.

MEXICAN WOODRAT   *Neotoma mexicana*

Widespread in the southwest, mainly in rocky places in the mountains amid pinyon-juniper or pine-oak woods. Less apt to build a bulky stick nest than most woodrats, instead placing its nest in a sheltered spot such as a tree hollow or rock crevice. ▶ Occurs in two color morphs, with the upperparts either grayish brown or reddish brown. White-throated Woodrat is more of a medium pale brown above; Southern Plains Woodrat (next page) is more purely gray.

STEPHENS'S WOODRAT   *Neotoma stephensi*

Has a remarkably close association with juniper trees, usually building its nest under them and feeding heavily on their foliage. Few mammals regularly eat the foliage of conifers; this woodrat and the tree voles (p. 226) are the only ones in North America that are known to specialize on such fare. ▶ A small woodrat, with a *bushier tail* than others in its range (but see Bushy-tailed Woodrat, next page). Color varies, darker brown above in southern part of range.

ARIZONA WOODRAT   *Neotoma devia*

Range poorly known because of confusion with Desert Woodrat; may extend into Utah and western Colorado. Generally around rocky areas in desert. Usually builds smaller nests than most woodrats. ▶ Smaller than most woodrats, with larger ears. Pale buffy brown overall, whiter on belly, gray in center of throat. Compare to Desert and White-throated Woodrats (both generally larger and darker).

young

White-throated Woodrat
L 13"   W 7½ oz

Desert Woodrat
L 12"   W 5 oz

Mexican Woodrat
L 14"   W 7 oz

Stephens's Woodrat
L 11½"   W 5 oz

Arizona Woodrat
L 11"   W 4 oz

EASTERN WOODRAT *Neotoma floridana*

Common in southeastern woodlands and sometimes in more open country provided there is dense ground cover. Like most woodrats, it builds a bulky stick nest on the ground, where it collects an odd assortment of inedible curiosities as well as food. ▶ Distinguished from other woodrats mostly by range. Brown Rat and House Rat (p. 190) have darker bellies, coarser fur, and mostly hairless tails.

ALLEGHENY WOODRAT *Neotoma magister*

Mainly limited to the central Appalachian region, around rocky places in the woods. Has recently disappeared from a number of places for reasons not fully understood. This species does not usually build large nests like other woodrats, but it will build stick middens for food storage. ▶ The only woodrat in its range. Compare to Brown Rat and House Rat (p. 190).

SOUTHERN PLAINS WOODRAT *Neotoma micropus*

Favors grasslands and plains, especially areas that include a mix of cacti and shrubs. Like most woodrats, it feeds on plant material, consuming a wide variety of seeds, nuts, berries, leaves, cactus pads, and other items. ▶ Medium-sized, gray above, usually much grayer than other woodrats in its range. Differs in habitat preference as well: Eastern Woodrat is usually in wooded areas, White-throated and Mexican Woodrats (previous page) are usually in more arid or rocky places.

DUSKY-FOOTED WOODRAT *Neotoma fuscipes*

Common in the Pacific states, in woodland and chaparral with dense ground cover. Females usually have one litter per year of two to four young. ▶ Gray-brown above, pale gray to white below. Dusky hairs on top of feet are hard to see. Compared to others in its range (previous page), Desert Woodrat is usually smaller, White-throated Woodrat is usually paler and browner.

BUSHY-TAILED WOODRAT *Neotoma cinerea*

Widespread and common, mainly in cooler climates of the northwest or the mountains and generally in wooded areas. Like other woodrats, it builds a bulky stick nest, where it usually lives alone. ▶ Color varies from brown to gray. Easily separated from other woodrats by its *very bushy tail;* the only species that comes close to this appearance is Stephens's Woodrat of the southwest (previous page).

WOODRATS

Eastern Woodrat
and
Allegheny Woodrat

L 14–16″   W 9–12 oz

Dusky-footed Woodrat

L 15″   W 10 oz

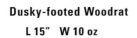

Southern Plains Woodrat
L 14″   W 9 oz

Bushy-tailed Woodrat

L 15″   W 13 oz

use their huge hind feet to hop about like tiny kangaroos, their long tails providing balance; the larger species may cover more than five feet in a single leap. All are active mainly at night, resting by day in burrows underground. They feed mostly on seeds, carrying them in fur-lined external cheek pouches and storing them in their burrows.

ORD'S KANGAROO RAT   *Dipodomys ordii*

The most widespread kangaroo rat, living in a variety of open habitats on sandy soil, from grassland to sagebrush flats to pinyon-juniper woodland. Females may raise two litters per year, averaging three or four young per litter. ▶ Medium-sized, variable in overall color. Tail relatively *shorter* than on most kangaroo rats. Check range maps: over much of its range, especially on the Great Plains, this is the only kangaroo rat. Overlaps with two species below, and with Chisel-toothed (next page) and Panamint (p. 204) as well as two Texas species (p. 206); see those for comparisons.

MERRIAM'S KANGAROO RAT   *Dipodomys merriami*

A denizen of the desert southwest, adapted to very arid conditions and able to survive without drinking water. Lives in a variety of lowland habitats, including some with hard rocky soil, where it digs relatively shallow burrows. ▶ Small and pale, usually buffy above, with a relatively long tail that is dark at the tip. Some kangaroo rats that overlap its range, including Desert (next page) and Banner-tailed, have white tail tips. Ord's has proportionately shorter tail. Also compare Chisel-toothed, Agile (next page), and Panamint (p. 204) Kangaroo Rats.

BANNER-TAILED KANGAROO RAT   *Dipodomys spectabilis*

A large and spectacularly marked rodent of the arid southwest, found in areas of grassland with scattered creosotebush or mesquite. Most easily detected by the large mounds that it builds, containing multiple entrances to its system of underground burrows; these mounds may be more than a foot high and more than 12 feet in diameter. Like other kangaroo rats, Banner-taileds often communicate with others of their own kind by drumming with their big hind feet, sitting on top of their mounds and drumming the hard-packed earth. ▶ Large and strongly marked; tail mostly *black,* with conspicuous *white tip.* Most others in its range have dark-tipped tails. Desert Kangaroo Rat (next page) is usually paler, with less contrast on the tail.

KANGAROO RATS

Ord's Kangaroo Rat
L 8–13" W 2–4 oz

variable in size and color

Merriam's Kangaroo Rat
L 9" W 1–2 oz

Banner-tailed Kangaroo Rat

L 13" W 3–4½ oz

KANGAROO RATS

These all occur in California, but two of them are also found farther east.

CHISEL-TOOTHED KANGAROO RAT   *Dipodomys microps*

Common in the Great Basin region, mainly in low desert dominated by saltbush. Named for its unusually flattened lower incisors, which it uses to peel back the outer layer of saltbush leaves to get at the inner layers — a major part of its diet, but eaten by few other animals. Unlike most kangaroo rats, often climbs shrubs to reach more leaves. ▶ Medium-sized, with a dark-tipped tail and an overall *gray tinge*. Next species has white-tipped tail. Compare to Ord's and Merriam's (previous page) and Panamint Kangaroo Rat (p. 204).

DESERT KANGAROO RAT   *Dipodomys deserti*

This well-named animal lives in our driest deserts, including Death Valley, in areas with loose sandy soil and scattered plants. Although it will drink water when available, it can survive long periods without, extracting moisture from the seeds it eats. ▶ Large, usually pale brown, with a long *white-tipped tail*. Banner-tailed Kangaroo Rat (previous page), which overlaps range in Arizona, is usually darker, with more contrasting tail (black and white, not brown and white).

CALIFORNIA KANGAROO RAT   *Dipodomys californicus*

Found in wetter regions than most kangaroo rats, throughout most of northern California and into southern Oregon, but only where there is open ground mixed with chaparral or scrub habitat. ▶ Medium-sized to large, with a *white-tipped tail*. Very little overlap in range with other kangaroo rats. Ord's (previous page) has dark-tipped tail. Heermann's (next page) occurs immediately to the south of this species and can have tail white-tipped. Heermann's has five toes on each hind foot (this species usually has four).

AGILE KANGAROO RAT   *Dipodomys agilis*

Fairly common in southern California, in open sandy areas (such as the edges of washes) in chaparral and coastal sage scrub, often living in colonies. Like other kangaroo rats, will gather seeds in its cheek pouches and store them in underground burrows. ▶ Medium-sized to large, with dark and white lengthwise stripes on tail sharply defined. Comparing other kangaroo rats in its range, Stephens's and Dulzura (p. 204) average smaller, and Stephens's has smaller ears. Merriam's (previous page) is smaller and usually paler.

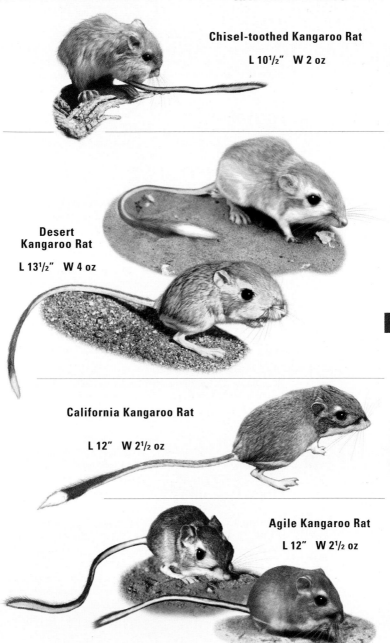

KANGAROO RATS

Chisel-toothed Kangaroo Rat

L 10½" W 2 oz

Desert Kangaroo Rat

L 13½" W 4 oz

California Kangaroo Rat

L 12" W 2½ oz

Agile Kangaroo Rat

L 12" W 2½ oz

201

HEERMANN'S KANGAROO RAT   *Dipodomys heermanni*

Although its range is limited to the central third of California, this kangaroo rat is widespread within that region, inhabiting grassland, brushy savannah, and other open habitats from sea level up to middle elevations in the mountains. The subspecies *morroensis* from along Morro Bay is considered to be endangered. ▶ Fairly large, somewhat variable in color. (Morro Bay race may lack the white hip stripe.) Tip of tail may be bushy and white or thin and dark. Compare to the three species below. Narrow-faced Kangaroo Rat (next page) averages larger and darker, with darker face markings and larger ears.

SAN JOAQUIN VALLEY KANGAROO RAT   *Dipodomys nitratoides*

Much of its former habitat has been converted to farmland, and this kangaroo rat is now considered endangered. It still survives on open alkaline flats with scattered grasses, saltbush, and other plants, mostly around the edge of the San Joaquin Valley. Formerly called Fresno Kangaroo Rat. ▶ Noticeably smaller than the other kangaroo rats in its range (and has four toes on each hind foot, not five). White stripe on side of tail is narrow and ends well before tail tip. Merriam's Kangaroo Rat (p. 198), similarly small but paler, approaches range in southern California but does not overlap.

GIANT KANGAROO RAT   *Dipodomys ingens*

Restricted to dry grassland at southwestern edge of San Joaquin Valley and adjacent inner Coastal Ranges. Individuals defend small territories, clearing away plants from around mounds that build up above their shallow burrows. They gather large numbers of grass and weed seeds and dry them in the sun before storing them underground. Now considered endangered because of habitat destruction. ▶ The largest kangaroo rat, *noticeably larger* than the two species above (the only ones that overlap its range).

BIG-EARED KANGAROO RAT   *Dipodomys elephantinus*

Highly localized in San Benito and Monterey Counties, from the Pinnacles to near Hernandez, in brushy habitats in the southern Gabilan Mountains. ▶ Range is best clue: overlaps with only two other kangaroo rats. Narrow-faced (next page) is darker, with much stronger markings on face. Heermann's (above) is a bit paler, averages smaller, has much smaller ears, and is usually found in more open habitats.

KANGAROO RATS

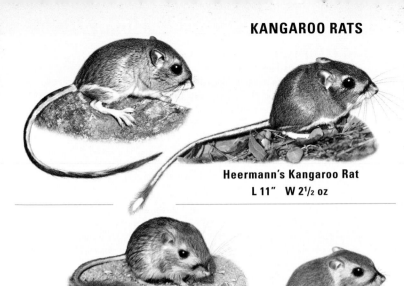

Heermann's Kangaroo Rat
L 11"   W 2¹/₂ oz

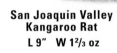

**San Joaquin Valley
Kangaroo Rat**
L 9"   W 1²/₃ oz

Giant Kangaroo Rat
L 13"   W 5 oz

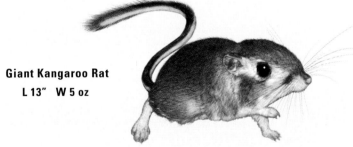

Big-eared Kangaroo Rat
L 12¹/₂"   W 3 oz

NARROW-FACED KANGAROO RAT   *Dipodomys venustus*

In coastal regions of central California, this kangaroo rat is an uncommon resident of hills covered with chaparral, open woods, or abandoned farmland. It feeds mainly on seeds, storing up large quantities in chambers in its underground burrows. ▶ Relatively large and dark. Heermann's Kangaroo Rat (previous page), which overlaps much of range, is slightly smaller and paler, with smaller ears. Big-eared Kangaroo Rat (previous page) has paler ears and face markings and very limited range.

DULZURA KANGAROO RAT   *Dipodomys simulans*

Common in grassland and chaparral in coastal regions from southern California south through Baja. May breed at any season but most often does so in winter or spring; females raise one litter per year, of two to four young per litter. ▶ Medium-sized with a long dark-tipped tail. Overall color varies from reddish brown to grayish brown. Stephens's (below) has smaller ears. Agile Kangaroo Rat (p. 200) quite similar but averages larger, may have broader white stripe on side of tail. Merriam's Kangaroo Rat (p. 198) averages much smaller and is usually paler buffy brown.

STEPHENS'S KANGAROO RAT   *Dipodomys stephensi*

Native to open habitats of coastal sage scrub and grassland in a limited area of southern California, this species has lost much of its former habitat to the growth of cities and agricultural land, and it is now considered endangered. ▶ Medium-sized, with relatively narrow white stripe on side of tail. Dulzura (above) and Agile Kangaroo Rats (p. 200) have larger ears and tend to be in denser habitats. Merriam's Kangaroo Rat (p. 198) averages notably smaller and somewhat paler.

PANAMINT KANGAROO RAT   *Dipodomys panamintinus*

Common in arid country of eastern California and adjacent Nevada, in very open habitats with scattered Joshuatrees, pinyon pines, junipers, cacti, or other plants. Like other kangaroo rats, they often engage in vigorous dustbathing. ▶ Medium-sized and long-tailed, usually pale warm brown above. Overlaps with several other kangaroo rats. Ord's (p. 198) is relatively shorter-tailed, Merriam's (p. 198) is smaller, Chisel-toothed (p. 200) is grayer overall, and Desert (p. 200) averages larger, with a white-tipped tail.

Narrow-faced Kangaroo Rat
L 12⅓″   W 3 oz

Dulzura Kangaroo Rat
L 11″   W 2 oz

Stephens's Kangaroo Rat
L 11″   W 2 oz

Panamint Kangaroo Rat

L 12″   W 2½ oz

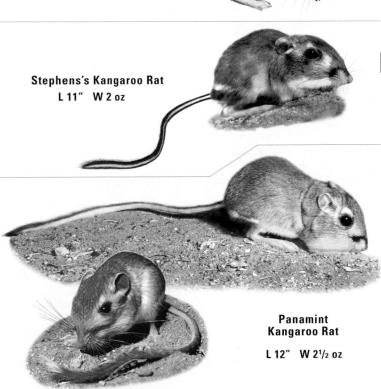

GULF COAST KANGAROO RAT *Dipodomys compactus*

A specialty of south Texas, locally common in sand dune areas of Padre Island and Mustang Island. Also occurs on the mainland, in areas of deep sandy soil and sparse plant life. ▶ Notably *short-tailed* compared to most kangaroo rats. Barrier island populations have two color morphs, buffy gray and orange-yellow, both quite pale; easily identified by range, as no other kangaroo rats occur with them. The slightly darker yellow-brown populations on the south Texas mainland overlap with Ord's Kangaroo Rat (p. 198), which has a slightly longer and more bushy-tipped tail.

TEXAS KANGAROO RAT *Dipodomys elator*

This species has always had a rather limited range in northern Texas and adjacent Oklahoma, but with loss of its natural habitat it may now be restricted to just three Texas counties, where it lives in areas of grassland and mesquite. ▶ Fairly large for a kangaroo rat, with *white-tipped tail.* Ord's Kangaroo Rat (p. 198), the only other species that approaches its range, has a shorter, dark-tipped tail and has five toes on each hind foot, not four.

DARK KANGAROO MOUSE *Microdipodops megacephalus*

Aside from their differently shaped tails, kangaroo mice look like pint-sized kangaroo rats — and act like them, hopping about in areas of sparse plant life. The thickened area at the center of the tail is a deposit for fat and increases in size toward fall, as the animal stores up fat prior to hibernation. The Dark Kangaroo Mouse is widespread in the Great Basin region, in upland sandy desert dominated by big sagebrush. ▶ Smaller than any kangaroo rat in its range, with narrowly pointed tail. Some pocket mice (beginning on next page) look somewhat similar but are not such accomplished hoppers. Compare to next species.

PALE KANGAROO MOUSE *Microdipodops pallidus*

Limited to western Nevada, barely crossing the line into eastern California. Usually not in the same habitats as Dark Kangaroo Mouse (above), favoring lowland sandy desert dominated by greasewood and saltbush. ▶ Like Dark Kangaroo Mouse but with slightly larger hind feet. Much paler overall; best identified by tail color, about the same color as the back (Dark Kangaroo Mouse has tail darker above, black at the tip).

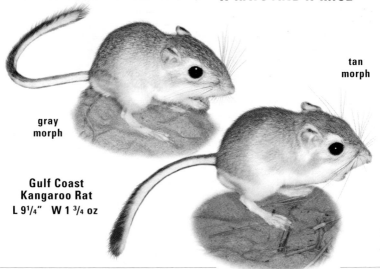

tan
morph

gray
morph

**Gulf Coast
Kangaroo Rat**
L 9¹/₄" W 1 ³/₄ oz

Texas Kangaroo Rat
L 11¹/₂" W 2³/₄ oz

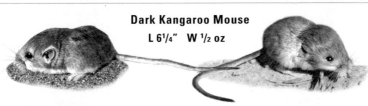

Dark Kangaroo Mouse
L 6¹/₄" W ¹/₂ oz

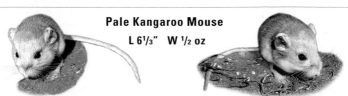

Pale Kangaroo Mouse
L 6¹/₃" W ¹/₂ oz

are named for their fur-lined cheek pouches, used for transporting seeds.

OLIVE-BACKED POCKET MOUSE *Perognathus fasciatus*

Fairly common on the northern Great Plains, in areas of dry grassland or open low scrub. ▶ Pocket mice have large hind feet and long tails; when alarmed they may escape by hopping, but they are not great leapers like the kangaroo rats (preceding section). This species has a yellowish stripe on its sides and is more *olive on the back* than others on this page. In northern parts of its range, this is the only pocket mouse.

PLAINS POCKET MOUSE *Perognathus flavescens*

This variable mouse occupies areas of sandy soil, from grassland to pinyon-juniper woodlands. Like other pocket mice, it eats mostly seeds but will also consume many insects when available. ▶ Varies in overall color, generally matching the color of local soil, with a few populations very pale or almost black. Narrow buffy line along sides. Larger than the next two species, and not olive above like Olive-backed Pocket Mouse.

SILKY POCKET MOUSE *Perognathus flavus*

A resident of dry short-grass plains and desert areas of the southwest. Like other pocket mice, it spends the day in its underground burrows, coming to the surface only at night. ▶ Very small, relatively shorter-tailed than the two preceding species, with distinct buffy patch behind each ear. Variably brown above, often with a buffy stripe along sides.

MERRIAM'S POCKET MOUSE *Perognathus merriami*

A close relative of the Silky Pocket Mouse, sometimes treated as belonging to the same species. Merriam's is locally common on short-grass plains and dry brushland. Like several of its relatives, it can survive without drinking water, obtaining moisture from its food. ▶ Almost identical to Silky Pocket Mouse, averaging paler and more yellowish above. Most readily separated by range (see maps).

GREAT BASIN POCKET MOUSE *Perognathus parvus*

Widespread in the Great Basin region, mainly in open sandy areas dominated by big sagebrush. Can survive on a diet of dry seeds but will eat insects and green vegetation when available. ▶ Of the silky-haired pocket mice (genus *Perognathus*), this is the largest. Rather dark brown above, with an olive-brown stripe on sides; tail bicolored (dark above, light below).

POCKET MICE

Olive-backed Pocket Mouse
L 5–5½" W ½ oz

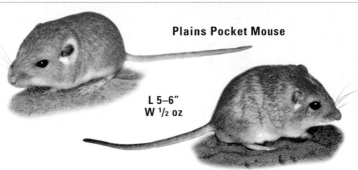

Plains Pocket Mouse

L 5–6"
W ½ oz

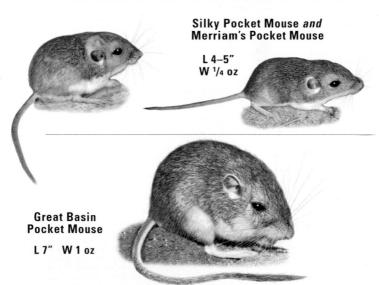

Silky Pocket Mouse *and*
Merriam's Pocket Mouse

L 4–5"
W ¼ oz

**Great Basin
Pocket Mouse**

L 7" W 1 oz

209

HISPID POCKET MOUSE *Chaetodipus hispidus*

Widespread on the Great Plains and in the southwest, from prairies to oak or pinyon-juniper woods, wherever there is a good understory of grass. ▶ Large for a pocket mouse, with a long bicolored tail that is thin at the tip. Olive-brown above and white below, with distinct *buffy stripe* on sides. Some on preceding page have similar color pattern but are smaller with much smoother fur ("hispid" means coarse or bristly).

BAILEY'S POCKET MOUSE *Chaetodipus baileyi*

Active all year in the Sonoran Desert, favoring shrubby areas on pebbly soil at the edges of hills. Able to eat the seeds of jojoba, which are poisonous to most mammals. ▶ Large for a pocket mouse, with long bicolored tail tufted at the tip. Drab grayish above, with coarse fur. Hispid Pocket Mouse (above) has buff side stripe; most other pocket mice in range are smaller.

LONG-TAILED POCKET MOUSE *Chaetodipus formosus*

In the Great Basin and in the Mojave and Colorado River Deserts, this pocket mouse inhabits rocky places with a good growth of shrubs such as sagebrush or creosotebush. Like other pocket mice, it is active only at night. ▶ Medium-sized, with conspicuously long bicolored tail tufted at the tip. Has soft fur and lacks contrasting stripe of color on sides. Compare to Desert Pocket Mouse and others on next page.

ARIZONA POCKET MOUSE *Perognathus amplus*

Found only in Arizona and Mexico, most commonly on open flats with grasses and low-growing shrubs. Generally inactive in winter, remaining in its burrow and mostly in a torpid condition, but not truly hibernating. ▶ Small, with a long tail that is thin at the tip. Usually orange-brown above but darker in areas with darker soil. Proportionately longer-tailed than Silky Pocket Mouse (previous page).

LITTLE POCKET MOUSE *Perognathus longimembris* (not illustrated)

Tiny but tough, surviving in extremely arid deserts and grasslands with no water and nothing but dry seeds to eat. Like some other desert creatures, likely to raise more young in wetter years when there is more plant growth. ▶ Very small, with a long tail that is thin at the tip. Color of upperparts varies from brown to gray. Averages smaller than other pocket mice in its range.

POCKET MICE

Hispid Pocket Mouse
L 8¹/₄" W 1¹/₃ oz

Bailey's Pocket Mouse
L 8¹/₄" W 1 oz

Long-tailed Pocket Mouse
L 7¹/₂" W ³/₄ oz

Arizona Pocket Mouse
L 6" W ¹/₂ oz

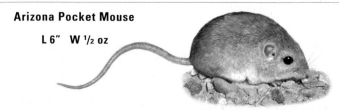

ROCK POCKET MOUSE   *Chaetodipus intermedius*

Common but inconspicuous in dry rocky country of the southwest. Like other pocket mice, active only at night; by day it remains in its burrow, which often has the entrance hidden under a rock. ▶ A medium-sized pocket mouse with coarse fur, including some stiff, spiny hairs on the rump. Long tail is tufted at the tip. Compare to next three species.

DESERT POCKET MOUSE   *Chaetodipus penicillatus*

In deserts of the southwest, this pocket mouse is common in areas with mesquites or palo verdes growing on fine sandy soils. Like other pocket mice, it stores seeds in chambers in its underground burrow and defends them against intruders. ▶ Medium-sized and long-tailed, with coarse fur but without spiny hairs on rump. Very similar to Rock Pocket Mouse (above) but less likely to show a contrasting buff stripe on sides.

CHIHUAHUAN POCKET MOUSE   *Chaetodipus eremicus* (not illustrated)

An inhabitant of the Chihuahuan Desert (pronounced chee-WAH-wahn), found commonly on open flats with creosotebush or mesquite growing on fine sandy soils. Only recently determined to be a separate species from the Desert Pocket Mouse. ▶ Very similar to Desert Pocket Mouse but averages a little larger. Best recognized by range, as they apparently do not overlap.

NELSON'S POCKET MOUSE   *Chaetodipus nelsoni*

A mouse of Mexico's central plateau, extending north through western Texas. Favors rocky places with sparse growth of desert shrubs and cacti. ▶ A medium-sized pocket mouse with coarse fur and numerous spines on the rump. Tail is long and is tufted at the tip. Grayer overall than most pocket mice, with white spots below the ears. Soles of hind feet are black (this is hard to see in the field!).

MEXICAN SPINY POCKET MOUSE   *Liomys irroratus*

Common in Mexico, this mouse barely enters the U.S. in south Texas, where it lives in remnants of native habitat such as subtropical brush or sabal palm groves. Classified in a separate subfamily from our other pocket mice, it differs from them in having an odd spoon-shaped claw on each hind foot. ▶ Large, with coarse spiny fur. The only other pocket mice in south Texas are the smaller Merriam's (p. 208) and the paler, less spiny Hispid (p. 210).

POCKET MICE

Rock Pocket Mouse
L 6³/₄" W ¹/₂ oz

Desert Pocket Mouse
L 6²/₃" W ³/₅ oz

Nelson's Pocket Mouse
L 7¹/₃" W ³/₅ oz

**Mexican Spiny
Pocket Mouse**
L 9" W 1¹/₂ oz

CALIFORNIA POCKET MOUSE *Chaetodipus californicus*

In coastal and foothill regions of California, this pocket mouse is still locally common in areas of dense chaparral and other scrub. Although it is mostly terrestrial like its relatives, it will also climb about in shrubs in search of food. ▶ Large for a pocket mouse, with coarse fur and with *stiff, whitish, spiny hairs* on its lower back and rump. Compare to next two species.

SAN DIEGO POCKET MOUSE *Chaetodipus fallax*

Limited to southwestern California and northern Baja, where it lives in various habitats from coastal sage scrub to rocky desert hills. Like other pocket mice, it hoards food for itself by storing seeds in chambers in its underground burrow system. ▶ Similar to California Pocket Mouse (above) but averages smaller. Differs from other pocket mice in its range in having a broad yellow or buff stripe along the sides.

SPINY POCKET MOUSE *Chaetodipus spinatus*

Widespread in Baja, extending north into very arid regions of southern California, where it lives in rocky desert with scattered low plants. Related to Rock Pocket Mouse (previous page), which replaces it just east of the Colorado River. ▶ A fairly large pocket mouse with coarse fur and with stiff, whitish, spiny hairs concentrated on its lower back and rump. Lacks buffy side stripe of San Diego Pocket Mouse and has slightly smaller ears than California Pocket Mouse.

SAN JOAQUIN POCKET MOUSE *Perognathus inornatus*

Like other creatures limited to California's central valleys, this species has lost much of its original habitat to development and agriculture. It is still locally common in some areas of grassland and arid scrub. ▶ A medium-small pocket mouse with smooth fur and with a long tail lacking an obvious tuft at the tip. Narrow buff stripe on sides, separating brown back from white belly.

WHITE-EARED POCKET MOUSE *Perognathus alticolus*

A rare and poorly known mouse with a very limited range, found only at a few spots in mountains on the edge of the Mojave Desert, at elevations between 3,000 and 6,000 feet. ▶ A medium-small pocket mouse with smooth fur. Compared to Little Pocket Mouse (p. 210) and San Joaquin Pocket Mouse (above), averages larger, with a more obvious dark tuft at tip of tail. Whitish or yellowish hair on ears is hard to see.

POCKET MICE

California Pocket Mouse
L 8¹/₂″ W ⁴/₅ oz

San Diego Pocket Mouse
L 7¹/₂″ W ²/₃ oz

Spiny Pocket Mouse
L 7²/₃″ W ¹/₂ oz

San Joaquin Pocket Mouse
L 5²/₃″ W ¹/₃ oz

White-eared Pocket Mouse
L 6″ W ²/₃ oz

are in a separate family (**Dipodidae**) from all other North American rodents. With large hind feet and very long tails, they somewhat resemble kangaroo rats (previous section), but they live in wetter habitats and do not have such a big-headed look. Jumping mice are omnivores, with diets that include seeds, berries, and insects; they also feed heavily on fungi. Their winter hibernation often lasts six months or more.

MEADOW JUMPING MOUSE   *Zapus hudsonius*

Common in open fields of rank grass or weeds but also enters forests with dense undergrowth, especially outside the range of the Woodland Jumping Mouse (below). When alarmed, may leap two to three feet. Like other jumping mice, active mainly at night. ▶ Known as a jumping mouse by shape and by tricolored pattern (dark back, yellow-buff sides, white belly). Tail is strongly *bicolored* (dark above, light below) and has *no white tip*. Compare to Western and Woodland Jumping Mice.

WESTERN JUMPING MOUSE   *Zapus princeps*

Mainly a mouse of western mountains, generally in damp habitats such as streamsides, wet meadows, or marshes. At high elevations it may be active for only three months of the year, hibernating for the other nine months. ▶ Similar to Meadow Jumping Mouse (above), which overlaps its range, but it averages larger, and its back may have a more grizzled or variegated look. The ears have a thin border of white hairs.

PACIFIC JUMPING MOUSE   *Zapus trinotatus*

Common in very humid habitats of the Pacific Northwest, from the understory of redwood groves to streamside alder thickets and wet mountain meadows. Like other jumping mice, it usually nests underground, but it will sometimes nest in trees. ▶ In most of its range, this is the only jumping mouse. Could be difficult to distinguish from Western Jumping Mouse (above) in areas where they occur close to each other, but this species lacks the white border on the ears.

WOODLAND JUMPING MOUSE   *Napaeozapus insignis*

An uncommon mouse of the forest understory, seldom coming out into open habitats. When alarmed, may live up to its name by leaping 10 feet or farther. ▶ Similar to Meadow Jumping Mouse (which sometimes enters woodlands) but tail has *white tip* (not always easy to see). Averages larger, and usually looks more reddish or orange on the sides, not so yellow.

JUMPING MICE

Meadow Jumping Mouse
L 8″   W ⅔ oz

Western Jumping Mouse
L 9″   W ¾ oz

Pacific Jumping Mouse
L 9″   W 1 oz

Woodland Jumping Mouse
L 9″   W ¾ oz

color variations

217

MEADOW VOLE   *Microtus pennsylvanicus*

Abundant in fields and grasslands over much of the continent. Famed as "the world's most prolific mammal," with females able to give birth to a new litter every three weeks; not surprisingly, it has frequent population cycles, peaking and crashing every two to five years, and affecting the populations of the many predators that rely on it. ▶ Stocky body, with relatively short tail and short muzzle. Brown above, pale gray below.

BEACH VOLE   *Microtus breweri* (not illustrated)

Found only on little Muskeget Island, Massachusetts, west of Nantucket Island. ▶ Like Meadow Vole but larger, paler, sometimes with white on the forehead or elsewhere on the head. The only vole on the island.

TUNDRA VOLE   *Microtus oeconomus*

Widespread in northern Russia, reaching our continent in the far northwest. Lives on tundra and in damp meadows in boreal forest regions. Active all year, even in high arctic climates, storing seeds and other food in fall to feed on during winter. ▶ Large for a vole, with small ears and short tail. Variable in color, reddish brown to gray, whitish below. Compare to Meadow, Taiga, and Singing Voles on this page.

TAIGA VOLE   *Microtus xanthognathus*

This vole lives on the edge of the Arctic, often in patchy habitats such as streamsides, bogs, and the new growth after fires. It feeds mainly on grasses and other simple plants. Like other voles, it travels regular runways through dense grass. ▶ Large for a vole and dusky brown, similar to some Tundra Voles (above) but identified by the *yellow-orange tinge* around its nose.

SINGING VOLE   *Microtus miurus*

An odd rodent of relatively dry tundra, named for its habit of sitting in the open in late summer and making a low metallic trilling. Another notable habit is its construction of "haypiles," sometimes quite large, consisting of willow shoots and many other plants, during late summer to serve as a food source in winter. ▶ Averages smaller and shorter-tailed than most voles in its range. Usually strongly tinged *buff,* especially below.

INSULAR VOLE   *Microtus abbreviatus* (not illustrated)

A relative of Singing Vole (above), found only on Hall and St. Matthew Islands in the Bering Sea, Alaska. (A bird, McKay's Bunting, shares the same very limited range.) ▶ The only rodent in its range. Like Singing Vole but averages slightly larger.

Meadow Vole
L 6²/₃″   W 1³/₄ oz

Tundra Vole
L 7¹/₂″   W 2 oz

Taiga Vole
L 7¹/₂″   W 4 oz

Singing Vole
L 5³/₄″   W 1¹/₂ oz

Insular Vole
L 6″   W 2 oz

219

WATER VOLE *Microtus richardsoni*

Our largest vole sticks close to streams and ponds in mountain meadows of the northwest. It swims well, including underwater. Active at all seasons, it digs tunnels under the snow in winter; in summer it travels well-established runways through dense low growth and digs burrows in the soil. ▶ Larger than other voles, brown above and grayish below. Noticeably *large* hind feet (about an inch long).

TOWNSEND'S VOLE *Microtus townsendii*

A vole of marshes and wet meadows, abundant in lowlands of the Pacific Northwest (but also found well up into the mountains of the Olympic Peninsula, Washington). Active all year, it feeds on a wide variety of marsh plants. ▶ Larger than most voles, dark brown overall, with relatively large ears. Water Vole mostly occurs farther east and at higher elevations. California Vole (next page) can be very similar.

CREEPING VOLE *Microtus oregoni*

This small vole favors grassy and weedy areas in wet coniferous forests of the northwest. It often burrows underground or under the accumulated leaf litter on the forest floor, spending less time aboveground than most voles. ▶ Smaller.than most of the voles in its range, very dark brown above, paler gray below. Its *eyes* look *very small.*

SAGEBRUSH VOLE *Lemmiscus curtatus*

Most voles are found in moist habitats, but this one lives in colonies in dry brushy places, often where sagebrush or bunchgrasses are the dominant plants. Most active around dawn and dusk, but it may be active at any hour year-round. Females may produce three or more litters per year. ▶ *Dull buff to gray* overall, with short tail. Other rodents in its habitat are longer-tailed or more strongly patterned.

LONG-TAILED VOLE *Microtus longicaudus*

Widespread but usually uncommon in the west, in areas with good cover such as forest edges, streamsides, or thickets. Restricted to mountains toward the south. Individuals range over larger areas than most voles and are less likely to travel established runways. ▶ Dusty gray to brownish gray, with a relatively long tail (about half of its head-plus-body length). Most voles in its range have shorter tails or richer brown colors.

WESTERN VOLES

Water Vole
L 10″ W 4 oz

Townsend's Vole
L 8″ W 2⅓ oz

Creeping Vole
L 5½″ W ⅔ oz

Sagebrush Vole
L 5″ W 1 oz

Long-tailed Vole
L 7″ W 1⅔ oz

221

PRAIRIE VOLE *Microtus ochrogaster*

Widespread and common in the heartland, on prairies, meadows, and farmland. Its abundance varies, with peaks in population every two to four years. A subspecies restricted to coastal Louisiana and Texas may now be extinct. ▶ Brown above, pale gray below. Meadow Vole (p. 218) averages longer-tailed; bog lemmings (p. 228) look distinctly shorter-tailed.

MONTANE VOLE *Microtus montanus*

An abundant rodent of the mountain west, favoring damp prairies, streamsides, and forests, and extending from low valleys up to above treeline. Active all year, even breeding in midwinter under the snow. ▶ Small and brown, pale gray below. Very similar to various other voles in its range. Long-tailed Vole (previous page) averages longer-tailed (appropriately); Meadow Vole (p. 218) may average darker.

CALIFORNIA VOLE *Microtus californicus*

Found mainly in meadows at low elevations but also in grassland with scattered oaks and in coastal marshes. In much of its range the main breeding season is during the wetter, cooler winter, when more green plants are available, not the dry summer. ▶ Similar to other voles in its range. Montane Vole is usually at higher elevations; Long-tailed Vole (previous page) has longer tail; Townsend's Vole (previous page) averages larger.

GRAY-TAILED VOLE *Microtus canicaudus*

Found only in the Willamette Valley of Oregon and a small area of Washington. Common in this limited range, in grasslands, pastures, and farm fields. Uses extensive burrow systems in summer but often forced out in the open by flooding in winter. ▶ Short tail is gray below, brown above. Eyes are relatively large. Townsend's and Water Voles (previous page) are larger, Creeping Vole (previous page) is smaller, with smaller eyes.

MOGOLLON VOLE *Microtus mogollonensis*

Limited to high-elevation habitats in the southwest, mainly in grassy areas and meadows surrounded by coniferous forest. Formerly considered to belong to same species as Mexican Vole, which lives south of the border. ▶ Montane Vole (above), Long-tailed Vole (previous page), and Western Red-backed Vole (next page) all occur in its range, but the first two are larger with longer tails and the latter is more colorful; they all tend to occur in wetter habitats in the mountains.

VOLES

Prairie Vole
L 6"
W 1½ oz

Montane Vole
L 7" W 2 oz

California Vole
L 7" W 2 oz

Gray-tailed Vole
L 6" W 1½ oz

Mogollon Vole
L 5¼" W 1 oz

SOUTHERN RED-BACKED VOLE   *Clethrionomys gapperi*

"Southern" only by comparison to the next species, this vole is common in damp forests of all kinds, willow thickets, and sedge meadows, especially where the ground is cluttered with logs and stumps. ▶ Has a medium-length tail for a vole. Variable in color, but the brighter morph is among the most colorful of rodents, with a distinct *reddish band* from the top of the head down the back, contrasting with grayish sides.

NORTHERN RED-BACKED VOLE   *Clethrionomys rutilus*

This species essentially replaces the Southern Red-backed Vole in northwestern Canada, where their ranges meet but barely overlap. It inhabits both open tundra and the edges of boreal forest. Its varied diet includes many leaves, seeds, berries, fungi, and lichens. ▶ Similar to Southern Red-backed Vole but somewhat paler, and the reddish may extend farther down on the sides. More colorful than other small arctic rodents.

WESTERN RED-BACKED VOLE   *Clethrionomys californicus*

Common in a limited region, from the coast into the mountains, mostly in very dense coniferous forest with little undergrowth. It spends much of its time in burrows underground, and it feeds heavily on fungi and lichens. ▶ Generally gray-brown, with a more reddish brown stripe down the center of the back. Coastal individuals tend to be darker and duller than those inland.

WOODLAND VOLE   *Microtus pinetorum*

Common in the east, mainly in moist deciduous or mixed forest, where it spends much of its time underground or under leaf litter. Its complexes of tunnels are often quite extensive, and several families may share a burrow system. It feeds on a variety of plant materials, especially seeds, berries, bulbs, roots, and bark. ▶ Small but chunky, with short tail, small eyes, and relatively large front feet, an adaptation for digging. Warm reddish brown above, grayish below.

ROCK VOLE   *Microtus chrotorrhinus*

A denizen of rocky places and streamsides in deciduous and mixed forests of the northeast, especially in moist areas with good ground cover. It feeds on green vegetation, such as the leaves and stems of bunchberry, and often stores up caches of food under rocks. ▶Medium-sized and mostly dark brown, with a distinct *yellow-orange wash* around the nose.

VOLES

Southern Red-backed Vole

L 5½″   W 1 oz

Northern Red-backed Vole

L 5½″   W 1 oz

Western Red-backed Vole

L 5½″
W 1 oz

Woodland Vole

L 5″
W 1 oz

Rock Vole

L 6″ W 1⅓ oz

RED TREE VOLE   *Arborimus longicaudus*

Tree voles are mysterious little rodents that spend most of their lives far above the ground in tall trees. This species is essentially restricted to western Oregon and is probably declining in numbers with the loss of the old-growth forest that it favors. It feeds mainly on the needles of Douglas-firs. ▶ Rather long tail for a vole; long soft fur is bright reddish brown. Best identified by range and habits.

SONOMA TREE VOLE   *Arborimus pomo*

Limited to a strip of northern California, mainly in old-growth forest with much Douglas-fir, feeding on large quantities of conifer needles. Like the Red Tree Vole, it builds a bulky nest for itself, often more than a foot in diameter and sometimes more than 100 feet above the ground. Males seem to come to the ground more often than females. ▶ Like Red Tree Vole (above) but slightly brighter reddish, best separated by range.

WHITE-FOOTED VOLE   *Arborimus albipes*   (not illustrated)

Rare and poorly known, apparently living in streamsides and alder thickets in the northwest, active only at night. Considered less arboreal than the tree voles, and may dig burrows. Feeds on a variety of green plants and roots. ▶ Long soft fur, duller and browner than that of the tree voles; tail is long and bicolored (dark above, white below). Feet are contrastingly *whitish above.*

EASTERN HEATHER VOLE   *Phenacomys ungava*

Widespread in the north but not often seen and seemingly rather scarce. This vole lives in underground burrows with several hidden entrances. It feeds on a wide variety of plant materials, including leaves, bark, berries, fungus, and lichens, and will often store food in piles near its burrows. ▶ Small, with short tail and small ears. Variably grayish brown overall, usually with a yellow wash, especially around the nose and rump.

WESTERN HEATHER VOLE   *Phenacomys intermedius*

With a limited range in the western mountains, usually at higher elevations, this vole is uncommon and poorly known. Like its eastern relative, it feeds on a variety of plant matter and caches extra food in piles outside its burrow entrances. ▶ Small and short-tailed, grayish brown above and paler below. Resembles a small version of Montane Vole (p. 222) but has a patch of short, stiff *orange hairs* inside ears.

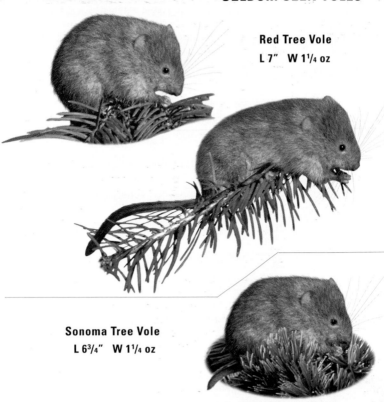

Red Tree Vole
L 7"   W 1¼ oz

Sonoma Tree Vole
L 6¾"   W 1¼ oz

Eastern Heather Vole
L 5½"   W 1 oz

Western Heather Vole
L 5½"   W 1 oz

LEMMINGS

are famous, although the best-known things about them are actually fictions. In northern Europe, the Norwegian Lemming sometimes reaches a peak population and then engages in mass movements, and during these movements some may drown while trying to swim across rivers or fjords. This is probably the source of the pervasive myth about suicidal lemmings jumping off cliffs.

BROWN LEMMING   *Lemmus trimucronatus*

Common on the tundra and active year-round, feeding on a variety of green plants in summer and eating many mosses in winter. One of the most important animals of the Arctic, affecting the lives of most of its neighbors. It goes through population cycles, hitting a peak of abundance every three or four years. Some predators, such as Snowy Owls and Least Weasels, are more likely to breed during peak lemming years; many nesting birds of the tundra are more likely to succeed in raising young during these peak years, when the predators are preoccupied with lemmings. ► Stocky and brown, with a very short muzzle, short tail, and often a *reddish area* on the rump. Northern Collared Lemming (next page) typically has more gray; Meadow Vole (p. 218) is not so short-tailed or blunt-faced.

SOUTHERN BOG LEMMING   *Synaptomys cooperi*

Bog lemmings look like small voles with large blunt heads. Despite the name, this species lives in various habitats, including mixed and coniferous woodlands, fields, and clearings, as well as bogs. It feeds on grasses, sedges, and other green plants as well as bark, roots, fungi, mosses, and other items. ► Small and short-tailed, dark brown overall. Most voles in its range have tails that are at least a little longer. Difficult to distinguish from next species where their ranges overlap.

NORTHERN BOG LEMMING   *Synaptomys borealis*

Widespread in the north but usually uncommon and seldom seen, despite its ability to live in a variety of habitats, from actual bogs to streamsides, meadows, forests, and alpine tundra. Active all year, using tunnels and nests beneath the snow in winter. ► Small, short-tailed, with short muzzle. Shorter-tailed and with different head shape than most voles in its range. Very similar to Southern Bog Lemming but averages grayer and usually shows a patch of *yellowish or buff hairs* at the base of the ears.

Brown Lemming
L 6″   W 3 oz

Southern Bog Lemming
L 5″   W 1¼ oz

Northern Bog Lemming
L 5″   W 1 oz

are well adapted to arctic life. Most populations have a seasonal color change, molting to white fur in winter (not illustrated here) that provides effective camouflage against snow. They also develop specialized claws on the front feet in winter, formed by enlargement and stiffening of the pads under two of the toes, making these lemmings more effective at digging through snow or frozen ground. Classification of this group is both complicated and unsettled; some authorities divide the North American populations into as many as nine species.

NORTHERN COLLARED LEMMING   *Dicrostonyx groenlandicus*

A lemming of open tundra, favoring relatively high, dry areas in summer. It extends north throughout the islands of the Canadian high Arctic, farther north than any other rodent. Active at all seasons, it lives mostly beneath the snow in winter, feeding on bark, buds, and twigs of willow thickets. ► A chunky little lemming with long fur and a very short tail. In summer, varies from brownish to blue-gray, with reddish brown accents and often with a hint of a *darker collar* on the neck. Turns white in winter. Populations on the Aleutian Islands, Alaska, are larger and do not develop the digging claws or the white pelage in winter; they may constitute a separate species.

UNGAVA COLLARED LEMMING   *Dicrostonyx hudsonius*

Limited to northern Quebec and Labrador and to a few adjacent islands. Usually in tundra and other open habitats, often in dry or rocky situations. ► Stocky and short-tailed. Dusty gray to brownish gray in summer, often with a dull *reddish brown patch* around the ears. Molts to white fur for the winter. No overlap in range with other collared lemmings. Northern Bog Lemming (previous page) is mostly in wetter habitats, and Meadow Vole (p. 218) has a longer tail; neither turns white in winter.

RICHARDSON'S COLLARED LEMMING   *Dicrostonyx richardsoni*

This lemming is limited to a region west of Hudson Bay, where it is often common in dry open tundra and rocky ridges. Like its relatives, it is active all year, using burrows in the ground in summer and burrows through the snow in winter. ► Similar in size and shape to other collared lemmings but usually *warmer reddish brown and buff* in summer; molts to white fur in winter. Range barely meets that of Northern Collared Lemming. Brown Lemming (previous page) averages larger and is often more reddish brown on rump area.

COLLARED LEMMINGS

**Northern
Collared Lemming**

L 5¹/₂" W 1¹/₂ oz

**Ungava
Collared Lemming**

L 5²/₃" W 2 oz

Richardson's Collared Lemming

L 5¹/₃" W 2 oz

SMALL BURROWERS

Some animals in this category are considered pests, as they dig in our fields and gardens, uprooting crops and sometimes eating them, and mounding up soil. Pocket gophers (and the odd Sewellel) are vegetarians and can cause a lot of damage at times, while moles are insectivores, eating insects and grubs that may be detrimental to our crops.

Members of three distinct families are included in this section.

Sewellel (family **Aplodontidae**): p. 234. Considered the world's most primitive living rodent, with no close relatives. (Despite its traditional name of "Mountain Beaver," it is not related to the beavers, nor is it usually found in mountains.) It burrows underground, coming out on the surface mainly at night. The Sewellel feeds on a wide variety of plants, including some that are toxic to other animals; it also reingests its own feces, as rabbits do, to make efficient use of all available nutrients.

Pocket gophers (family **Geomyidae**): pp. 234–240. Rodents specialized for a life underground, they are named for the fur-lined "pockets," or pouches,  in their cheeks, which have openings outside their mouth. They use these to carry food and nesting material but never dirt, and they can turn the pouches inside out for cleaning. All are solitary, digging extensive systems of burrows in which they spend virtually all their time.

Pocket gophers are built for digging and living underground, with large front claws on powerful forelegs, small ears and eyes, slim hips, and a short tail. Their ever-growing front incisors allow them to dig through soil with their mouth closed to keep out the dirt. These incisors are also good for cutting through the roots of plants. Pocket gophers are vegetarian, eating roots, tubers, and bulbs, as well as leaves and stems. Sometimes the first sign of a gopher's presence is the eerie sight of a whole plant slowly disappearing into the ground as the gopher pulls it under. Pocket gophers come to the surface only briefly (and usually only at night) to shovel out dirt from a burrow or to harvest vegetation near the burrow entrance. They store enough food in their burrows to last them through the winter, excavating the soil under snow cover and storing the soil in tunnels made in the snow. When the snow melts in the spring, these soil casts are distinctive indications of the work of a gopher.

When one pocket gopher accidentally connects to another's tunnel underground, it will plug the connection with soil. The entrances to their burrows are plugged with dirt on the surface — preserving the microclimate within the burrow while keeping out predators. Males visit the burrows of females only to mate with them. Females raise their young alone, and the young grow quickly and leave their mother's burrow. All pocket gophers require open areas and deep enough soil in which to construct their burrows; they push soil to the surface, forming fan-shaped or flattened mounds. They also require lots of low-growing vegetation for food.

Because pocket gophers tend to eat whatever plants are available, they can become pests in gardens or farm fields. In natural areas, however, their digging is beneficial in breaking up and aerating hard soils.

Populations of pocket gophers are sedentary and often isolated from other populations by stretches of unusable habitat, so they have evolved many local variations. Although most pocket gophers look very similar overall, individuals from one area may look different from members of their own species in other areas. This has made it difficult for biologists to classify these animals, and it is certainly difficult for naturalists to tell them apart, even on those uncommon occasions when we can actually see them! The information in this guide will allow you to make educated guesses about the pocket gophers in your area, but do not expect to identify them to species unless you are prepared to examine their skulls or their DNA.

Moles (family **Talpidae**): pp. 242–244.
These are not rodents but members of the order Insectivora, which also includes the shrews (next section) and hedgehogs. Like pocket gophers, moles are burrowing animals commonly found in our gardens, but moles eat great quantities of insects and grubs, not plant food. This means that they must range over much wider areas to find food and thus do not  tend to become so inbred. Also like pocket gophers, they are streamlined in shape, and their forelimbs are shaped for digging, but moles are smaller and they lack external ears. Their velvety fur bends both ways, allowing them to move forward or backward in their burrows with little hindrance. Their paddle-shaped feet do not come under them but move out to the side. A digging mole moves like a swimmer doing the breaststroke. Most species are solitary, defending their burrows from other moles, except during mating and raising of young. Their feeding and burrowing habits may actually be beneficial for gardens, as they aerate the soil and consume harmful insect pests.

SEWELLEL or MOUNTAIN BEAVER   *Aplodontia rufa*

An avid burrower, seldom seen because it ventures aboveground mainly at night. Lives in moist northwestern forests with deep enough soil for its burrows and enough dense underbrush to hide the six-inch-wide burrow entrances. Feeds on a wide variety of plant material, including ferns, nettles, rhododendron leaves, tree seedlings, and bark. Does not hibernate but stores food in its burrows. Mates in late winter, and two to four young are born in early spring. ▶ Good-sized rodent with short hairy tail, small eyes and ears, large claws, and long whiskers. Dark brown with whitish spot below each ear. Suggests an oversized pocket gopher with a hairier tail.

BOTTA'S POCKET GOPHER   *Thomomys bottae*

Found over a large area and in a wide variety of habitats, from desert to high mountain meadows, wherever the soil is deep enough for burrowing. Females may breed in their first year, having one or more litters of four to six (up to 10) pups, the numbers varying according to food availability. ▶ Variable in size and extremely variable in color, more or less matching the soil color where they live. Ranges from pale tan (almost white) to dark brown (almost black); short stubby ears have black around the bases. Many in Arizona have a white spot under the chin. Resembles Southern and Townsend's Pocket Gophers (next page) and interbreeds with them where their ranges overlap; they may all belong to the same species.

CAMAS POCKET GOPHER   *Thomomys bulbivorus*

Common in its limited range in the Willamette Valley of Oregon, where it sometimes becomes a pest by feeding on agricultural crops. Builds extensive burrows in which it lives a solitary life except when mating and raising young. ▶ Largest pocket gopher in the northwest. Dark brown with black on the muzzle and around the ears, gray below, usually with white patch on chin.

WYOMING POCKET GOPHER   *Thomomys clusius*   (not illustrated)

Limited to south-central Wyoming, in southeastern Sweetwater and southwestern Carbon Counties. It lives in gravelly soil dominated by greasewood on the tops of dry ridges or along the edges of eroded washes. ▶ Small and pale yellowish. Range is best clue. Overlaps only with Northern Pocket Gopher (next page), which averages larger and darker, with black spot behind ear.

SMALL BURROWERS

adult

young

Sewellel
L 14″ W 2¹/₃ lbs

at burrow
entrance

Botta's
Pocket Gopher

L 8¹/₂″ W 6 oz

Camas
Pocket Gopher

L 11″ W 14 oz

NORTHERN POCKET GOPHER *Thomomys talpoides*

Our most widespread pocket gopher, from deep rich soils to poor rocky soils, but must have enough soil for its extensive burrows and enough low-growing plants for food. Although it aerates the soil as it digs, thus encouraging plant growth, many farmers consider it a pest because it consumes crops. ▶ Gray-brown to yellow-brown, with black spot behind the ear.

IDAHO POCKET GOPHER *Thomomys idahoensis* (not illustrated)

Formerly considered the same species as Northern Pocket Gopher. Found in shallow, rocky soils; active all year, storing its excavated soil in burrows made in the snow during winter. ▶ Small, pale yellow-brown in Idaho and Montana, darker brown in Wyoming. Dark gray around the nose. Differs from Northern Pocket Gopher in its smaller size and lack of black ear patch.

WESTERN POCKET GOPHER *Thomomys mazama*

Found only west of the Cascades. May spend more time aboveground than most of its relatives. Feeds on roots, leaves, and seeds of various plants. ▶ Light to dark red-brown, gray underneath. Black patch behind ear is five times the size of the ear. Some individuals are all black. Northern Pocket Gopher is mostly separated by range. Mountain Pocket Gopher usually is duller.

TOWNSEND'S POCKET GOPHER *Thomomys townsendii*

Lives in deep moist soils of valleys in the Great Basin. May interbreed with Botta's Pocket Gopher where they meet. ▶ Varies from gray to brown, with dark nose and usually a black spot behind ear. Sometimes has white on top of head. Averages larger than other gophers in its range. Botta's (previous page) tends to be in drier habitats; Northern is usually at higher elevation.

SOUTHERN POCKET GOPHER *Thomomys umbrinus*

Only in Huachuca, Santa Rita, Pajarito, and Patagonia Mountains, Arizona, and Animas Mountains, New Mexico. Usually at higher elevations than Botta's Pocket Gopher (but they interbreed where they meet). ▶ Pale brownish at lower elevations, dark red-brown in mountain meadows, with a darker stripe from the nose down the middle of the back.

MOUNTAIN POCKET GOPHER *Thomomys monticola*

Found above 5,000 feet in the Sierra Nevada of central and northern California and extreme western Nevada. Prefers deep soils near edges of montane meadows, but also lives under open forests and near treeline. ▶ Reddish brown with black ear patch about three times the size of the ear. Similar to Western Pocket Gopher (above) but perhaps duller.

POCKET GOPHERS

young

**Northern
Pocket Gopher**
L 8²/₅" W 4 oz

**Western
Pocket Gopher**
L 8¹/₃" W 3¹/₂ oz

**Townsend's
Pocket Gopher**
L 10¹/₂" W 9 oz

**Mountain
Pocket Gopher**
L 8¹/₅" W 3¹/₅ oz

**Southern
Pocket Gopher**
L 8¹/₂" W 4¹/₂ oz

237

Genetic studies have shown that Plains, Attwater's, Baird's, Llano, and Knox Jones's Pocket Gophers (this page and next) are actually separate species. Formerly they were all treated as one wide-ranging species. All pocket gophers of the genus *Geomys* look very much alike: they cannot be identified in the field except (in some cases) by range.

PLAINS POCKET GOPHER   *Geomys bursarius*

Common in sandy soils across the Great Plains and has adapted well to altered habitats such as cemeteries and roadsides. It feeds on roots, stems, and leaves of weeds and grasses, also acorns. Solitary in its extensive burrows like all pocket gophers, it gets together with others of its kind only to mate. Females have one or two litters each year of up to eight young. ▶ Medium-sized, variable in color (generally matching local soil), sometimes with a white blaze on top of its nose. The only pocket gopher in parts of its range (see maps).

ATTWATER'S POCKET GOPHER   *Geomys attwateri* (not illustrated)

This gopher is very common on the Texas coastal plain, especially in areas of sandy soils of clay loam with good growth of grass and weeds. Its burrows have looping tunnels, unlike those of most pocket gophers. Feeds on all parts of grasses and perennial weeds. ▶ Adults are some shade of brown to match local soil, juveniles are gray. Overlaps with Baird's (below) and Texas (next page) Pocket Gophers, not safely separated in the field.

BAIRD'S POCKET GOPHER   *Geomys breviceps*

Found only in sandy soils, this pocket gopher sometimes builds its nesting mounds aboveground to reduce flooding of its living quarters and the stored food during rainy months. It feeds on roots, stems, and leaves of many plants. ▶ Variable, pale brown to black. The only pocket gopher in parts of its range, but not safely identified where it overlaps with Plains or Attwater's Pocket Gophers (above).

YELLOW-FACED POCKET GOPHER   *Cratogeomys castanops*

Tolerant of more arid conditions than other gophers, expanding its range in some areas. Lives in deep sandy or silty soils with mesquite, cactus, or grassland. Digs very long burrows, with a shallow level for feeding and a deeper level for nesting and storing food. In some areas females produce litters year-round of up to five young. ▶ Moderately large, pale buff to dark reddish brown, lighter below. Distinguished from other pocket gophers in the U.S. by its larger eyes.

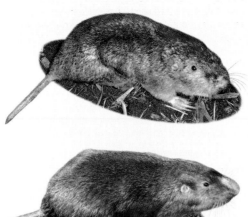

**Plains
Pocket Gopher**

L 10¹/₂"   W 6¹/₂ oz

Baird's Pocket Gopher

L 8"   W 3¹/₂ oz

**Yellow-faced
Pocket Gopher**

L 10¹/₂"   W 11 oz

SOUTHEASTERN POCKET GOPHER *Geomys pinetis*

This gopher of the southeastern piney woods is locally called "sandy mounder" for its habit of mounding up sandy earth at its burrow entrances. Lives in deep, dry, sandy soils on the coastal plains, under open stands of pine and oak. Feeds on roots and tubers of local plants, including crops such as sweet potatoes and peanuts. Females produce one or two litters per year of up to three young. ▶ Tan to gray-brown, with paler feet and underparts. The only pocket gopher in its range.

TEXAS POCKET GOPHER *Geomys personatus*

In the U.S., restricted to deep sandy soils of the lower Rio Grande Valley and south Texas. ▶ Moderate size, but size varies with soil density. Dull gray-brown, lighter below. Yellow-faced Pocket Gopher (previous page), which may overlap in range, has larger eyes. Not safely distinguished from Attwater's Pocket Gopher (previous page) where their ranges meet.

LLANO POCKET GOPHER *Geomys texensis* (not illustrated)

Also called Central Texas Pocket Gopher, but we prefer the shorter Llano (pronounced YAH-no). Limited to two isolated areas of the Texas Hill Country, in oak-juniper habitats in the north and mesquite scrub toward the south. ▶ Mostly reddish brown above, paler below, with whitish feet and short tail. May be identified by range, but it looks just like related pocket gophers.

DESERT POCKET GOPHER *Geomys arenarius*

Locally common in regions of deep sandy soils, not in extreme desert, despite the name. The subspecies of the Tularosa Basin, New Mexico (White Sands region), is perhaps being displaced by the Yellow-faced Pocket Gopher (previous page), which is more tolerant of arid conditions. ▶ Light sandy brown, paler below. Yellow-faced Pocket Gopher is larger, with larger eyes. Botta's Pocket Gopher (p. 234) is smaller.

KNOX JONES'S POCKET GOPHER *Geomys knoxjonesi* (not illustrated)

Found in open grasslands on sandy soil in western Texas and southeastern New Mexico. May interbreed with Plains Pocket Gopher (previous page) where their ranges meet. Some scientists believe it belongs to same species as Desert Pocket Gopher. ▶ Buff-brown on back, paler on sides, light below. Not safely distinguished from other members of genus *Geomys*. Yellow-faced Pocket Gopher (previous page) has larger eyes.

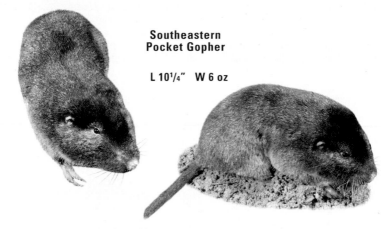

**Southeastern
Pocket Gopher**

L 10¼″   W 6 oz

**Texas
Pocket Gopher**

L 10³/₅″   W 10 oz

**Desert
Pocket Gopher**

L 10″   W 7²/₅ oz

Moles have tubular bodies, tiny eyes, no external ears, and paddle-shaped feet for digging. Look for the raised ridges they leave when they tunnel just below the soil's surface.

EASTERN MOLE   *Scalopus aquaticus*

Our most widespread and common mole, living in moist loamy or sandy soils in much of the eastern U.S. Active year-round, it rarely comes to the surface. Human activities actually benefit the mole, by breaking up hard soils and providing needed moisture. Eastern moles eat insects and grubs but especially like earthworms. They construct extensive burrows with a deep level of tunnels for living and shallower tunnels for feeding. Adults are solitary and territorial, defending their burrows from other moles, except when mating happens in the fall. Females bear one litter each spring of two to five young. ▶ Varies in size and color, generally smaller and paler toward the south. Compare to next two species.

HAIRY-TAILED MOLE   *Parascalops breweri*

This northeastern mole inhabits sandy loam soils under various types of forest, as well as under meadows and fields with good plant cover. Like other moles, it eats earthworms and a variety of insects. In winter, deeper burrows are expanded and individuals live alone. Males leave their winter burrows to join females in spring for mating. Females remain solitary after mating and construct a leaf-lined nest far below the surface. More gregarious in late summer, when several may be found together in the same burrow system. ▶ Gray, black, or dark brown with a very hairy tail. Eastern Mole has a longer snout and its tail is less hairy.

STAR-NOSED MOLE   *Condylura cristata*

Its space-alien face makes this mole unique. The 11 pairs of fleshy protuberances surrounding the nostrils are good for more than looks: extremely sensitive to touch, they allow the mole to feel its way in the dark, and they may be able to detect electrical fields given off by certain prey in the water. The Star-nosed Mole prefers very wet habitats. Active all year, it tunnels in mud or snow, travels surface runways at night, and swims very well: its streamside burrows often have openings underwater. Females bear one litter of about five young in nests lined with leaves and grass. ▶ Blackish, with long scaly tail and starlike nose appendages.

MOLES OF THE EAST

emerging from hole
using broad feet

color
variations

Eastern Mole
L 6″
W 2⁴/₅ oz

Hairy-tailed Mole
L 6¹/₃″   W 1⁴/₅ oz

Star-nosed Mole

L 7″   W 2¹/₅ oz

TOWNSEND'S MOLE   *Scapanus townsendii*

Our largest mole lives in deep loam in meadows only from the Cascade Mountains westward. Feeds on earthworms and insects like other moles, but also consumes much plant material. Compared to other moles, this species constructs deeper burrows, with more molehills, and fewer shallow foraging tunnels. ▶ Large and grayish black, with very few hairs on its short tail. Compare to the very similar Coast Mole (below). Broad-footed Mole (below) has a hairier tail.

COAST MOLE   *Scapanus orarius*

Common in a wide variety of habitats (not just near the coast). Feeds on insects and other invertebrates year-round but is most common where there are lots of earthworms. ▶ Very similar to Townsend's Mole (which overlaps western part of its range), but prefers well-drained soil near beaches or streams or in forests, which Townsend's avoids. However, these two species can be found in the same field. Coast Mole averages a bit smaller. Broad-footed Mole (below) has hairier tail.

BROAD-FOOTED MOLE   *Scapanus latimanus*

Widespread in and near California. Common from sea level up to 9,000 feet, mostly in moist soils but also in boulder fields with dry soil. Prefers earthworms but also eats insects, snails, slugs, spiders, centipedes, and some plant material. Forms molehills on the surface as it burrows. ▶ Gray or black, with short hairy tail. The only mole in most of its range. Distinguished from the two preceding species by its hairier tail.

AMERICAN SHREW MOLE   *Neurotrichus gibbsii*

This odd little mole suggests a shrew in some ways: it is agile and often aboveground, even climbing bushes in search of insects. Most common in shady ravines and along streams, in loose soils with good cover of leaf litter, grass, or shrubs. Constructs shallow runways under the leaf litter, where it forages for insects, pillbugs, and earthworms. Also digs deeper burrows, which lack mounds and have many entrances. Unlike other moles, it may live in small groups. Females may nest aboveground, raising litters of up to four young. ▶ Dark gray to black. Much smaller than other moles and may look proportionately longer-tailed. Might be confused with a shrew (next section) but note the smaller eyes, broader forepaws, and lack of external ears.

MOLES OF THE WEST

emerging from burrow

not to scale

Townsend's Mole
L 8¼″ W 4 oz

Coast Mole

L 6⅓″
W 2¾ oz

Broad-footed Mole

L 6½″
W 1⅗ oz

American Shrew Mole

L 4½″
W ⅓ oz

245

SHREWS

(family **Soricidae**) are often mistaken for small mice, but they are not related to mice or other rodents; they belong to the order Insectivora. Shrews range from small to tiny, with the smallest adult shrews measuring only three inches from head to tail tip and weighing only $^6/_{100}$ of an ounce (about half as much as a penny). Compare such shrews to the Blue Whale, at 110 feet long and some 200 tons, and it is difficult to believe that they both belong to the same group of vertebrates, the mammals!

Not only are they the smallest mammals in North America, shrews are also the most active. Because of their small size, their surface area is large relative to their body volume, so they lose heat rapidly. Only their high metabolic rate allows them to keep warm in cool weather. Therefore, shrews must be constantly refueling themselves to avoid starving to death, and they may consume an amount of food up to more than half their body weight each day. They eat mostly insects and a wide variety of other invertebrates, such as earthworms, centipedes, slugs, and snails. They are not limited to invertebrates, however: as voracious hunters, they take almost any kind of prey they can overcome, such as mice, fish, reptiles, and amphibians, and they also feed on carrion. Poisonous secretions in the saliva of some species help them subdue their prey. Because their teeth are not designed for injecting this poison, they must chew it into whatever they are attacking; the toxins may immobilize small prey such as mice and may paralyze some kinds of invertebrates (such as snails) so that they remain fresh longer than if they had been killed immediately. Some species of shrews are known to use echolocation, making high-pitched sounds and listening for the echoes off of nearby objects, allowing them to navigate through their surroundings and perhaps to find food.

Shrews mostly live solitary lives in the leaf litter of forest floors or in underground burrows. They lose water rapidly because of their frenetic life style, so they prefer moist habitats, even aquatic ones like streams, ponds, and marshes. The mating season is from early spring to late fall, and short pregnancies and large litters allow populations to grow rapidly during the summer. Shrews are active all winter, burrowing under the snow. They reduce their weight in winter — possibly to lower their food intake needs.

Shrews have very small eyes and small ears that are mostly buried in their fur. They apparently have poor eyesight but keen senses of hearing and smell. Their snouts are long and mobile with long whiskers, allowing them to feel their way along and find hidden insects. Shrews have musk glands that give off an odor when handled. These glands produce odors that are probably important in social interactions such as attracting mates, but they may also deter predators by making the shrew taste bad. Shrews live short lives, about one and a half years at the most.

Field identification of the different species of shrews ranges from very difficult to impossible. In many cases, even scientists who study these animals can separate the species only by examining the structure of the teeth, the amount of red-brown pigment on the tips of certain teeth, or the structure of the skull. Some shrews can be reliably identified only by chromosome number. And there are

still a number of unresolved issues of classification: there are probably still some cryptic species of shrews in North America that have not yet been recognized. So even if you see a shrew that looks exactly like one of the pictures in this book, it may not be that species! Still, by studying the range maps in this guide, by considering habitat clues, and by paying attention to details like the length of the tail, you should be able to make an educated guess about the identity of a shrew when you are lucky enough to see one well.

Shrews are harmless and interesting animals that can survive even in gardens and suburbs in some areas if their human neighbors do not make it impossible for them. Keep housecats indoors, as they take a serious toll on shrews and other small mammals. Also, avoid using pesticides in the garden, because these poisons generally kill off far more than just the intended targets, and they will certainly reduce the amount of insect food available for shrews (as well as for songbirds and other popular creatures).

WATER SHREW   *Sorex palustris*

Most common along swift streams but also found at ponds and marshes. A good swimmer and diver, it has large feet edged with fringes of stiff hairs, enabling it to run for several seconds across the water's surface. Feeds on aquatic insects and other invertebrates as well as some small fish and salamanders. ▶ Large for a shrew, dark gray above, whitish below, with fringed feet. Compare to next species. Other shrews in its range are smaller.

MARSH SHREW   *Sorex bendirii*

Usually around marshes or streamsides. Like Water Shrew, can run on surface of water briefly, swim and dive well. ▶ Large, sooty gray all over. Very similar to Water Shrew but has a darker belly (except on Olympic Peninsula, Washington, where Marsh Shrews are pale-bellied). Lacks the fringe of hair on the feet of Water Shrew. Other shrews in its range are smaller.

TROWBRIDGE'S SHREW   *Sorex trowbridgii*

Common and widespread in mature coniferous forests. Constructs burrows in loose soils and runways in leaf litter, where it forages for a wide variety of foods. Eats insects, spiders, centipedes, worms, fungi, and Douglas-fir seeds, which it hoards. ▶ Body dark gray above and below, with distinctly bicolored tail. Marsh Shrew is larger; other shrews in its range are paler on the belly.

MERRIAM'S SHREW   *Sorex merriami*   (not illustrated)

More tolerant of dry conditions than most shrews. Widespread in sagebrush scrub, also in prairies, pinyon-juniper woods, and coniferous forests. ▶ Small, grayish brown, darker on back and whitish below. Tail is distinctly bicolored, grayish on top and whitish below. Probably not safely separable from Montane Shrew (p. 256) in the field, although habitat is a clue.

ARIZONA SHREW   *Sorex arizonae*

Only in Chiricahua, Huachuca, and Santa Rita Mountains, Arizona; Animas Mountains, New Mexico; and in Mexico. Mainly near water in rocky canyons. ▶ Pale brown, paler below. The only shrew in the Huachucas and Santa Ritas. In the Chiricahuas, Montane Shrew (p. 256) averages larger.

PREBLE'S SHREW   *Sorex preblei*   (not illustrated)

Uncommon to rare, reported from scattered points in arid shrublands in Oregon, California, Idaho, Montana, Nevada, and Wyoming; also oak grasslands in New Mexico and Colorado, wetter alkaline habitat in Utah, and forests of eastern Washington. ▶ Very small, gray above and silvery below, with bicolored tail darker toward tip. Not safely identified in the field.

SHREWS

Water Shrew

L 6″ W ½ oz

Marsh Shrew

L 6″ W ½ oz

Trowbridge's Shrew

L 4³/₅″ W ⅕ oz

Arizona Shrew

L 4″ W ³/₁₀ oz

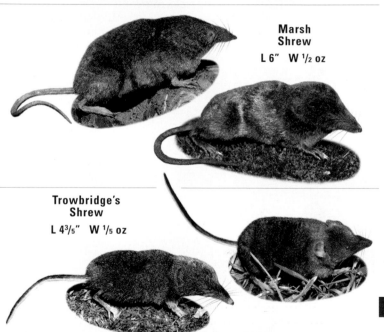

SMOKY SHREW — *Sorex fumeus*

Common in moist forests, sometimes in bogs and swamps. Active at night in all seasons, it runs about frenetically through the leaf litter, over boulders and under rotten logs, feeding on insects, earthworms, centipedes, and sometimes fungi or even salamanders. Constantly twitches its nose and twitters as it runs about foraging, perhaps using echolocation to navigate in the dark. ▶ Medium-sized shrew, brown above in summer, dark gray above in winter (and in juveniles), paler below. Moderately long tail, but not proportionately as long as in Long-tailed Shrew (below). Water Shrew (previous page) is much larger and is whiter below.

SOUTHEASTERN SHREW — *Sorex longirostris*

Common in a variety of wet to dry habitats with dense ground cover, but not often seen. Forages in leaf litter and in burrows of other animals, seeking spiders (its main prey) as well as insects, slugs, snails, centipedes, and other creatures. Females bear two or more litters of one to six young. ▶ Small, reddish brown, with a long narrow snout. Tail is fairly long (at least half as long as head and body combined). In parts of its range, other shrews have shorter tails. Not safely separated from Pygmy Shrew (p. 254) where they overlap. Compare to Cinereus Shrew (p. 254).

LONG-TAILED SHREW — *Sorex dispar*

Also called Rock Shrew for its preference for cool shaded areas under talus slopes or near rocky streams. Once considered rare, this species is just not often observed, since it spends most of its time under boulders. ▶ Small, slender, and slaty gray all over, including the very long tail, which is almost as long as the head and body combined. Smoky Shrew (above) in winter is similar but paler gray, with a tail only two-thirds as long. Water Shrew (previous page) is larger, white underneath, and has a distinctive fringe of hairs on its feet.

GASPÉ SHREW — *Sorex gaspensis* (not illustrated)

Closely related to Long-tailed Shrew, replacing it in the Maritime Provinces of Canada (the population of Gaspé Shrews in New Brunswick is only about 30 miles from a population of Long-tailed Shrews in Maine). Prefers habitat along rocky streams and in mixed forests. ▶ Very much like Long-tailed Shrew; slightly smaller and paler. Gray color and tail length separate it from other shrews in its range.

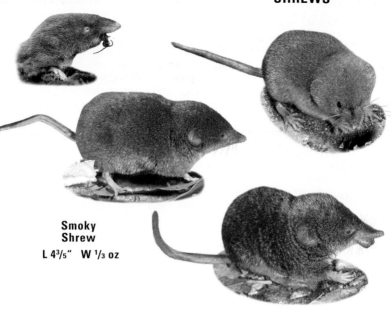

Smoky Shrew
L 4³/₅" W ¹/₃ oz

Southeastern Shrew
L 3¹/₂"
W ¹/₇ oz

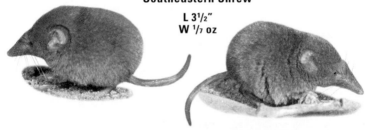

Long-tailed Shrew
L 4⁷/₁₀" W ¹/₅ oz

LEAST AND NORTHERN SHREWS

LEAST SHREW   *Cryptotis parva*

Common in brushy fields but also occurs in marshes and woods. Apparently more social than most shrews; several may be found in the same nest. Eats many insects as well as spiders and earthworms. ▶ Small, brownish in summer, grayish in winter (and in juveniles). Short tail, less than 45 percent as long as head and body. Most shrews in its range have longer tails. Compare to short-tailed shrews (p. 258).

ARCTIC SHREW   *Sorex arcticus*

Common in boreal forest regions, favoring marshy clearings and meadows. It is active day and night, foraging primarily for insects. ▶ Fairly large. Adults in summer are distinctly tricolored, while juveniles and winter adults are more uniformly brown with paler underparts. Similar to Tundra and Barren Ground Shrews but averages larger; best separated by range.

MARITIME SHREW   *Sorex maritimensis*   (not illustrated)

Until recently, considered a subspecies of Arctic Shrew (above). Occurs only at overgrown edges of freshwater marshes in Nova Scotia and New Brunswick. ▶ Similar to Arctic Shrew but no overlap in range. Tricolored pattern more distinct than on other shrews in the Maritime Provinces.

TUNDRA SHREW   *Sorex tundrensis*

Our most colorful shrew, common in alder thickets and other dense growth at the edges of tundra hillsides. Habits are poorly known, but females probably have several litters of young in a season. ▶ Tricolored pattern in summer, with rich brown back, tan sides, pale gray belly (pattern less distinct in winter). Barren Ground Shrew (below) is similar but averages smaller and duller. No range overlap with Arctic Shrew (above).

BARREN GROUND SHREW   *Sorex ugyunak*   (not illustrated)

Widespread on the tundra north of treeline, across the arctic slope of Alaska and Canada; apparently sometimes common, but its habits are poorly known. Has been found in sedge meadows and in thickets of dwarf willows. ▶ Tricolored pattern like that of the Tundra Shrew, with brown back sharply set off from tan sides (grayer in winter) and paler belly, but averages much smaller and perhaps duller brown above.

PRIBILOF ISLAND SHREW   *Sorex pribilofensis*   (not illustrated)

Found only on St. Paul Island in the Pribilof Islands, west of mainland Alaska, a treeless island with lush grasses and tundra plants. ▶ The only shrew in the Pribilofs. Resembles Barren Ground Shrew (above).

SHREWS

Least Shrew
L 3″   W 1/5 oz

young

Arctic Shrew
L 4 1/2″   W 3/10 oz

Tundra Shrew
L 3 7/10″   W 1/4 oz

PYGMY SHREW *Sorex hoyi*

Very common in the north, in forests, marshes, and clearings with dense understory; less common farther south. Often stands up on its hind legs. ▶ Very small, especially in southern part of range (where it may weigh only ⁷/₁₀₀ of an ounce). Warm brown to gray-brown above, paler below; muzzle is paler than top of head. Tail makes up about a third of total length. In southern part of range, tiny size is diagnostic. In the north, compare to Cinereus Shrew (below).

CINEREUS SHREW *Sorex cinereus* (Masked Shrew)

Widespread and common, especially in moist habitats with dense low cover, but active mainly at night and seldom seen. ▶ Small, brownish above, pale gray below. Tail is long (makes up about 40 percent of total length), with blackish tip (can be hard to see). Pygmy Shrew and Prairie Shrew have shorter tails without dark tips, but not always safely identified by sight. Vagrant and Montane Shrews (next page) have shorter muzzles.

MT. LYELL SHREW *Sorex lyelli* (not illustrated)

Rare. Lives above 6,000 feet in the the central Sierra Nevada of California (Tuolumne and Mono Counties). ▶ Very similar to Cinereus Shrew (no range overlap). Not reliably separated from other shrews in its range.

PRAIRIE SHREW *Sorex haydeni* (Hayden's Shrew)

An uncommon shrew of the northern plains, found in grasslands, dry pine woods, marshes, grassy bogs, and lake and river edges. ▶ Small, brown with short tail. Once considered a subspecies of Cinereus Shrew (above), and it is difficult even for experts to distinguish these two species except by dental differences. However, Cinereus Shrew has a black tuft on the tip of its longer tail.

DWARF SHREW *Sorex nanus*

As the smallest ones are less than ⁶/₁₀₀ of an ounce, this species rivals Pygmy Shrew (above) as the tiniest mammal in North America. Widepread in the Rockies region in a variety of habitats, sometimes far from water. ▶ Very small, brown above in summer, grayer in winter. Smaller than most shrews in its range, but probably not reliably identified except by dental characteristics.

INYO SHREW *Sorex tenellus* (not illustrated)

Localized in southwestern Nevada and the slopes of the Sierra Nevada in Mono and Inyo Counties, California. Mostly in rocky places in coniferous forest. ▶ Similar to Dwarf Shrew (no range overlap). Smaller than other shrews in its habitat, but reliably identified only by dental characteristics.

SHREWS

Pygmy Shrew

L 3³/₅″ W ¹/₅ oz

Cinereus Shrew

L 3⁴/₅″ W ¹/₁₀ oz

Prairie Shrew

L 3²/₅″ W ¹/₁₀ oz

Dwarf Shrew

L 3³/₅″
W less than ¹/₁₀ oz

MONTANE SHREW   *Sorex monticolus* (Dusky Shrew)

One of the most common shrews in moist habitats, with dense low cover throughout its range. ▶ Large, dusky brown to gray above, silvery white to grayish below; tail is bicolored. This shrew is larger than the other shrews in its range except Water Shrew (p. 248). Montane Shrew and the next four species are all closely related, difficult to separate except by differences in the structure of their teeth.

VAGRANT SHREW   *Sorex vagrans*

Apparently named for typical frenetic activity; no more of a "vagrant" than other shrews. Lives in moist, dense habitats, such as marshes and streamsides. ▶ In summer, rusty or brown above, paler below. In winter, gray or almost black, paler below. Ornate Shrew averages smaller, others on this page average larger, but they are not safely identified except by dental characteristics.

ORNATE SHREW   *Sorex ornatus*

Mainly in California marshes and streamsides but also found in woods and chaparral with dense low cover. Some salt marsh populations are now threatened by loss of habitat owing to continuing development along the coast. ▶ Despite the name, not very ornate: drab gray-brown above fading to paler below. Subspecies in salt marshes may be much darker gray. Usually the smallest shrew in its habitat but not safely separated from Vagrant Shrew where they overlap.

BAIRD'S SHREW   *Sorex bairdii* (not illustrated)

Only in northwestern Oregon, in wet coniferous forests. ▶ Very similar to Vagrant Shrew, averages larger but not reliably identified in the field.

PACIFIC SHREW   *Sorex pacificus*

Mainly in western Oregon, in moist areas with rotting logs and brushy thickets in coniferous forests and along streams. Mostly nocturnal. Eats insects, centipedes, snails, and other invertebrates, small amphibians, fungi, and other items. ▶ Big (for a shrew), dark cinnamon brown all over. Long tail, more than three-quarters the length of head and body combined. Similar to others on this page but might be recognized by size and color.

FOG SHREW   *Sorex sonomae* (not illustrated)

Common in the fog belt along the Pacific Coast from Lincoln County, Oregon, south to Marin County, California. Found in damp habitats with dense low cover. ▶ Averages about as large as Pacific Shrew but is often a duller brown. Reliably identified only by dental details.

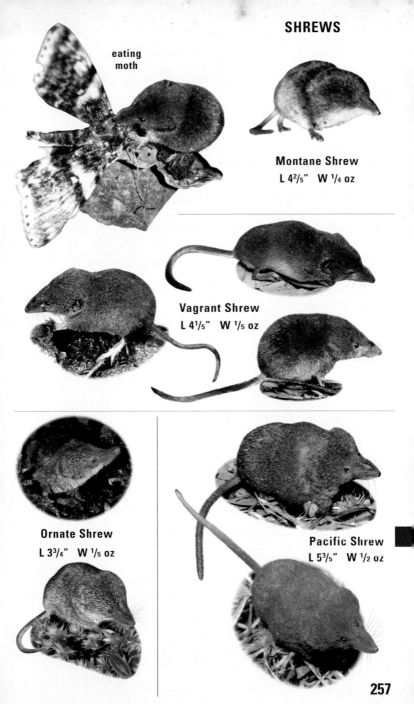

SHREWS

eating moth

Montane Shrew
L 4²/₅" W ¹/₄ oz

Vagrant Shrew
L 4¹/₅" W ¹/₅ oz

Ornate Shrew
L 3³/₄" W ¹/₅ oz

Pacific Shrew
L 5³/₅" W ¹/₂ oz

257

The short-tailed shrews (genus *Blarina*) were all formerly regarded as one species, and differences among them are still poorly known. They differ mainly in chromosome number and slightly in average size. In most places they can be separated by range, but where they overlap, they cannot be distinguished in the field.

NORTHERN SHORT-TAILED SHREW   *Blarina brevicauda*

Common in woods and clearings with dense ground cover and well-drained soil. Feeds on a variety of small creatures; it has poisonous saliva, which may help it to kill small animals or to paralyze some invertebrates for later consumption. ▶ Compared to most shrews, the three short-tailed species have shorter, broader snouts, a more robust body shape, and proportionately shorter tails. Uniformly silvery gray to blackish, with brownish tips to the fur; generally darker in winter.

SOUTHERN SHORT-TAILED SHREW   *Blarina carolinensis*

A shrew of moist woods in well-drained soil, especially under dead wood. Nocturnal, feeds on insects and other invertebrates. Apparently eats more nuts, berries, and other vegetation than most shrews. Its short snout and enlarged front feet are helpful in digging; like other short-tailed shrews, it digs extensive burrows. ▶ Averages smaller than the other two short-tailed shrews but not identifiable where their ranges overlap.

ELLIOT'S SHORT-TAILED SHREW   *Blarina hylophaga*

Found in mature floodplain forest, grassy woods of oak or pine, or along wet ditches or streams. Does not require much ground cover if the soil is soft enough for it to burrow deeply. Mostly in south-central states, with an isolated population on central Texas coast. Feeds on invertebrates but also small animals that it subdues with its poisonous saliva. ▶ Averages intermediate in size between Northern and Southern Short-tailed Shrews but not identifiable where their ranges overlap.

DESERT SHREW   *Notiosorex crawfordi*

The only shrew found in the deserts and semiarid ponderosa pine or pinyon-juniper woodlands of the southwest. Well adapted to its desert environment, does not require drinking water. Does not burrow, constructing its nests in woodrat middens or under brush piles. Probably eats mostly invertebrates and carrion in the wild. ▶ Brownish gray or silvery gray above, paler underneath, with long pointed muzzle, large ears for a shrew, and medium-length tail. Other shrews in its range are restricted to the mountains.

SHREWS

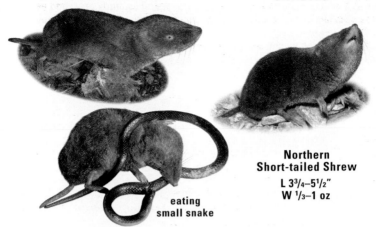

eating
small snake

**Northern
Short-tailed Shrew**
L 3³/₄–5¹/₂″
W ¹/₃–1 oz

**Southern
Short-tailed Shrew**
L 3–4¹/₄″
W ¹/₅–¹/₂ oz

**Elliot's
Short-tailed Shrew**
L 3¹/₂–4³/₄″
W ¹/₂ oz

Desert Shrew
L 3²/₅″   W ¹/₅ oz

eating
grub

BATS

are the only mammals with wings, and the only ones capable of true flight (the so-called flying squirrels are really gliders). They are classified in the order Chiroptera, a group with more than 900 species worldwide. Bats live in almost all habitats on land, including many remote oceanic islands, and are absent only from the coldest regions. Among land mammals, only the rodents are more diverse and widespread.

Bats have been surrounded by superstitions and have been much maligned and persecuted by humans as a result. But in fact, these animals are almost always harmless, or even beneficial to human interests. For example, most of our bats are insect-eaters, providing vast amounts of insect control over North American farmlands. Nectar-feeding bats play an important role in pollinating many plants in our southwest. But beyond such material considerations, these are fascinating little creatures with amazing behaviors and adaptations, and they are worthy of protection for their own sake. In recent years, organizations such as Bat Conservation International (www.batcon.org) have done much to change public perceptions, and we are finally seeing welcome support for conservation of bats.

There are many threats to bat populations. As with birds and other insectivores, many bats have probably been affected by indiscriminate use of pesticides. Molestation of bats in their roosting colonies is also a major problem. Disturbance of hibernating bats can cause them to fly about the cave or other roost, losing weight and depleting stored fat that they need to survive the winter. The closing off of abandoned mine shafts is also a problem, as bats often use mines as substitutes for natural caves; it is preferable to install bat-friendly gates across these mine openings, thus allowing the bats to enter freely while other creatures are excluded.

Unwanted bats roosting in attics of houses may be evicted by closing their entrance holes after they have left to forage in the evening. Doing this either early or late in the year, when flightless young are not present, reduces needless killing of bats by humans unwilling to share space. However, those who are enlightened enough to want these animals around can erect bat houses to encourage the roosting of bats and their natural insect-controlling activities near gardens and yards.

Many bats use *echolocation,* or sonar, to navigate and to locate flying insects in the dark. They emit ultrasonic pulses of sound (through their open mouth or through their nose) while flying; sounds that bounce off of objects and are reflected back to the bats' ears allow them to echolocate both obstacles and potential prey. Most of the sounds that they use to echolocate with are very high-pitched, above the range of human hearing. Their outer ears are large and are often specially shaped to help pick up and funnel the reflected supersonic pulses to the inner ear. Bat ears have a projecting flap of skin, called the *tragus,* from the base of the ear, which may help them to determine the direction of the reflected sound.

Bats are usually adept at maneuvering in flight. Some can even hover virtually stationary in the air. The elongated bones of the fingers, hand, and arm are connected between the digits and to the body and hind limbs and tail by a flight membrane made of skin and reinforced by elastic connective tissue. Bat wing design differs from that of birds, allowing the greater maneuvering abilities necessary to catch insects in midair within a short distance. Wing design also varies among bats, being generally longer and narrower in those that fly long distances in foraging. Bats hang upside down when roosting, and in that posture, tendons lock their toes into a grasping position. Males and females usually roost separately from each other, and females often form maternity colonies that allow sharing of body warmth by the young while the mother is away at night feeding.

Identifying bats in flight is usually difficult, even for experts. Some experts can recognize some bats by sound using a bat detector, a device that receives the supersonic calls of bats and converts them to sounds audible to humans. And some bats have calls that are audible to the unaided human ear. Mostly, however, bats can be recognized only with a very close look at a stationary individual. Here the shape of the face, and the presence or absence of a tail extending past the interfemoral membrane that connects the tail to the legs, are important features. Next, the overall colors, the size of ears, and the shape of the tragus are important. Finally, the calcar, the cartilage that is attached to the ankle to support the tail membrane, may have a piece of extra cartilage that juts out to form a keel, and the presence of this keel is an identifying mark for some bats.

(**NOTE: DO NOT PICK UP AND HANDLE BATS**. They can carry rabies, and a bat allowing itself to be handled may be sick. If you are bitten by any mammal, seek medical attention. The modern rabies vaccine is now a series of small injections in the arm, replacing the painful old stomach shots. Biologists studying bats regularly update their rabies vaccinations.)

FREE-TAILED BATS

Free-tailed and Mastiff bats (family **Molossidae**) have a long tail extending out beyond the tail membrane, broad ears, and fur that is usually short and velvety. The long narrow wings of these bats are ideal for fast, long-distance flight, allowing them to seek their food — mostly flying insects — many miles from their colonies. They forage higher than most bats, sometimes flying thousands of feet above the ground and in large groups. They are mostly subtropical and tropical, but some species reach our southern and southwestern states.

MEXICAN FREE-TAILED BAT *Tadarida brasiliensis*

Tourists visiting caves in Texas, New Mexico, and Arizona may see huge clouds of these bats departing on summer evenings. This is the most abundant and conspicuous bat in North America, and it lives in the largest colonies of any mammal (up to 20 million individuals). Some southwestern populations migrate to central and southern Mexico in winter, while some from other regions of the U.S. may stay put, entering a torpid state during cold weather. Sometimes found resting in manmade structures. Feeds on moths, beetles, and other insects caught in flight. ▶ Medium-sized, with long tail extending beyond tail membrane. Uniformly brown. Has deep vertical grooves in upper lip. Ears *not* joined at the midline of the forehead.

POCKETED FREE-TAILED BAT *Nyctinomops femorosaccus*

Uncommon and local in desert lowlands of the southwest. Colonies are usually of fewer than 100 bats, roosting in caves, cliff crevices, and buildings. Feeds mostly on moths and other insects. ▶ Small to medium-sized. Brown, gray-brown, or red-brown above, slightly paler below, with hairs white at the base. Like other Molossids, has a long tail extending beyond the tail membrane. The bases of the ears join in the middle of the head, unlike those of Mexican Free-tailed (above).

BIG FREE-TAILED BAT *Nyctinomops macrotis*

This long-tailed bat summers in the southwest, up to about 6,000-foot elevations, and migrates south to Mexico in winter. Roosts in small colonies in buildings, caves, and tree cavities. Feeds on moths and other flying insects. A strong flyer, sometimes recorded far outside normal range. ▶ Larger than the two species above. Glossy pale red-brown or dark brown fur, with hairs white at base. Ears broad and large, joined at the midline of the head, extending beyond the snout when laid forward. Lips are wrinkled at sides. Voice: echolocation notes sounding like loud clicks.

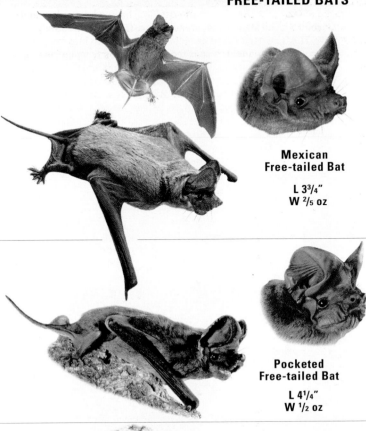

**Mexican
Free-tailed Bat**

L 3³/₄"
W ²/₅ oz

**Pocketed
Free-tailed Bat**

L 4¹/₄"
W ¹/₂ oz

**Big
Free-tailed Bat**

L 5¹/₅–6"
W ⁹/₁₀ oz

MASTIFF BATS

GREATER BONNETED BAT   *Eumops perotis* (Western Mastiff Bat)

Forms small colonies in rock crevices, buildings, and tunnels in arid canyons and cliffs of the southwestern U.S. Does not migrate. Must roost 15–20 feet above the ground, as it cannot take flight from a flat surface. Feeds on moths and other large insects, foraging up to 15 miles from its roost. ▶ Largest bat in North America, with enormous ears joined at base and protruding in a bonnet over the face. Dark chocolate brown, generally darker than next species. Voice: frequent, piercing chips, audible more than 1,000 feet away.

UNDERWOOD'S BONNETED BAT   *Eumops underwoodi*

A subtropical bat occurring in the U.S. mainly in Pima County, Arizona, where it flies low over desert pools to drink. Habits of this bat are not well known, but one Arizona colony evidently roosts in a deep cave. Probably eats beetles, grasshoppers, and other hard-bodied insects. ▶ Cinnamon brown. Jaws are more massive than those of Greater Bonneted Bat, and ears are smaller, reaching only to the nose when laid forward. Long guard hairs on rump. Voice: audible high-pitched chips emitted several times a minute while flying.

WAGNER'S BONNETED BAT   *Eumops glaucinus*

Widespread in the neotropics, reaching the U.S. only in southeastern Florida, where it is listed as endangered. Roosts singly or in small colonies, in tree hollows, palm foliage, and under roof tiles. Unlike other mastiff bats, can take flight from a flat surface. ▶ Medium-large, with long tail, ears joined at base. Few similar species occur in its range; Mexican Free-tailed Bat (previous page) is smaller and has lips deeply furrowed, not smooth. Voice: high, piercing cries that can be heard even above Miami's downtown traffic noise.

PALLAS'S MASTIFF BAT   *Molossus molossus*

Widespread in the American tropics, reaching the U.S. only in the Florida Keys. Roosts in colonies under the roofs of buildings. Also known as Velvety Free-tailed Bat and Cuban House Bat. ▶ Medium-small, brown, with fairly pointed ears and a tail that extends beyond the tail membrane. Smaller than the preceding species. Similar in size to Mexican Free-tailed Bat (previous page), but upper lip lacks deep wrinkles. **Note:** Three other tropical bats are reported as having been identified recently in far southern Florida: Jamaican Fruit Bat *(Artibeus jamaicensis)*, Buffy Flower Bat *(Erophylla sezekorni)*, and Cuban Flower Bat *(Phyllonycteris poeyi)*. The status of these species in Florida is still uncertain.

MASTIFF BATS

**Greater
Bonneted Bat**

L 6–7″   W 2–3 oz

**Underwood's
Bonneted Bat**

L 6″   W 1–2 oz

**Wagner's
Bonneted Bat**

L 5–6″   W 1–2½ oz

**Pallas's
Mastiff Bat**

L 3¾″   W ½ oz

265

are very small bats with rather small ears. Their size and their weak, erratic flight make them distinctive.

EASTERN PIPISTRELLE   *Pipistrellus subflavus*

A small bat seen most often at dusk and in early morning, along river bottoms, over open pastures, or along woodland edges, fluttering slowly after flying insects. During the spring and summer, females form small maternity colonies in old buildings, caves, or hollow trees, where they will raise their twin young; males roost separately during this season. Winter roosts are often larger, with up to several thousand individuals, and the pipistrelles may migrate hundreds of miles to reach the caves where these communal roosts are located. During hibernation they are in a deep state of torpor and tend not to react to intrusions. Solitary roosting individuals may be covered with dew. ▶ Very small, pale yellowish brown to gray-brown overall; face does not contrast with the fur as much as on Western Pipistrelle. Individual hairs on body are pale in the middle with a darker base and tip. The leading edges of the wing and tail membranes are lighter in color than the main parts of the membranes. Compare to smaller species of Myotis on next few pages. Pipistrelles do not have the long pointed tragus (structure in front of the ear opening) that all Myotis do.

WESTERN PIPISTRELLE   *Pipistrellus hesperus*

This tiny bat flies earlier in the evening and later in the morning than most other bats. It may be recognized by its diminutive size and by its slow, fluttery flight, suggesting a large butterfly. Most common in open country, such as grassland, desert, open woods, and the edges of suburbs, it occurs from sea level up to 8,000 feet. Unlike some bats, not very gregarious; tends to roost singly or in groups of fewer than a dozen individuals, in crevices in cliffs or buildings. Roost sites chosen are near permanent sources of water, including rivers, ponds, stock tanks, or even swimming pools. Feeds on small swarming insects such as mosquitoes, moths, and winged ants. Does not migrate, instead hibernating through the winter. ▶ The smallest bat in North America, and one of our smallest mammals of any sort. Body fur uniformly buffy gray or yellowish gray, contrasting sharply with the leathery black face, black ears, and black wing membranes. Compare to California Myotis and Western Small-footed Myotis (p. 270).

PIPISTRELLES

hibernating bat
covered in dew

**Eastern
Pipistrelle**

L 3¼″
W ¼ oz

**Western
Pipistrelle**
L 2⁹⁄₁₀″
W ⅛ oz

BIG BROWN BAT *Eptesicus fuscus*

Common and widespread, foraging at night over wooded areas, rivers, farmland, and cities. By day, rests under loose tree bark, in tree hollows, rock crevices, buildings, or caves. In spring and summer, maternity colonies of up to a few dozen females form in sheltered places such as tree cavities. For winter, migrates short distances to hibernate in caves, mines, or sometimes buildings. Aggressive when handled and will definitely bite. Feeds on flying insects, with an apparent preference for beetles. ▶ Medium-sized with long chestnut brown or pinkish tan fur. Ears, face, and wing and tail membranes are black and mostly hairless. Ears are thick, short, and round. The tragus (the structure in front of each ear) is short and rounded, unlike the long pointed tragus of all Myotis.

LITTLE BROWN MYOTIS *Myotis lucifugus*

The bat most commonly seen in residential areas in the east. Daytime roosts and maternity colonies are frequently found in buildings. Females are very faithful to their maternity colony, returning to the same site year after year. Migrates up to 600 miles to hibernate in abandoned mines and caves. Does much foraging over water. ▶ Small and brown with long glossy fur. Quite similar to some other species of myotis (on following pages); with a close look, note the long toe hairs (five to seven per toe) that extend to the toenail or beyond. Sparse hair on tail membrane from above to about the knees.

EVENING BAT *Nycticeius humeralis*

This bat has been found roosting in hollow trees, under palm fronds, and in buildings, but not in caves. Females migrate north to maternity colonies in spring, leaving males to summer in southern latitudes. ▶ Similar to Big Brown Bat but with shorter forearm. Light cinnamon to blackish brown above, tawny below. Blunt, rounded ears are dark and leathery; tragus (structure in front of ear) is short and curved forward as in Big Brown Bat.

EASTERN SMALL-FOOTED MYOTIS *Myotis leibii*

Uncommon to rare in eastern forests. Hibernates in small numbers in crevices of caves or mines. Daytime roosts have been found in buildings, old swallow nests, bridges, and under rocks, as well as in caves. ▶ One of the smallest eastern bats, with a slow and erratic flight. Thick fur yellow-tan to blackish brown with a golden sheen, face and ears black with pointed tragus.

SMALL BATS

Big Brown Bat

L 4²/₅"
W ¹/₂–⁴/₅ oz

echolocating

with moth

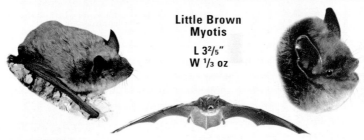

Little Brown Myotis

L 3²/₅"
W ¹/₃ oz

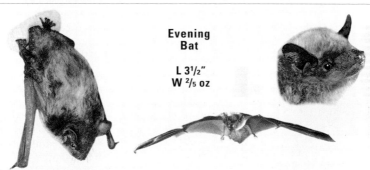

Evening Bat

L 3¹/₂"
W ²/₅ oz

Eastern Small-footed Myotis

L 3"
W ¹/₅ oz

CALIFORNIA MYOTIS *Myotis californicus*

Common and widespread in the west, from deserts to pine forest. Active all year in warmer climates, but will hibernate during winter at higher elevations or north-ward. Roosts singly or in small numbers in a variety of situations. Forages for insects in erratic flight, often close to the ground or over waterholes. ▶ Dull, pale yellow-orange in arid areas and lower elevations, brown to dark brown with orange tinge in Pacific Northwest and mountains of southwest. Ears, wings, and tail membrane are dark, and the tail membrane is sparsely furred from elbow to knee. Very small feet. Calcar (spur extending from ankle) has a keel. Compare to next species and to Long-legged Myotis (next page).

WESTERN SMALL-FOOTED MYOTIS *Myotis ciliolabrum*

Widespread in the west in rocky areas in varied habitats, from dry grassland to oak-juniper woods. Not found in the most arid habitats used by California Myotis; apparently not so well adapted to conserve water. Roosts singly or in small groups in crevices on cliffs, or in mines or caves. Hibernates in winter. ▶ Very similar to California Myotis but tends to have a flatter head and longer muzzle. Calcar (spur extending from ankle) has a keel. Paler and with less fur on underside of wings than Long-legged Myotis (next page).

INDIANA MYOTIS *Myotis sodalis* (Indiana Bat)

Listed as endangered throughout its range, best known for its tendency to hibernate in very dense congregations in cold caves with high humidity. In November, it swarms at cave entrances for two to three weeks before settling into torpor in colonies with thousands of individuals. In March, females leave the caves for wooded areas to form maternity colonies under the loose bark of trees. ▶ Similar to Little Brown Myotis (previous page) but fur is less glossy; toes have fewer and shorter hairs.

GRAY MYOTIS *Myotis grisescens*

Listed as endangered, dependent upon a few wet limestone caves in the southeast and very susceptible to human disturbance. Females and young live separately from males in large maternity colonies from April until July or August. In October, flocks move hundreds of miles to the winter hibernating caves. Forages mostly over water. ▶ Uniformly gray or gray-brown fur, short ears. Unlike any other myotis, wing membrane is attached at ankle rather than to the base of the toes.

California Myotis
L 3¹/₅″ W ¹/₅ oz

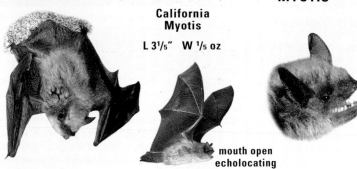

mouth open
echolocating

Western Small-footed Myotis
L 3¹/₄″ W ¹/₅ oz

mouth open
echolocating

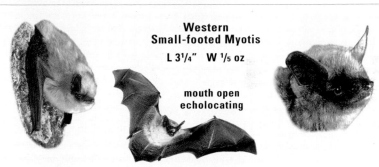

colony on cave ceiling

Indiana Myotis
L 3²/₅″ W ¹/₄ oz

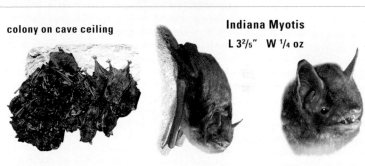

Gray Myotis
**L 3¹/₂″
W ²/₅ oz**

271

LONG-LEGGED MYOTIS *Myotis volans*

Widespread in the west but most common in coniferous forest above 6,000 feet. Fast in flight, feeding on flying insects, especially moths. Can fly at cooler temperatures than many other bats, but during the winter hibernates in caves and abandoned mines. The single young is born in the summer. ▶ Dark reddish brown to almost black, with shorter, more rounded ears than most Myotis. The calcar (spur extending out from ankle) has a raised keel. Fur on underside of base of wing, from elbows to knees, is longer and denser than on any other Myotis.

YUMA MYOTIS *Myotis yumanensis*

Dependent upon access to water, this bat is frequently seen skimming the surface of ponds and rivers. Roosts during the day in buildings, under roof shingles, under bridges, and in mines and caves; will also roost in abandoned Cliff Swallow nests. ▶ Color varies from light to dark brown, and ears are short. Very similar to Little Brown Myotis (p. 268), but Yuma Myotis has duller (less glossy) fur, and the ears are paler brown.

CAVE MYOTIS *Myotis velifer*

This bat has a stronger, less fluttery flight than most Myotis, enabling it to forage over a wider area. Inhabits caves at lower elevations, in colonies of up to 20,000 individuals. Also found roosting in buildings, in rock crevices, and under bridges. Hibernating during the winter in Kansas, Texas, and Arizona, it probably migrates south during winter from western part of U.S. range. ▶ Larger than most Myotis. Upperparts pale brown in the eastern part of the range to darker brown in more western regions, underparts paler. Has short ears and short, stubby nose.

KEEN'S MYOTIS *Myotis keenii*

Uncommon and with a limited range in the Pacific Northwest. Roosts in trees and caves, usually singly but sometimes in small groups. Hibernates in colonies, sometimes with other species of bats. Formerly thought to be the same species as Northern Myotis (next page). ▶ Small but with longer ears than the average Myotis, extending beyond the nose if bent forward. Reddish to dark brown, with distinctly darker patches on the back just where the wing attaches to the body.

Long-legged Myotis

L 3½″   W ¼ oz

L 3⅕″   W ⅕ oz

Yuma Myotis

Cave Myotis

L 3⁹⁄₁₀″   W ⅖ oz

Keen's Myotis

L 3″   W ⅕ oz

MYOTIS WITH LONGER EARS

LONG-EARED MYOTIS   *Myotis evotis*

Longer eared than other Myotis, this bat sometimes stops using its sonar in order to listen for sounds made by its insect prey. Often forages by hovering above vegetation, picking insects off the leaves. ▶ Pale dull brown to light yellow with large, glossy, black or dark brown ears, longer than those of its relatives. Bigger overall than many Myotis. Compare to others on this page.

FRINGED MYOTIS   *Myotis thysanodes*

Common at low to middle elevations in the west. Forages for insects sitting on vegetation, using its short broad wings to maneuver among the foliage. The wings are particularly tough to withstand piercing by thorns. Eats many small beetles, but it also takes other insects. ▶ Yellowish brown to khaki brown. Similar to other long-eared species of Myotis, but in a very close view, identified by the fringe of hair on the trailing edge of its tail membrane.

NORTHERN MYOTIS   *Myotis septentrionalis*

This bat does not catch and eat insects in midair but picks them off foliage while hovering and then hangs up to eat them. Occurs in woods and streamside areas, roosting under tree bark and in buildings. Up to 350 individuals can hibernate in a single cave or mine, preferring moist cool situations for hibernation. ▶ Dull brown with dark shoulder spots, and its ears are shorter than those of Long-eared Myotis.

SOUTHWESTERN MYOTIS   *Myotis auriculus*

A bat of southwestern mountains, most often found in forests of ponderosa pine. A gleaner like the similar Long-eared and Fringed Myotis, feeding mainly on moths. ▶ Brown like other Myotis on this page, it lacks the tail fringe of Fringed Myotis. It has shorter ears and paler wing membranes than Long-eared Myotis, and the bases of its back hairs are brown rather than black.

SOUTHEASTERN MYOTIS   *Myotis austroriparius*

This bat loves water, foraging low over streams and ponds, often roosting in damp caves. Hibernates in winter in the northern part of its range, but can be active intermittently all winter in Florida. Unlike our other Myotis, the female gives birth to twins, catching them in her tail membrane as they emerge feet first. ▶ Dull woolly gray-brown or orange-brown fur, with shorter ears than Northern Myotis and duller fur than the glossy Little Brown Myotis.

MYOTIS

Long-eared Myotis

L 3⁷/₁₀″
W ¼ oz

mouth open echolocating

Fringed Myotis

L 3½″ W ³/₁₀ oz

Northern Myotis

L 3²/₅″
W ¼ oz

Southwestern Myotis

L 3²/₃″
W ¼ oz

Southeastern Myotis

L 3¹/₃″
W ⅕ oz

mouth open echolocating

CALIFORNIA LEAF-NOSED BAT   *Macrotus californicus*

This bat of the Sonoran and Mojave Deserts neither hibernates nor migrates, spending winters in warm humid caves or mine tunnels. Forages at night mostly by flying slowly, close to the ground, locating perched insects by sight. Most of its time is spent hanging from its long legs and feet, sometimes holding on with one foot while it grooms with the other. As with other bats, females segregate from males into maternity colonies while raising their young. ▶ Light gray with large ears. Conspicuous leaf-shaped extension on its nose.

TOWNSEND'S BIG-EARED BAT   *Corynorhinus townsendii*

Mostly a wide-ranging western bat, mainly in forested regions. It feeds mostly on moths. In summer, forms maternity colonies of up to a thousand or more individuals. In winter, it hibernates in small numbers or alone in mines and caves not far from its summer roosts. When hibernating, large-eared bats curl their ears back in the shape of a ram's horns to conserve heat. Uncommon in most of its range; the two eastern populations are listed as endangered. ▶ Pale cinnamon to blackish brown, with very large ears and two fleshy lumps on the muzzle. Lacks the forward-projecting brow flap of Allen's Big-eared Bat (below). In the east, compare to Rafinesque's Big-eared Bat (below).

ALLEN'S BIG-EARED BAT   *Idionycteris phyllotis*

An uncommon bat of wooded areas in southwestern mountains, also extending into the Mojave Desert. It maneuvers well in flight, feeding on soft-bodied insects that it gleans from vegetation or catches in mid-air. Drinks on the wing from pools of water. ▶ Medium-small with huge ears. Separated from Townsend's Big-eared Bat by *lappet,* an extra brow or forehead flap projecting forward from base of ear.

RAFINESQUE'S BIG-EARED BAT   *Corynorhinus rafinesquii*

Lives in forested regions of the east and southeast, foraging at night in very maneuverable flight. Where it roosts in caves with other bats, it tends to roost closer to the entrance, making it more vulnerable to predators. Females give birth to a single young, which is able to fly at three weeks of age. ▶ Smoky gray with very large ears and fleshy lumps on both sides of its muzzle. Townsend's Big-eared Bat is browner. No other huge-eared small bat occurs in its range.

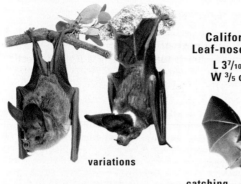

California Leaf-nosed Bat
L 3⁷/₁₀″
W ³/₅ oz

variations

catching cricket

Townsend's Big-eared Bat
L 4″
W ²/₅ oz

Allen's Big-eared Bat
L 4¹/₃″   W ²/₅ oz

Rafinesque's Big-eared Bat
L 3³/₄″   W ²/₅ oz

277

SPOTTED BAT *Euderma maculatum*

This striking bat is widespread in the west, from low deserts to mountain forests, but seems uncommon everywhere, and its habits are not well known. Feeds on the wing on moths and other soft-bodied insects, but also known to take June beetles. Roosts during the day in rock crevices. Has been seen foraging in the winter in low deserts, but a few individuals have also been found hibernating. Call audible to human ears as a high-pitched metallic squeak. ▶ Back black with *three large white spots*, belly white. *Very large* pinkish ears and a small muzzle.

SEMINOLE BAT *Lasiurus seminolus*

This southeastern bat is often fairly common in wooded areas, especially where the trees are heavily hung with Spanish moss, its favored daytime roosting site. Generally roosts alone. Forages mostly just above forest canopy, taking flying insects as well as insects perched on vegetation or the ground. ▶ Mahogany red overall with white tips on the fur of the back, yellowish fur on face, rounded ears, and long tapered wings. The tail membrane is densely furred on top. Essentially identical to female of next species.

EASTERN RED BAT *Lasiurus borealis*

Common in woodlands, streamsides, and towns. Usually roosts singly among the foliage of trees or shrubs. At least some individuals migrate southward in winter; some hibernate in trees or in leaf litter on the ground, wrapping themselves up in their tail membranes and rousing periodically to feed when it is warm enough to fly. ▶ Males are bright orange-red, females are rusty red with frosting on the tips of their back fur. Tail membrane is densely furred over the entire upper surface. Flies with tail straight out behind.

WESTERN RED BAT *Lasiurus blossevillii*

Only recently determined to be a separate species from Eastern Red Bat (above). Solitary like that species, roosting alone in cottonwoods along streams. Hibernation behavior is poorly known, but some individuals do move to warmer areas for the winter. Females bear up to four young, which cling to their mother's fur while she roosts and stay behind when she forages. ▶ Similar to Eastern Red Bat but rusty red rather than brownish red, and hind edge of tail membrane is only sparsely haired at most. Best distinguished by range.

COLORFUL BATS

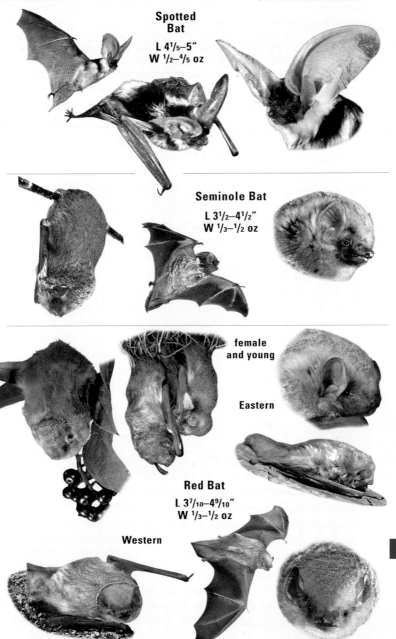

Spotted Bat
L 4¹/₅–5″
W ¹/₂–⁴/₅ oz

Seminole Bat
L 3¹/₂–4¹/₂″
W ¹/₃–¹/₂ oz

female and young

Eastern

Red Bat
L 3⁷/₁₀–4⁹/₁₀″
W ¹/₃–¹/₂ oz

Western

HOARY BAT   *Lasiurus cinereus*

Our most widespread bat, found in forests over most of North America and south into the tropics. Most from northern latitudes are believed to migrate south for winter. Solitary, roosting alone in trees. Feeds on many flying insects but prefers moths. Dense fur on its body provides good insulation, and it wraps the heavily furred tail membrane around itself like a blanket. Females have up to four young (usually two) in late spring. ▶ Large, with yellow and brown fur heavily tipped in white, giving it a frosted or hoary look. Somewhat similar to Red and Seminole Bats (previous page) but larger, a duller shade of brown, and with contrasting yellow face. Large size and fast, direct flight are distinctive over most of its range.

SILVER-HAIRED BAT   *Lasionycteris noctivagans*

A common forest bat, preferring to roost alone in tree snags in old-growth coniferous and mixed forests. Hibernates in tree hollows, under bark, and sometimes in caves, but many apparently migrate south before hibernating. Takes insects in flight, foraging over water and in clearings. Females form small maternity colonies where they raise their two young. ▶ Dark brown to black with silvery tips to hairs, especially on young bats. Older individuals may lack this frosted effect. Smaller than Hoary Bat and lacks the contrastingly pale face.

PETERS'S GHOST-FACED BAT   *Mormoops megalophylla*

A unique bat with the most unusual face of all our bats. Roosts in large colonies in caves and mine tunnels in Texas and farther south. Does not hibernate. A fast and high flier, specializing in eating large moths. ▶ In Texas, this bat has long blond-brown fur (although populations in South America are deep cinnamon red with a purple sheen). A close look at the face distinguishes this species from all our other bats.

HAIRY-LEGGED VAMPIRE   *Diphylla ecaudata*

Several species of vampire bats live in Mexico, but only this one has reached the U.S. — once in 1967 in southwestern Texas, evidently a lone wanderer from the typical range about 500 miles farther south. While all vampire bats feed on blood, this one takes blood mainly from birds. This species also differs from other vampire bats in being solitary. Vampire bats appear more four-legged than most bats while walking around supported by their wrists and toes. ▶ Dark brown with flattened face and round nose. Not easily confused with other bats in the U.S.

DISTINCTIVE BATS

Hoary Bat
L 4³/₄″
W 1 oz

Silver-haired Bat
L 4″
W ¹/₃ oz

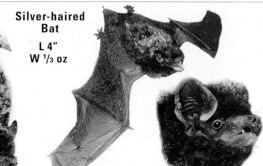

Peters's Ghost-faced Bat
L 3¹/₂″
W ¹/₂ oz

profile

Hairy-legged Vampire
L 3¹/₄″ W 1¹/₁₀ oz

NORTHERN YELLOW BAT *Lasiurus intermedius*

A southeastern bat (despite the name) of forests near water, preferring to roost in Spanish moss or dead palm fronds. Excessive tidying of woodlots, with clearing of dead fronds and Spanish moss, may reduce the populations of these beautiful bats. Somewhat social, roosting in small groups and forming maternity colonies. Migrates south from the northernmost parts of its range in winter. ▶ Has yellow-brown or yellow-orange long silky fur, pointed ears, and fur on about the basal half of the upper surface of the tail membrane. Larger than Southern Yellow Bat, with which it sometimes roosts where their ranges overlap.

SOUTHERN YELLOW BAT *Lasiurus ega*

A tropical bat reaching the U.S. only in southern Texas. Roosts in dead palm fronds, usually singly or in small numbers. Forages on the wing, taking insects. Females usually bear three young. ▶ Dull yellow with pointed nose and ears. About one-third to one-half of the tail membrane is furred on the upperside. Easily confused with Northern Yellow Bat but averages much smaller.

WESTERN YELLOW BAT *Lasiurus xanthinus* (not illustrated)

Formerly considered part of same species as Southern Yellow Bat. Widespread in southwestern deserts, usually associated with sources of permanent water such as streams, cattle ponds, and swimming pools. It roosts among dead palm fronds and may be expanding its range with the planting of ornamental palms. ▶ Like Southern Yellow Bat (may be slightly brighter yellow on tail membrane), best identified by range.

PALLID BAT *Antrozous pallidus*

Mostly found in deserts, preferring areas near rocky outcrops and water. Pallid Bats are known for eating centipedes and scorpions, but they usually take various large insects found on the ground or on vegetation, including sphinx moths coming to cactus flowers. Their large ears help them to detect sounds made by the arthropods they hunt. Better able to walk on the ground than many bats, supporting themselves on wrists and hind feet. Social, roosting in groups of 20 or more. Among their vocalizations are high-pitched trilling calls, used for recognition signals rather than echolocation. ▶ Pale straw color with large ears, large eyes, and hairless muzzle. A musky odor is emitted by glands on the nose.

PALE BATS

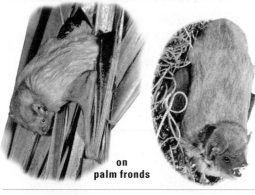

on
palm fronds

**Northern
Yellow Bat**

L 5″   W ³/₅ oz

**Southern
Yellow Bat**

L 4¹/₂″
W ³/₅ oz

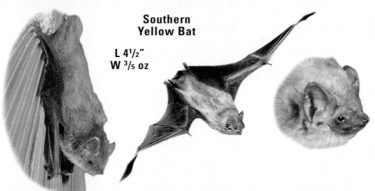

with centipede

with
katydid

Pallid Bat

L 4¹/₂″
W ³/₄ oz

LONG-NOSED, NECTAR-FEEDING BATS

have longer muzzles and tongues than insect-eating bats, enabling them to reach the nectar deep in flowers. They are strong, long-distance fliers, migrating to follow the seasons of blooming and fruiting plants.

MEXICAN LONG-TONGUED BAT   *Choeronycteris mexicana*

A nectar- and pollen-feeding bat that summers in the southwestern U.S., coming north to feed at succulents that bloom in summer, such as agaves and saguaro cacti, and migrating to Mexico and Central America for the winter. These bats frequently flock to hummingbird feeders in Arizona and may drain them overnight. They hover briefly as they feed, darting in quickly to a flower or feeder and darting away in less than a second. Also feeds on fruit and insects. Roosts by day in caves, mine tunnels, and drainage culverts. Females have one young, born well-furred. ► Buffy brown or gray-brown, with a very long muzzle with a short leaflike extension on top. Compare to next two species and to California Leaf-nosed Bat (p. 276).

LESSER LONG-NOSED BAT   *Leptonycteris curasoae*

An endangered species. Summer resident in the south-west, migrating north from Mexico and Central America. Feeds on nectar, pollen, cactus fruit, and possibly insects. Visits hummingbird feeders in southern Arizona like the preceding species. In Arizona, feeds mainly on blossoms and fruit of saguaro and organ pipe cactus in early summer, switching to agave nectar and pollen when the agaves bloom in late summer. Roosts in caves and abandoned mines in maternity colonies up to 10,000 strong (or up to 100,000 in Sonora). It has had a confusing history of names, having been known as Southern Long-nosed Bat, North American Long-nosed Bat *(Leptonycteris yerbabuenae),* and Sanborn's Long-nosed Bat. ► Similar to others on this page but has a shorter muzzle and lacks the external tail of Mexican Long-tongued Bat. Mexican Long-nosed Bat (below) is larger, grayer, and has longer wings.

MEXICAN LONG-NOSED BAT   *Leptonycteris nivalis*

An endangered species, found only in southwestern Texas in June and July, coming north to feed on blooming agaves. Roosts in colonies, sometimes very large, in caves and abandoned mines. ► Dark brownish gray with no external tail and a narrow tail membrane. Although all three species on this page overlap in range in Mexico and often roost together there, no other nectar-feeding bat overlaps this species in its Texas range.

NECTAR-FEEDING BATS

pollen on face

female

nectaring at yucca blossom

Mexican Long-tongued Bat
L 3³/₅″ W ³/₅ oz

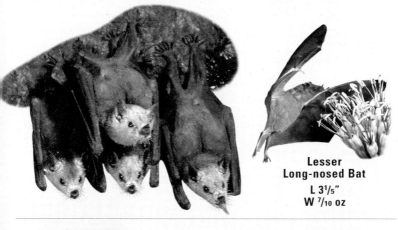

Lesser Long-nosed Bat
L 3¹/₅″
W ⁷/₁₀ oz

Mexican Long-nosed Bat
L 3¹/₄″
W ⁴/₅ oz

represent two unrelated groups, often seen in coastal waters.

Seals are thought to have evolved from bearlike, meat-eating ancestors and to have gone back to the sea roughly 25 million years ago. Thus classified in the order Carnivora (with dogs, cats, bears, raccoons, and weasels), seals and walruses belong to the suborder Pinnipedia, meaning *wing-foot* or *fin-foot*, a reference to their front limbs, which are flattened into flippers. All pinnipeds live at sea most of the year. However, unlike whales and dolphins, they are still tied to the land, as they must haul out of the water onto land or pack ice to give birth and nurse their pups.

The animals in this section are classified in four families.

Sea lions and fur seals (family **Otariidae**), pp. 288–290. Also known as eared seals, they differ from the true seals in having small external ears. They also have the ability to rotate their hind flippers forward underneath them, allowing them to walk on all fours like a land mammal. In the water, the front flippers provide propulsion and the hind flippers are used as a rudder for steering. Their greater mobility on land and playful nature make them popular as trained acts in zoos and aquaria. Found in cold or temperate waters, eared seals in North America include two fur seals and two sea lions. They are highly gregarious in the breeding season, hauling out on land to gather in thousands in large herds called *rookeries*, where the largest and most mature males compete with other males for the right to mate with multiple females.

Guadalupe Fur Seal is listed as threatened, probably owing to over-hunting in the 1700s and 1800s. The western population of Steller's Sea Lion is listed as endangered. As these aquatic mammals depend on fish and crustaceans, they are affected by human competition for food. Some estimates claim that 90 percent of the populations of large fishes have been fished from the world's oceans, thus depleting the prey base. Miles-long drift gill nets also are a threat as they entangle these air-breathing mammals below the surface, drowning them.

True seals (family **Phocidae**), pp. 292–298. Also called earless seals or hair seals, they lack external ears. They also lack the ability to rotate their hind flippers under them, compelling them to flop along on their belly when moving about on land. There are nine species in North American waters, ranging from the small

Ringed Seal to the very large Northern Elephant Seal. In the water, true seals are very agile, using their hind flippers for propulsion and steering with their front flippers. Most species are gregarious, still coming to shore in groups to give birth and nurse their pups. Most mate in the water, except for gray and elephant seals. Although many earless seals were over-hunted in the past, driving them almost to extinction, populations are mostly increasing or stable at the moment.

Walrus (family **Odobenidae**), p. 300. Walruses resemble eared seals in shape and locomotion but are easily distinguished by their tusks (enlarged canine teeth). Males have longer and less curved tusks than females. The tusks of males are useful in signaling dominance, and both sexes use them for hauling out on the ice, battling

other Walruses, and fending off Polar Bears and Killer Whales (especially in defense of the young). Adult males have thickened and hardened skin on their neck and shoulders which may act as a shield in battles with other males. Commercial hunting of Walruses is banned worldwide now, and only subsistence hunting by native peoples continues. However, these unusual animals, once heavily hunted for their blubber oil, tusk ivory, and skins, continue to be threatened by water pollution, decreases in their food supply, and the retreat of sea ice that goes along with global warming.

Manatees (family **Trichechidae**), p. 300. More closely related to elephants than they are to other marine mammals, manatees belong to their own order (Sirenia), which contains only three species of manatees and two species of dugongs. Like dolphins, and unlike seals and Walruses, manatees give birth and nurse their young in the water, never hauling out on land. Members of this group are the only vegetarian marine mammals, eating aquatic plants (one nickname for these animals is "sea cow"). Listed as endangered, the slow-moving West Indian Manatee is placed at risk by its habit of sleeping barely submerged in shallow water, where the propellers of fast-moving boats can damage them. About one-fourth to one-third of the annual deaths in Florida are from boat propeller damage.

287

STELLER'S SEA LION   *Eumetopias jubatus*   (Northern Sea-Lion)

This largest eared seal ranges along the rim of the North Pacific Ocean from California to Japan, feeding mostly in waters less than 600 feet deep. It eats mainly fish, squid, and octopus. In recent decades, its populations have declined by more than 90 percent in some regions, and it is now listed as endangered in parts of Alaska. Reasons for the decline are not well understood; it may be linked to climate change, or it may involve the decreasing availability of its favored fish prey.

Each spring, breeding adults haul out on offshore rocky islands. Mature males fast for two months while they defend space and a harem of up to 20 females. The females, already pregnant from the previous year, haul out in these rookeries three days before giving birth. Males roar loudly and make ritualized threat displays, even biting to establish and maintain their territories. The voices of females are higher, and pups bleat like sheep. ▶ Adults are buffy to reddish brown, turning blonder as they age, with *contrastingly darker flippers*. Snout is broad and straight, ears are small and pointed. Males are much larger and bulkier than females, with a mane of long coarse hair, hence the "lion" in the name. Paler and larger than California Sea Lion.

CALIFORNIA SEA LION   *Zalophus californianus*

The trained antics of this playful creature in aquaria and zoos make this our most familiar sea lion. In the wild, limited to the west coast of the U.S. and Canada, and the Galapagos Islands. California Sea Lions breed only in the southern part of their range, but adult males move north in fall, overwintering as far north as British Columbia. Feeds on a wide variety of fish, octopus, squid, and abalone, sometimes foraging more than 200 feet deep and staying down for up to 20 minutes. Rookeries on sandy or rocky beaches are defended by territorial males, but females come and go across territories as they like, choosing the male with whom they mate. Females give birth to a single pup, which they nurse for up to eight months. Males and females bark, and pups bleat like sheep. ▶ Males are black when wet, but when dry are buff to chocolate brown with a bulky neck and a paler prominent bump on the top of the head. Females are blonder and smaller. No sharp contrast between flippers and body on adults, and more pointed snout than Steller's Sea Lion (above).

SEA LIONS

bull with harem

bull

female nursing pup

Steller's Sea Lion

male L 9' W 1,250 lbs
female L 7¹/₂' W 580 lbs

bull with harem

California Sea Lion

male L 7' W 825 lbs
female L 5¹/₂' W 200 lbs

underwater

juvenile

bull

have thick and soft waterproof underfur (50 times more dense than that of land mammals) that was once harvested commercially, but now only subsistence hunting is allowed. There are nine species of fur seals, two of them occurring in the northern hemisphere.

NORTHERN FUR SEAL *Callorhinus ursinus* (Alaska Fur Seal)

Tourists visiting the Pribilof Islands of Alaska in summer enjoy the spectacle of tens of thousands of Northern Fur Seals crowding the beaches. Commercial hunting of these seals was halted in the 1980s, but their numbers have continued to decline since, and the world population has dropped by about 60 percent since the 1950s. Reasons for the decline are not well understood, but they may be related to loss of food supplies because of overfishing of the Bering Sea. Away from the Pribilofs, this species colonized San Miguel Island, California, beginning in the 1950s and Bogoslof Island, Alaska, beginning in the 1970s; those populations are in the low thousands but increasing.

Mature males establish territories in island rookeries in early summer, defending their harems of up to 100 females from other males. Females give birth to a single pup and then mate with the territorial male within two or three days. By November, all seals have gone to sea and stay at sea until the following summer unless sick or injured. ▶ Distinctive shape, with small head and short pointed snout. Males are much larger than females. Both sexes are uniformly black when wet. When dry, adult males are brownish black with a lighter head and mane, while females are brown. In California, compare to next species.

GUADALUPE FUR SEAL *Arctocephalus townsendii*

Hunted almost to extinction before it was even recognized as a species in 1897, this rare fur seal breeds on Guadalupe and San Benito Islands off the coast of Baja California. Increasing numbers have been spotted in their former range in the southern Channel Islands and north to central California; in 1997, a pup was born on San Miguel Island off California. As with its relatives, males defend territories and up to a dozen females, but unlike other fur seals, those territories contain shady caves and hollows for shelter from the sun. Feeds on squid and fish. ▶ Resembles Northern Fur Seal, but male has larger head and longer snout. Females are more similar, but note that Guadalupe Fur Seal has fur extending along the top of the larger front flippers. Compare to California Sea Lion (previous page).

FUR SEALS

male with harem

male

female

pup

Northern Fur Seal
male L 7′ W 460 lbs
female L 4 ¹/₂′ W 90 lbs

male

Guadalupe Fur Seal
male L 7′ W 420 lbs
female L 5′ W 110 lbs

juvenile

females

NORTHERN ELEPHANT SEAL   *Mirounga angustirostris*

dashed lines: orange is typical foraging range for females; pale blue is typical foraging range for adult males

This huge seal was once hunted relentlessly for the oil in its blubber and was actually thought to be extinct for a time in the late 1800s, until a few were discovered on Guadalupe Island off the west coast of Baja. Since then the population has increased again and the species has reoccupied former haunts along the California coast and its offshore islands; the total population may now be as many as 150,000, with the largest colonies on the Channel Islands. When not ashore for molting and breeding, mature elephant seals are solitary, foraging far offshore in the North Pacific Ocean. Males range northward through the Gulf of Alaska and near the eastern Aleutian Islands, while females mostly range farther south. This seal feeds on squid, octopus, and fish (including rays and skates), diving 1,000 to 2,500 feet or deeper and sometimes remaining below the surface for 20 minutes (females) or up to two hours (males).

From December to March, males haul out on sandy beaches where they snort and bellow and threaten each other, competing for the attention of groups of up to 60 females. The males fast for up to three months during this breeding season. When an elephant seal is fasting, it sleeps and periodically stops breathing for up to 20 minutes, reducing its heart rate and metabolism in the process and presumably conserving energy. Females come ashore after the males do and bear a single pup, which they nurse for up to four weeks while they themselves fast, losing more than 40 percent of their weight. Their milk is among the richest of all mammal milk, being more than 50 percent fat. The females then mate and abandon the pup, going to sea to feed. The pup (now weighing almost 600 pounds) fasts for up to eight weeks, practicing swimming, before going to sea independent of its mother.

In June and July, males return to shore to molt their fur, again fasting as they do so. Adult females, juveniles, and subadult males molt earlier onshore. After the molt they return to the sea until December. ▶ Brown or gray above, paler below. Adult males are easily recognized by their large size and by the swollen long snout drooping forward over the muzzle. Females, not as large, differ from the sea lions and fur seals (pp. 288–290) in head shape and in the absence of external ears. Compare to Harbor Seal (next page).

ELEPHANT SEAL

bulls
fighting
in the surf

bulls
roaring

**Northern
Elephant Seal**

male L 12½′   W 3,970 lbs
female L 8′   W 1,430 lbs

pair
courting

female
nursing pup

293

SMALL SEALS

Along with the Northern Elephant Seal on the preceding page, these are classified as true seals (family **Phocidae**), lacking both external ears and the ability to rotate their hind flippers forward. When moving about on land, they must flop along on their belly.

HARBOR SEAL *Phoca vitulina*

Common and often seen on the Pacific and northern Atlantic coasts, this seal is well-named for its preference for coastal waters. For resting, breeding, and nursing pups, it uses many haul-out sites, including sea ice, ledges exposed at low tide, sandbars, and even man-made piers. Harbor Seals do not migrate like some other seals, but young individuals may wander widely, and the species sometimes follows salmon or other fish upriver many miles inland. Able to dive to almost 1,500 feet and stay submerged for more than 20 minutes. Feeds on a wide variety of fish. Bounty hunts that were once used to reduce competition for fish have now been eliminated, and populations of Harbor Seals are growing. ▶ Variable in color, but two main types: light background with dark spots, and dark background with light rings. *Newborn pups are dark.* On land, often in a typical "banana-like" posture with head and tail both lifted. Short muzzle with V-shaped nostrils. In the northeast, Gray Seal (next page) averages larger, with a longer muzzle. In the north, Ringed Seal is smaller with a shorter, more rounded appearance. Spotted Seal, (below) which overlaps in Alaska, is very similar and best distinguished by habitat, preferring open sea with pack ice from fall to early summer rather than coastal areas. However, it can be found hauled out with Harbor Seals when no ice is available.

SPOTTED SEAL *Phoca largha*

From autumn to early summer, found near the leading edge of pack ice, where it rests, breeds, and raises its young. When no ice is available, found in open waters and on land in the North Pacific; most commonly along the northwestern coast of Alaska. The diet varies according to age and food availability. Pups feed on crustaceans such as shrimp and crabs, while older seals feed on fish, squid, and octopus. Unusual in its monogamous habit of pairing up shortly before the female gives birth. The male stays with the female and pup until he mates with her after the pup is weaned. ▶ Varies in background color, but usually brownish yellow with dark spots. *Newborn pups are white.* Compare to Harbor Seal above and to Ringed Seal (p. 298).

SEALS

sunning on tidal rocks
in typical "banana"
posture

**Harbor
Seal**

L 5½'   W 250 lbs

mother
and
pup

wet seal

Spotted Seal

L 5'   W 200 lbs

white
pup

HARP SEAL   *Phoca groenlandicus*

With their big dark eyes, the furry white pups of this species are probably the most famous of seals, having been much publicized during efforts to halt the annual Canadian harvest of pups for their white coats. This hunt is gradually being replaced by increasing numbers of tourists viewing the seals. Closely associated with seasonal movement of pack ice, Harp Seals may migrate more than 6,000 miles, following Atlantic cod and other small fish on which they feed. They often hunt in groups of several hundred seals.

Thousands of Harp Seals gather on ice floes to breed in February. Females give birth to a single pup, which grows a long white coat ("whitecoat" stage) within four days. By the time it is weaned at the end of only two weeks, the "greycoat" now has gray spots of juvenile coat underneath the white fur and weighs almost a hundred pounds. The female then abandons the pup to go to sea and feed, replacing all the weight she lost fasting while nursing. ► Mature adults are white with a large dark horseshoe-shaped mark on the back and blackish on the head. Young develop spots on their silvery gray juvenile coat by the time they are one month old and keep this coat until they are more than four years old. Some males become dark gray instead of white. All of the other spotted seals are more densely and numerously spotted.

GRAY SEAL   *Halichoerus grypus*

A large long-nosed seal of the North Atlantic. More agile on land than other true seals and may go many yards inland to breed and give birth. It feeds mainly on bottom-dwelling fish. Females bear one pup each year, fasting while nursing the pup for only 18 days on a milk of 50 to 60 percent fat. Following weaning, the pups fast for up to a month before going to sea to hunt. After the breeding season, adults go to sea to fatten again before the summer molt. Populations of this species have been increasing in recent years. ► Largest seal on the east coast, with males larger than females. Adult males are blackish to dark gray with lighter splotches and have an elongated "Roman nose" with nostrils that are parallel when viewed from the front. Females have shorter noses and are light gray with dark patches. Best distinguished from other seals in its range by size and head shape. Pups are whitish to brown at first, molting to adultlike color after two to four weeks.

NORTHEASTERN SEALS

mother with pup
at
breathing hole

adult

sooty
male

**Harp
Seal**

L 6′ W 290 lbs

young

female
nursing pup

**Gray
Seal**

L 7′ W 530 lbs

male

swimming

female

whitecoat

pups

moulter

297

RINGED SEAL *Phoca hispida*

The smallest and most abundant true seal of the Arctic, and the only one that digs snow and ice caves for birthing pups and for resting. Usually solitary. A single, white-coated pup is born in early spring and is nursed for almost two months. Ringed Seals are frequent prey for Polar Bears. ▶ Dark gray to blackish above, paler below, with dark spots that have silvery rings around them scattered across the back and sides. Males secrete oil from face glands during spring, often coloring the face darker than the body. Compare to larger Harbor Seal (p. 294), which can have somewhat ringed pattern.

RIBBON SEAL *Phoca fasciata*

This striking seal rarely comes to land, molting, pupping, and mating on thick pack ice far offshore. Probably totally pelagic during the summer, when pack ice has melted. Feeds on walleye pollock and other fish, squid, shrimp, and crabs. Relatively unafraid of humans and ships. ▶ Adult males are dark brown to black with wide whitish bands around the neck and encircling the body. Females have the same ribbons of lighter color, but their background is lighter brown so the pattern does not show as well. No other seals have this pattern. Pups are bluish gray, lighter underneath.

BEARDED SEAL *Erignathus barbatus*

Mostly in open arctic and subarctic waters with pack ice; usually solitary or in small groups. Feeds mostly on bottom-dwelling crabs, shrimp, clams, snails, and some fish. A sign of spring in many parts of the Arctic is the birdlike trilling song of adult males, as they attract and then battle for females. ▶ Very large, with a *small* head, rectangular front flippers, and long whiskers. Dark gray to brown, sometimes stained reddish on face.

HOODED SEAL *Cystophora cristata*

The adult male of this species has an inflatable air sac on the top of the nose, which forms a black bi-lobed "hood." Males also can extrude the nasal membrane through one nostril to form a red balloon, presumably rendering them irresistible to females! Migratory, following the edge of the pack ice in the central and western North Atlantic, feeding on fish, squid, octopus, starfish, and mussels. ▶ Adults are light gray with black patches, although males are darker. Females lack the head decorations and may resemble the Gray Seal (previous page), but have shorter snouts.

NORTHERN SEALS

Ringed Seal
L 4¹/₄′ W 150 lbs

adult

female nursing pup

pups

Ribbon Seal
L 5¹/₄′ W 165 lbs

male

female with pup

Bearded Seal
L 7¹/₂′ W 495–790 lbs

pup

color variations

female
L 7′
W 400–770 lbs

Hooded Seal

with pup

male
L 8¹/₃′
W 550–960 lbs

Two unrelated but distinctive mammals, from very different climates.

WALRUS   *Odobenus rosmarus*

This hulking arctic beast is famous, even though most people will never see one. Walruses often gather in herds. Males haul out on land, while females tend to rest on ice floes, gathering in groups of up to 50. Such groups are likely to be courted by one or more displaying bulls, posturing and calling in the water nearby. Unlike most seals, Walrus females do not mate shortly after giving birth but wait until the following year, as they bear one pup that they nurse and shelter for up to two years. The pup often rides on its mother's back as she swims. Walruses forage in a piglike manner on the sea floor, using their snouts to grub for clams and other invertebrates; they also eat some fish and even small seals. Their impressive tusks apparently are not used in feeding, but play a part in displaying for dominance and in fights. Older males may bear many scars from such encounters. Walruses also use their tusks to help them move about on land or ice. ▶ Unmistakable. Males have longer, straighter tusks than females. Pacific Walruses are larger and have more wrinkled skin and longer snouts than do those in the Atlantic. Apparent color of an individual may vary as its sparsely haired skin flushes with blood for temperature regulation.

WEST INDIAN MANATEE   *Trichechus manatus*

This unique aquatic herbivore lives in warm tropical and subtropical waters off the eastern coastlines of North, Central, and South America. Manatees have a low metabolic rate and cannot tolerate waters below 60°F. The main U.S. population occurs in Florida, but in summer, manatees range west to Louisiana and north to the Carolinas and Virginia. Harmless, gentle, and fascinating to watch, it has become a symbol for conserving coastal waters. Feeding on aquatic floating and submerged plants, it consumes up to 150 pounds of plant matter per day. Evidently not totally adapted to a saltwater environment, the manatee is often found drinking fresh water at springs and up rivers. Manatees are social, communicating in squeaks and squeals, nuzzling snout to snout, embracing with their flippers, and playing by bumping and chasing each other. Females give birth in the water, bearing a single calf (occasionally twins) every two or three years. ▶ Very large with large front flippers, tail flattened horizontally. Uniformly dull gray with occasional pinkish patches.

WALRUS AND MANATEE

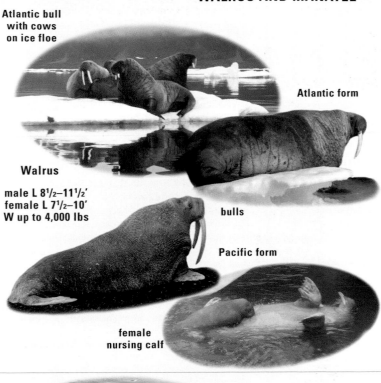

Atlantic bull with cows on ice floe

Atlantic form

Walrus

male L 8½–11½'
female L 7½–10'
W up to 4,000 lbs

bulls

Pacific form

female nursing calf

West Indian Manatee

L 9–13'
W up to 3,500 lbs

female nursing calf

underwater views

DOLPHINS, PORPOISES, AND WHALES

belong to the order **Cetacea** and collectively are called cetaceans. They are divided among a number of families, as described below. Porpoises make up a distinct group, but the term "whale" is applied to members of several families, including the largest of the marine dolphins (Killer Whales and pilot whales).

The fossil record indicates that whales arose from primitive land mammals that ventured back into the sea roughly 60 million years ago. The first cetaceans probably evolved from the same ancestors that gave rise to some of today's hoofed mammals. Some whales still have two pelvic bones, remnants of hind limbs lost long ago.

In the 1960s, the TV program *Flipper* brought a Bottlenose Dolphin into homes each week and taught the public about the intelligence of these marvelous creatures. Today whale watching has become a major industry and thousands of people venture out to sea each week to see whales and dolphins in their natural habitats. Marine parks and aquaria display Killer Whales, Bottlenose Dolphins, Belugas, and other cetaceans. In the past, relations between humans and cetaceans were far less benign. Large-scale commercial hunting drastically reduced the populations of most of the large whales worldwide, and many species still have not recovered; some populations are on the verge of extinction.

Identifying cetaceans at sea is difficult at best. Some species would be hard to distinguish even if we could study the whole animal, and, of course, we usually can't. With brief glimpses of parts of the animal, under harsh lighting and often difficult viewing conditions, we must put together clues to arrive at an identification.

Many aspects of shape are useful in identification. In particular, the size and shape of the dorsal fin, if any, and the shape of the head, flippers, and tail flukes should be noted. Some species, especially among dolphins, have an enlarged area called the *melon* on the forehead. Color patterns are also important, but it can be challenging to tell the difference between real pattern and illusions created by shadows and light reflections. Behavior also offers many clues. Some cetaceans regularly practice *bow-riding* (approaching a boat and then swimming just ahead in the bow wave). Some are quite active, *breaching* (leaping out of the water) at times, while others are slow-moving. Some are usually seen in *pods,* or groups, while others tend to be solitary. Finally, the shape of the *blow* (the visible spout of warm breath expelled by whales through the blowholes on top of the head) is distinctive for many whales, and we describe it in the text for most species.

Most of our illustrations in this section are photos showing the kinds of partial views that we usually get of cetaceans at sea. However, to help observers understand what they are seeing, for most species we have included small-scale paintings showing the whole animal.

As one final complication in identifying these animals, many cetaceans vary quite a bit among regions or among individuals. In some species, the variations are as diagnostic as human fingerprints and allow for individual identification, as in the tail flukes of Humpback Whales.

Here are the families of cetaceans included in this guide:

Marine dolphins (family **Delphinidae**): pp. 304–316. The most diverse group of cetaceans. Most are sociable, sometimes traveling in pods of hundreds of individuals; some practice cooperative hunting. A number of species have highly refined abilities at echolocation.

Porpoises (family **Phocoenidae**): p. 318. Our two species differ from most dolphins in having shorter fins, flattened teeth with narrow cutting edges, and no distinct "beak" separated from the forehead.

Beaked whales (family **Ziphiidae**): pp. 320–324. Mostly rather small whales, found mainly in deep waters. Several of the species are very poorly known and have never been positively identified in life.

White whales (family **Monodontidae**): p. 326. Two odd small whales, the Beluga and the Narwhal, limited to far northern waters.

Gray Whale (family **Eschrichtiidae**): p. 328. **Rorquals** (family **Balaenopteridae**): pp. 330–334. **Right whales** (family **Balaenidae**): p. 336. Collectively these make up the suborder Mysticeti, the baleen whales (all other cetaceans in this book belong to the suborder Odontoceti, or toothed whales). Their mouth structure and feeding behavior are totally different from those of other cetaceans. Instead of teeth, their mouths are lined with numerous long narrow plates called *baleen.* Most of these animals feed by opening their mouths wide, lunging into and enveloping entire schools of tiny prey, and then straining out the food by forcing the water out through their baleen plates.

closeup of baleen of Gray Whale

Sperm Whale (family **Physeteridae**): p. 338. Small sperm whales (family **Kogiidae**): p. 340. One large whale and two very small ones, with the shared characteristic of a hollow region in the head filled with a waxy oil called *spermaceti.* These are toothed whales, with a small underslung lower jaw on the bottom of the large head.

BOTTLENOSE DOLPHIN — *Tursiops truncatus*

Familiar to many for its frequent appearances in captivity and for its love of bow-riding with boats at sea. Common in temperate and tropical waters throughout the world, it is the most numerous dolphin along our Atlantic Coast. Various populations of this species differ in size, appearance, and range. Some groups are resident year-round and some are migratory; coastal populations tend to be smaller, with longer flippers, than those living farther offshore. Diet varies with location, usually whole fish swallowed head first but also squid and crustaceans. Very gregarious, living in long-term social groups called pods. Members of a pod often hunt cooperatively, for example herding fish in schools to trap them against sandbars. ► Streamlined body with broad head and short beak. Adult males are longer and heavier than females. Variably gray or gray-brown, shading to whitish below. Some older individuals have light spotting on the sides. Calves are darker than adults and have light lines on the body that disappear after six months. Longer flippers than other dolphins, except Rough-toothed Dolphin (next page).

SHORT-BEAKED COMMON DOLPHIN — *Delphinus delphis*

This and the Long-beaked (below) were formerly thought to constitute just one species. The Short-beaked is widespread in tropical and warm temperate waters, often farther offshore than the Long-beaked. Fastest of the small dolphins, it feeds on squid and small schooling fish. Gregarious, found in herds of hundreds or even thousands, often with other marine mammals. May come streaking in from a long distance away to ride the bow wave of a boat (also will ride the "snout wave" of baleen whales). ► Note the hourglass or crisscross pattern and the yellow or tan patch on the sides (may look grayish at sea). Very similar to next species, but unlikely to be confused with other dolphins if seen well.

LONG-BEAKED COMMON DOLPHIN — *Delphinus capensis*

More coastal than the Short-beaked, in shallower and warmer waters, and probably less abundant. Gregarious, found in herds from tens up to thousands of individuals. ► Very similar to Short-beaked and overlaps with it off southern California. Long-beaked tends to have a slightly longer rostrum (beak) and flatter forehead, its flippers and dorsal fin may be shorter, and the narrow dark flipper stripe often begins near the corner of the mouth, not the center of the lower jaw.

DOLPHINS

Bottlenose
Dolphin

Short-beaked
Common Dolphin

Long-beaked
Common Dolphin

Bottlenose
Dolphin
L 8¹/₂′   W 500 lbs

Short-beaked
Common Dolphin
L 6¹/₃′   W 200 lbs

Long-beaked
Common Dolphin
L 7¹/₃′   W 225 lbs

ATLANTIC SPOTTED DOLPHIN *Stenella frontalis*

Found only in warm temperate, subtropical, and tropical waters of the Atlantic Ocean, this dolphin feeds on small fish and squid. It usually travels in groups of 10 to 15, but sometimes up to 50. Very active on the surface: bow-riding, lob-tailing, and doing forward flips. Does not do well in captivity. ▶ Stockier with longer flippers and dorsal fin than Pantropical. Highly variable in amount of spotting; tends to be more heavily spotted in southern coastal regions than in northern populations off New England. Calves are born unspotted and sometimes adults are unspotted also. Conversely, can be so heavily spotted as to appear white from a distance. Light shoulder blaze sweeping up into the dark dorsal cape distinguishes unspotted individuals from Bottlenose Dolphin. See next species.

PANTROPICAL SPOTTED DOLPHIN *Stenella attenuata*

One of the most abundant dolphins in subtropical and tropical waters around the world. Frequently found with yellowfin tuna, Spinner Dolphins, and seabirds. It often gets ensnared and drowns in the nets of fishermen who pursue the dolphins in order to find tuna. Feeds on small fish and squid. ▶ Similar to preceding species (and similarly variable) but tends to be less robust, and tail stock is dark above and light below (dark above and below on Atlantic Spotted). Pantropical lacks the pale shoulder blaze, and adults usually lack dark spots below. Individuals living near the coast tend to be larger than those far out at sea. Unspotted at birth, calves at weaning (around two years old) grow dark spots on abdomen first, then light spots above.

ROUGH-TOOTHED DOLPHIN *Steno bredanensis*

Lives in warm seas worldwide but mainly in deep offshore waters, so its habits are poorly known. Often in schools of 50 or fewer, but sometimes in herds of several hundred. Fairly approachable by boats. Often associates with pilot whales and Bottlenose Dolphins, sometimes with Melon-headed Whales or Fraser's Dolphins. Feeds on octopus, fish, and squid. ▶ Distinctive head shape, lacking a crease in front of the melon, so the forehead is one long smooth line. White on lips, throat, and belly (sometimes tinged pink) contrasts sharply with dark gray top of beak. Dark gray cape shows mild contrast with light gray sides. Large flippers are set farther back on body than on most dolphins.

DOLPHINS

Atlantic Spotted Dolphin

Pantropical Spotted Dolphin

Rough-toothed Dolphin

Atlantic Spotted Dolphin

L 6½′ W 270 lbs

Pantropical Spotted Dolphin

L 7′ W 230 lbs

Rough-toothed Dolphin

L 7½′ W 270 lbs

SPINNER DOLPHIN *Stenella longirostris*

Named for its habit of leaping high out of the water and spinning on its longitudinal axis. Usually makes three or four rotations but may spin as many as 14 times before crashing back to the water. Reasons for this behavior are obscure, but it may aid in social communication; the display is visible from great distances. The Spinner Dolphin is common in tropical waters worldwide. Unlike most dolphins, it feeds mainly at night, resting in shallow waters by day. Offshore, it may rest among groups of Pantropical Spotted Dolphins and their associated yellowfin tuna; this habit makes it susceptible to being caught and drowned in tuna nets. Feeds on fish and squid. ▶ Slender, with a long slim beak. Populations vary in appearance, and the dorsal fin can be triangular, point forward, or curve backward. Some in eastern Pacific are uniformly gray with dorsal fins triangular or pointing forward. Others are mainly tricolored (dark above, white below, with sides pale gray or pinkish), with an even-edged dark stripe from eye to flipper. Compare to Clymene Dolphin.

CLYMENE DOLPHIN *Stenella clymene*

Formerly considered a subspecies of Spinner Dolphin, separated only in 1981, so habits not fully studied. Found in the Atlantic and the Gulf of Mexico, mostly in waters deeper than 800 feet. Its diet includes species of squid that surface only at night, so it may feed at night; it also eats some deep-water fish. Occurs in pods of fewer than 50, often with Spinner and Short-beaked Common Dolphins. Has been seen leaping and rotating in the air like Spinner Dolphin. ▶ Similar to Spinner Dolphin but usually has shorter beak, dark cape on back dips lower on sides below dorsal fin, and dark stripe from flipper becomes narrower toward eye.

STRIPED DOLPHIN *Stenella coeruleoalba*

Found in warm temperate, subtropical, and tropical waters worldwide. Often seen "roto-tailing," jumping high and furiously rotating its tail while in the air. Very social, often in groups of a few hundred. Feeds on midwater fish (especially lanternfish) and squid. ▶ Larger and stockier than the two species above. Has similar tricolored pattern but usually shows pale blaze from shoulder up into dark cape (compare to unspotted individuals of Atlantic Spotted Dolphin, previous page). Narrow dark stripe from eye to under tail is diagnostic.

DOLPHINS

Eastern Pacific
form

Spinner
Dolphin

Clymene
Dolphin

Striped
Dolphin

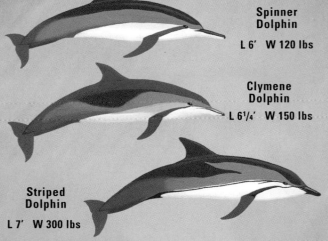

Spinner
Dolphin

L 6'   W 120 lbs

Clymene
Dolphin

L 6¼'   W 150 lbs

Striped
Dolphin

L 7'   W 300 lbs

The first three below are often called "lags," short for *Lagenorhynchus.*

PACIFIC WHITE-SIDED DOLPHIN   *Lagenorhynchus obliquidens*

A very common dolphin of the North Pacific. Highly acrobatic and gregarious, usually in groups of 50 to 100, often associated with other cetaceans. Feeds on small schooling fish, squid, and some deep-water fish that move close to the surface at night. Very inquisitive, often approaching ships, bow-riding or wake-riding. When traveling fast, frequently leaps clear of the water. ▶ Prominent recurved, bicolored dorsal fin and flippers are diagnostic. Short, blunt "beak." Pale gray streak on back from head to flanks is distinctive.

ATLANTIC WHITE-SIDED DOLPHIN   *Lagenorhynchus acutus*

This colorful North Atlantic species is often found in groups of several hundred over the continental shelf, ocean canyons, and other areas with much sea floor relief. Frequently feeds with Humpback and Fin Whales. Diet includes squid, hake, and smelt. ▶ Sharp pattern, and combination of white and bright yellow flank patches, make this species unmistakable if seen well. Often associates with White-beaked Dolphin, and with poor views the two can be confused.

WHITE-BEAKED DOLPHIN   *Lagenorhynchus albirostris*

Fairly common in the North Atlantic, mainly over the continental shelf. Varied diet includes bottom-dwelling species such as haddock, cod, and octopus as well as schooling fish like capelin and herring. May feed with Humpback, Fin, and Killer Whales. Frequently bow-rides and does acrobatics. ▶ Similar to preceding species but more heavy-bodied and with a larger dorsal fin. Pattern varies but usually has a very dark area on each side and a pale gray "saddle" crossing the back behind the dorsal fin; never has yellow flank patches. Despite the name, the "beak" is often gray or brown.

FRASER'S DOLPHIN   *Lagenodelphis hosei*

Described to science based on a skull found in Borneo in the late 1800s but never seen alive until 1971. Now known to be fairly numerous in tropical, deep-water haunts, usually in water over 3,000 feet deep. Highly gregarious, commonly in groups of 100 to 1,000, as well as much smaller groups. Sometimes with other cetaceans, such as Melon-headed Whale. ▶ Distinctive appearance with small dorsal fin and flippers, very short beak, and blackish side stripe running forward to beak and creating "bandit mask" appearance.

DOLPHINS

Pacific White-sided Dolphin

Atlantic White-sided Dolphin

Fraser's Dolphin

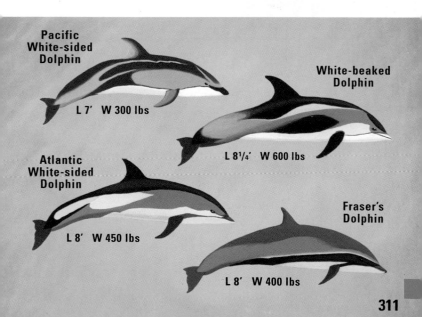

Pacific White-sided Dolphin
L 7′ W 300 lbs

White-beaked Dolphin
L 8¼′ W 600 lbs

Atlantic White-sided Dolphin
L 8′ W 450 lbs

Fraser's Dolphin
L 8′ W 400 lbs

Mariners often use the term "blackfish" for these three species, the pilot whales (next page), and the Killer Whale (p. 316). Most of these species are gregarious and easy to approach. Despite their names, they are more closely related to dolphins than to whales (and, of course, they're not fish).

FALSE KILLER WHALE *Pseudorca crassidens*

False Killer Whales are found throughout deep tropical and temperate waters, usually in groups of 10 to 20 that form loose aggregations with other groups. These whales use a unique foraging system in which the group spreads out in a line over more than a mile to increase their ability to locate food. Prey varies by region but includes octopus, squid, mahi mahi, and tuna. Individuals also share food. The name False Killer Whale comes from occasional attacks on whales larger than itself. ▶ Medium size, tall dorsal fin, and the sharp bend on the leading edge of the flippers are the best field marks for this species. On the pilot whales (next page), the dorsal fin is lower and more broad-based. Compare to next two species.

PYGMY KILLER WHALE *Feresa attenuata*

Widespread in tropical and subtropical waters but poorly known, frequenting deep waters well offshore. Generally in groups of fewer than 50. Appears to be naturally rare, but Hawaii is a good place to try to see this species. Tends to be less active than other dolphins. Feeds on squid, octopus, fish, and sometimes other dolphins. ▶ Can be very difficult to separate from the other species on this page. Smaller than False Killer and lacks the bend on the leading edge of the flippers. Very similar to Melon-headed Whale but has more rounded tips to flippers and more rounded head. Some individuals show a white chin.

MELON-HEADED WHALE *Peponocephala electra*

Generally far offshore, in deep waters off the continental shelf. Often travels in schools of several hundred to more than a thousand and frequently associates with other cetaceans, such as Fraser's Dolphin. May be wary of boats. Melon-headed Whales were once hunted in the Solomon Islands, where their teeth were used as currency and necklaces made from teeth were a woman's dowry. ▶ Very similar to Pygmy Killer Whale, but head and tips of flippers are more pointed. If seen from above, head of this species looks more triangular. Melon-headed Whale often travels in much larger groups than Pygmy Killer Whale.

BLACKISH DOLPHINS

False Killer Whale

Melon-headed Whale

Pygmy Killer Whale

False Killer Whale
L 11–19′ W 2,200–3,000 lbs

Pygmy Killer Whale
L 7 ½′ W 320 lbs

Melon-headed Whale
L 8′ W 410 lbs

The first two are called pilot whales because of the myth that one animal guides or "pilots" the group. Pilot whales form tight-knit pods of 10 to 30 animals (sometimes up to 60) that may be associated with other such groups. Strandings on beaches may involve very large numbers.

SHORT-FINNED PILOT WHALE *Globicephala macrorhynchus*

Common off both coasts. A deep diver, able to remain underwater for up to 15 minutes and dive to 1,600 feet in pursuit of its favorite prey, squid. Females may outnumber adult males in a pod by eight to one. ▶ The two pilot whales are distinguished from all other cetaceans by the bulbous head, dark color, and low, broad-based dorsal fin. Compare to False Killer Whale (previous page). Off Atlantic Coast, compare to next species.

LONG-FINNED PILOT WHALE *Globicephala melas*

Off our Atlantic Coast this species follows its food, squid and mackerel, in an east-west migration, moving from over the continental slope in winter and spring to the continental shelf in summer and fall. ▶ Off eastern Canada, easily recognized by shape of head and dorsal fin. From Massachusetts to South Carolina, may overlap preceding species, and the two are very hard to distinguish. The flippers of Long-finned average longer and more angled, those of Short-finned shorter and more evenly curved, but this is rarely obvious at sea.

NORTHERN RIGHT WHALE DOLPHIN *Lissodelphis borealis*

Common in deep, cold, North Pacific waters; may be farther offshore in spring and summer. Whalers named it the Right Whale Dolphin because, like right whale (p. 336), it lacks a dorsal fin. Groups of several hundred to a thousand often associate with other cetaceans. Their characteristic long, low leaps make them difficult to detect in rough seas. ▶ Easy to identify by its long, slender, bicolored body; lack of dorsal fin; large group size; and long, low leaps out of the water.

RISSO'S DOLPHIN *Grampus griseus*

Widespread off both coasts and in all temperate and tropical oceans. Usually in groups of a dozen to 25, but sometimes up to several hundred. Feeds on squid, mostly at night. Can be very playful during the day, breaching and tail-slapping. ▶ Similar in shape to pilot whales but usually paler, and its dorsal fin is much more erect and set farther back. Color varies from almost white to brown and dark gray. Older individuals heavily scarred, probably from the teeth of other Risso's Dolphins.

DOLPHINS

Short-finned
Pilot Whale

Long-finned
Pilot Whale

belly
up

Risso's Dolphin

Northern Right
Whale Dolphin

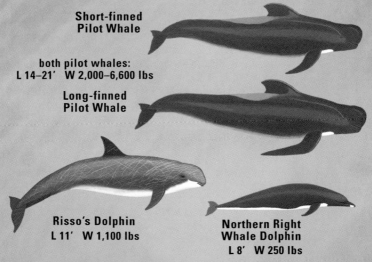

Short-finned
Pilot Whale

both pilot whales:
L 14–21'   W 2,000–6,600 lbs

Long-finned
Pilot Whale

Risso's Dolphin
L 11'   W 1,100 lbs

Northern Right
Whale Dolphin
L 8'   W 250 lbs

315

KILLER WHALE

KILLER WHALE

Orcinus orca (Orca)

Almost everyone knows the Killer Whale. Oceanariums, TV documentaries, and the *Free Willy* movies have made them the universally known dolphin. The name Killer Whale dates back to a time when these animals were persecuted and feared. However, their great public exposure has changed the negative image that they once had, and ecotourists are now eager to see them. Actually, Killer Whales are very curious and will often approach ships or allow themselves to be approached. Pods, the basic social unit of Killer Whales, are centered around a female and her offspring. Often animated behaviors such as breaching, spy-hopping, flipper-slapping, and lob-tailing are observed. Diving is seldom long or to great depths. Killer Whales may live as long as 70 years.

These are not only the largest of the dolphins, but also the most widespread of all dolphins and whales. They occur from the ice-laden Arctic and Antarctic to equatorial waters, coastally and far out at sea, but their center of abundance is in the higher latitudes and in nearshore waters. With this vast geographic range comes a wide variety of prey, including squid, fish, otters, seals, penguins, sea turtles, rays, sharks, and other whales and dolphins — and, oddly enough, deer and moose that they find swimming to islands.

Two distinct forms of Killer Whales are genetically discrete: transients and residents. Residents tend to form larger pods, up to 25 animals, while transient pods usually consist of one to seven animals. Residents have smaller home ranges, while transients move over large areas. Residents feed mostly on fish, transients on mammals. Residents vocalize more and dive for shorter periods. Some scientists believe that these forms should be classified as different subspecies or even different species. ▶ The unmistakable black-and-white pattern and tall dorsal fin of males is instantly recognizable. Females and young have shorter, more curved dorsal fins and narrower flippers. At a great distance a female or young one could be mistaken for a False Killer Whale, but the white patch behind the eye should be apparent on closer inspection. The highly variable "saddle" patch on the back, behind the dorsal fin, may be used to identify individuals (this patch is indistinct or absent in the first year). Newborns have an orange tint to the white areas of their pattern.

KILLER WHALE

pod or
family group

Killer Whale

male
L up to 30′
W up to 6 tons

breaching

spy-hopping

female and male
dorsal fins

female
L up to 25′
W up to 4 tons

PORPOISES

Although some people have used the terms "porpoise" and "dolphin" interchangeably, the porpoises actually belong to a separate family **(Phocoenidae)**, which includes only these two species in North American waters. They have relatively small flippers and no prominent beak.

HARBOR PORPOISE *Phocoena phocoena*

As the name implies, Harbor Porpoises are found in relatively shallow water close to shore and will swim up rivers. Despite living near shore, this species can be easy to overlook. Unlike most dolphins, it is usually seen individually or in groups of two to five. Frequently all that is seen of this species is its small triangular dorsal fin just clearing the surface as it moves away. Sometimes approachable when resting on the surface. Feeds almost exclusively on small, schooling fish, and sometimes squid and octopus. Still common overall, but some populations are endangered by bottom-set gillnets. ▶ The smallest North American cetacean. Does not bow-ride and is usually wary of boats. Relatively plain gray but has darker stripe from corner of mouth to base of flippers, pale sides, mottled gray on flanks. May show small tubercles or bumps on leading edge of dorsal fin. Separated from all dolphins by its small size; medium gray back; small, triangular dorsal fin; and low, smooth, rapid, rolling movements in the water. In the Pacific, compare to Dall's Porpoise.

DALL'S PORPOISE *Phocoenoides dalli*

A fast-swimming, abundant porpoise, endemic to the North Pacific. One of the most frequent bow-riding species, often crossing back and forth between one side of the ship and the other. Able to reach speeds of 35 miles per hour in its almost hyperactive antics. Usually in groups of 2 to 15, these porpoises seem to go out of their way to come to boats to play in the bow wave. Its heavy-bodied form is unique among porpoises, as is its penchant for inhabiting deep, open ocean waters. Has been known to hybridize with Harbor Porpoise. ▶ Unique in shape and pattern. The tiny head and flippers are out of proportion to the heavy body and appear to have been an afterthought of the committee that designed this species. Distinct bicolored appearance similar only to the much larger Killer Whale (p. 316). The "rooster tail" of water kicked up when this porpoise breaks the surface is distinctive and sometimes obscures the animal completely. Pacific White-sided Dolphins (p. 310) sometimes produce a similar rooster tail.

PORPOISES

Harbor Porpoise

"rooster-tail"

Dall's Porpoise

Harbor Porpoise

L 5' W 150 lbs

Dall's Porpoise

L 6' W 250 lbs

319

BEAKED WHALES

(family **Ziphiidae**) are among the most poorly known cetaceans. Much of what is known of these animals comes from stranded animals and specimens caught accidentally by commercial fishermen. Most beaked whales show numerous linear scars on their bodies, presumably from the teeth of other beaked whales during aggressive encounters. Beaked whales are deep divers and feed primarily on squid, fish, and crustaceans from the sea floor as deep as 10,000 feet below the surface.

NORTHERN BOTTLENOSE WHALE *Hyperoodon ampullatus*

Limited to the northern Atlantic Ocean, this is probably the best known of beaked whales, as it has been the subject of an extended study for several years. Easier to observe than most beaked whales, it appears to be quite curious about slow-moving or stationary ships and will often approach them closely. Usually occurs in groups of fewer than 10. Known to dive to more than 5,000 feet deep and sometimes stays underwater for more than an hour. Feeds mainly on squid. ► Large size, distinct melon on head, dolphin-like beak, and gray to brown color should separate this species from all others.

BAIRD'S BEAKED WHALE *Berardius bairdii*

The largest beaked whale, widespread in the North Pacific. Usually travels in pods of fewer than 10 but sometimes in aggregations of up to 50. At times, members of a pod will move together, diving and surfacing synchronously. Like most beaked whales, Baird's spends most of its time below the surface, often on the surface only a few minutes between 30- to 60-minute dives. Dives can be as deep as 6,000 feet. Its diet includes various fish, skates, octopus, and squid. ► A large, long, dark gray whale. The large size and fairly prominent melon separate it from other beaked whales in its range. In size it resembles some of the baleen whales, but with any kind of reasonable view, head shape will separate it from those.

CUVIER'S BEAKED WHALE *Ziphius cavirostris*

The most widespread beaked whale yet rarely seen, perhaps because it breathes only a few times between dives of 20 to 40 minutes. Eats mostly squid but also fish and crustaceans. Groups vary from two to seven individuals. ► Highly variable in color, from dark gray or tan to reddish brown to nearly white. Body size and coloration may lead to confusion with Bottlenose Whale, but note how the head of Cuvier's is more sloping.

BEAKED WHALES

Northern Bottlenose Whale

female and calf

breaching

Baird's Beaked Whale

Cuvier's Beaked Whale

Northern Bottlenose Whale

L 30′   W 9 tons

Baird's Beaked Whale

L 36′   W 10 tons

Cuvier's Beaked Whale

L 20′   W 3 tons

The whales on this page and the next are among the most mysterious animals on earth. Several species have never been seen alive and are known only from specimens washed up on shore or caught by fishing operations. Beaked whales of the genus *Mesoplodon* are identified largely by the shape and position of their two teeth. Only adult males have teeth, so females and young of most species cannot be identified on sight. Because so little information is available about these animals, our illustrations of their color patterns should not be taken too literally.

BLAINVILLE'S BEAKED WHALE   *Mesoplodon densirostris*

The most widespread *Mesoplodon* and the only one that has been studied at sea. Usually in small groups over the edge of the continental shelf, near deep waters. Usually comes to surface slowly, but then may slap its beak against surface of water. ► High arch of lower mandible is distinctive in Atlantic; in Pacific, compare to Ginkgo-toothed (next page) and Stejneger's Beaked Whales (below). Tooth of adult male juts forward and may be crusted with barnacles.

GERVAIS'S BEAKED WHALE   *Mesoplodon europaeus*

Seems to be stranded on our east coast more often than any other *Mesoplodon*, but apparently it has never been identified alive at sea. ► Has a relatively narrow beak, without the arching lower mandible of Blainville's. The single tooth on each side (in adult males only) is located two-thirds to three-fourths of the way out from the corner of the mouth to the tip of the beak.

STEJNEGER'S BEAKED WHALE   *Mesoplodon stejnegeri*

The Aleutian Islands seem to be this species' center of distribution. Groups of 5 to 15 have been seen mostly in deep waters over or near the continental shelf. This species was first described from a single skull, and nearly a century passed before anything else was learned about it. ► Much like Blainville's in head structure; prominent arch on lower jaw with teeth erupting from near the apex. Body mostly dark.

SOWERBY'S BEAKED WHALE   *Mesoplodon bidens*

Limited to the North Atlantic, occurring alone or in small groups. The first beaked whale to be described to science, in 1804, from a specimen stranded in Scotland. ► Long narrow beak, with the single tooth on each side (adult males only) erupting from the lower mandible about halfway out. Compare to True's (next page), Blainville's, and Gervais's Beaked Whales.

UNCOMMON BEAKED WHALES

female
with calf

**Blainville's
Beaked Whale**

young male

**Blainville's
Beaked Whale**

HEADS OF ADULT MALES TO SHOW TOOTH POSITIONS

**Blainville's Beaked Whale
L 15′   W 2,000 lbs**

**Gervais's Beaked Whale
L 16′   W 2,400 lbs**

**Sowerby's Beaked Whale
L 17′   W 2,500 lbs**

**Stejneger's Beaked Whale
L 17′   W?**

TRUE'S BEAKED WHALE   *Mesoplodon mirus*

Occurs mainly in warmer waters of the North Atlantic. Like several of its relatives, it has almost never been identified at sea. ▶ Dark above and light below, with a narrow beak and fairly straight mouthline. In adult males, two teeth erupt from the tip of the lower jaw. No other *Mesoplodon* has this tooth position, but see Cuvier's Beaked Whale (p. 320).

HUBBS'S BEAKED WHALE   *Mesoplodon carlhubbsi*

Known to occur only off the west coast of North America and in a limited area off Japan. ▶ Might be the easiest *Mesoplodon* to identify at sea, although it almost never has been seen in the wild. The adult male is very dark, with whitish beak and raised whitish "skull cap." Its lower jaw is sharply arched at the center and topped with a single wide tooth on either side. Females and young are gray but may show a paler beak.

GINKGO-TOOTHED BEAKED WHALE   *Mesoplodon ginkgodens*

The colorful name comes from Japanese scientists who thought the teeth of the male were shaped like leaves of ginkgo trees. Widespread in the Pacific and Indian Oceans, but known mainly from stranded specimens and from some taken by whalers. ▶ Males are dark gray, females paler. In adult males, the lower jaw is arched at the center, with the tooth erupting at the center of the arch. Males seem to lack the narrow body scars of many male beaked whales.

PERRIN'S BEAKED WHALE   *Mesoplodon perrini*

Known only from a few stranded specimens on the southern California coast and a couple of possible offshore sightings. Just described to science in 2002; previously the California specimens were thought to be Hector's Beaked Whale, a species of the Southern Hemisphere, until genetic analysis proved them distinct. ▶ Dark gray above, fairly pale on belly and head. The single tooth on each side (adult males only) is fairly wide and triangular and is located very near the tip of the beak.

PYGMY BEAKED WHALE   *Mesoplodon peruvianus* (not illustrated)

The smallest beaked whale, averaging less than 12 feet long. Little-known; described to science as recently as 1991. Its main range seems to be off the west coast of South America, but it has been reported once off California. ▶ Appearance of live individuals is poorly known. Apparently gray above, lighter below. Mouthline is strongly curved. Single tooth on each side in adult males may not erupt far enough to be visible above the gum tissue.

RARE BEAKED WHALES

True's Beaked Whale

breaching

beaked whales
(*Mesoplodon* sp.),
probably True's Beaked Whales

**True's Beaked
Whale**

HEADS OF ADULT MALES TO SHOW TOOTH POSITIONS

**True's Beaked Whale
L 16¹/₂' W 2,600 lbs**

**Hubbs's Beaked Whale
L 17¹/₂' W 3,000 lbs**

**Ginkgo-toothed Beaked Whale
L 16' W ?**

**Perrin's Beaked Whale
L 13¹/₂' W ?**

ARCTIC ODDITIES

Besides the Bowhead Whale, these two (the only members of the family **Monodontidae**) are the only cetaceans that are limited to the Arctic.

BELUGA OR WHITE WHALE   *Delphinapterus leucas*

These whales have adapted well to harsh conditions in the Arctic. Their white color proves amazingly difficult to see with a background of ice or white-capped waves. The large melon on their head may be part of the most well-developed sonar of any cetacean, helping them navigate in murky waters at depths from extreme shallows to deeper than 2,500 feet. Belugas are very social, especially in summer, when they gather in very large numbers (sometimes thousands) in estuaries to give birth and shed their skin. Females maintain strong ties to the estuary where they were born, returning there each summer. Several of these estuaries have become major whale-watching areas, including the mouth of the Churchill River in Manitoba and the lower St. Lawrence River. Belugas are commonly displayed at oceanariums and were among the first cetaceans to be brought into captivity. Unlike most cetaceans, their neck bones are not fused, so they can turn their heads and even nod. Belugas have a varied vocal repertoire that can sometimes be heard above the water. ▶ Unmistakable when seen well. The uniform white or light yellow color, large melon, "smiling" mouth line, and lack of a dorsal fin should separate them from any other species. Young are uniformly gray.

NARWHAL   *Monodon monoceros*

The northernmost of all cetaceans, tied to the edge of the pack ice year-round. In the Middle Ages, tusks of male Narwhal were sold as "unicorn horns." All males (and a few females) possess the tusk, which is actually a single left upper jaw tooth. The tusk can grow to nine feet and weigh 22 pounds. In an occasional individual, both teeth will erupt to form double tusks. Narwhals begin life as a uniform gray calf. After weaning they turn almost black and then slowly turn whiter with age. ▶Tusked males are unmistakable. Overall pattern varies, with the amount of dark spotting and streaking diminishing with age. Some old individuals are almost as white as Beluga, but Narwhals are almost always in groups, and some group members will show the characteristic dark streaking and spotting.

ODD ARCTIC WHALES

juvenile

Beluga

porpoising

Narwhal

males and female
in pod

males sparring

tail fluking

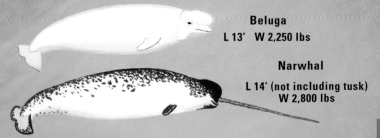

Beluga
L 13′   W 2,250 lbs

Narwhal

L 14′ (not including tusk)
W 2,800 lbs

belongs to its own family **(Eschrichtiidae)**. This is the first of the baleen whales, which continue through page 336.

GRAY WHALE *Eschrichtius robustus*

Gray Whales are probably the most-watched whales on earth. With their long migration routes up and down the west coast of North America and the fact that they feed in shallow water, these animals are visible from land for much of their lives. They are also the center of attention for commercial whale-watching boat trips out of several ports. Their migration is thought to be the longest of any mammal's: 10,000 to 12,000 miles one-way. At the northern end of this migration, the whales spend the summer in the Bering, Chukchi, and Beaufort Seas. At the southern end of the route is the calving and breeding ground, mostly on the outer coast of Baja California. Here females give birth to their young in the warm, shallow water. Usually one or two animals are seen traveling together. On the summering and wintering grounds they sometimes gather in larger groups. Feeding is done by scooping large quantities of bottom sediment and straining out shellfish and shrimplike animals, a behavior that has led to a vernacular name of "mussel-digger."

A population that formerly occurred in the North Atlantic is now extinct, possibly finished off by early whaling in the 17th or 18th century, and a population off the coast of Asia is perhaps on the verge of extinction. However, stocks along the west coast of North America, which were seriously depleted before receiving protection in 1937, have made a spectacular comeback. The recovery has been so good that several whale-watching companies in the San Diego area now guarantee a sighting or your money back! ▶ Overall medium to dark gray, with heavy pale mottling. Has no dorsal fin but shows a small hump on the back followed by "knuckles" (actually the backbone showing) down the back to the tail. Long, curving mouth line. Whale lice and barnacles are common on the whale's body and especially its head, forming yellowish or white patches. The flippers are broader and more paddle-shaped than those of most baleen whales.

GRAY WHALE

adult
with many
barnacles

breaching

calf
spy-hopping

whale watchers
with Gray Whale

Gray Whale
L 43'   W 12 tons

329

HUMPBACK WHALE

Along with the five species on pages 332–334, the Humpback belongs to the Rorqual family (**Balaenopteridae**). These are all baleen whales, their mouths lined with long narrow strips of baleen instead of teeth. *Rorqual* comes from the Norwegian word *rorhval,* meaning pleat or furrow. This refers to the pleats on the underside of the jaw, which expand to allow the whales to take in huge quantities of water to strain out their prey items. These are all big whales, and they all have two blowholes.

HUMPBACK WHALE   *Megaptera novaeangliae*

Found throughout most oceans of the world. Humpbacks migrate from their Arctic and Antarctic feeding grounds in summer to subtropical and tropical waters in winter for mating and calving. They do not feed in winter but are sustained by the huge fat reserves they put on during the long summer days. Humpbacks are among the most vocal whales. Males "sing" haunting songs that can last for hours. For their great bulk, they are also among the most active whales, often breaching over and over or slapping the water with their flippers or flukes. They frequently seem curious about boats and may approach, allowing close views. Their dives are short (usually less than 10 minutes), and they typically raise their tail flukes out of the water as they dive.

Humpbacks have been studied extensively. The patterns of their tail flukes are as unique as fingerprints, allowing individuals to be identified. Unlike toothed whales, Humpbacks do not form long-term social bonds. Groups form as needed to hunt prey or for mating. When feeding cooperatively, Humpbacks will use a "bubble net" to round up prey. Finding a large school of prey, several animals will swim around the school, releasing air bubbles that form a "wall" that the school will not go through. When the school is completely encircled with the "net" of air bubbles, the whales will swim up through the tightly packed prey with mouths agape in an action called lunge feeding. ▶ *Very long flippers,* knobs on top of the head, and low dorsal fin make this whale distinctive. The upperside of the flippers is mostly dark in Pacific populations, mostly white in the Atlantic. Right Whale (p. 336) lacks a dorsal fin. Fin Whale (p. 334) and Sei Whale (p. 332) are close in size but lack the long flippers, seldom show their flukes when diving, and are much more streamlined.

HUMPBACK WHALE

lunge
feeding

breaching

tail flukes

spy-hopping

front
flipper

North Atlantic form

Humpback Whale
L 50′   W 40 tons

RORQUALS

When these three species are at the surface, their blowholes and dorsal fins are usually visible above the water at the same time, unlike some other whales.

NORTHERN MINKE WHALE *Balaenoptera acutorostrata*

The smallest of the rorquals and the most common, usually found within 100 miles of land. Supposedly named for a young whaler named Meincke who cried out a sighting during an era when this species was considered too small to be worth hunting. Some individuals will approach ships. Feeds principally on small schooling fish and krill. ▶ The *white flipper patch* is probably the best field mark when present (but it is sometimes lacking). Snout distinctly pointed. If seen feeding, the baleen is whitish or yellow. Dorsal fin is set farther forward than on other rorquals.

BRYDE'S WHALE *Balaenoptera edeni* *(Balaenoptera brydei)*

The most poorly known of the baleen whales, partly because of past confusion with Sei Whale (below). It appears to be less migratory than most of its relatives. In some parts of the world there appear to be distinct forms of Bryde's whales in inshore and offshore waters, differing in habits and in some structural details. ▶ Similar to Sei Whale, including prominent dorsal fin, but has *three* longitudinal ridges on top of head, not just one. The dorsal fin is very curved, and its trailing edge may look ragged. When diving, it seldom raises its flukes above the water. The baleen is dark.

SEI WHALE *Balaenoptera borealis*

The Sei Whale (pronounced like "sigh") was heavily exploited by whalers during the 20th century and is now probably the rarest of rorquals. It is also one of the fastest, and it seems to be more unpredictable in its migrations than most whales — sometimes moving into a region in numbers, later to disappear for several years. It often feeds by skimming through patches of copepods at the surface, mainly at dawn. Tends to swim close to the surface and can often be followed while underwater by watching for "fluke prints" (calm areas of surface water created by the tail as it pushes toward the surface). ▶ Very large and dark, with noticeable dorsal fin. Has just one ridge on top of head, not three as in Bryde's Whale. Tends to not arch the tail as much as other whales when diving, appearing to sink rather than dive. Compare to Fin Whale (next page).

WHALES

Northern Minke Whale

Bryde's Whale

Sei Whale

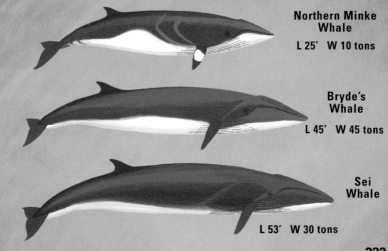

Northern Minke Whale
L 25′ W 10 tons

Bryde's Whale
L 45′ W 45 tons

Sei Whale
L 53′ W 30 tons

These two are the largest animals on earth. As far as we know, the Blue Whale is the largest and heaviest animal that has ever lived.

FIN WHALE *Balaenoptera physalus*

This massive creature is one of the fastest swimmers among whales (up to 25 miles per hour). Unlike most rorquals, Fin Whales occur in small groups fairly often. Found in all the world's oceans but prefers polar and temperate waters to more tropical ones. Seems to ignore boats and go about its business undisturbed by their presence. Both Fin and Blue Whales are capable of producing exceptionally loud, low-pitched sounds, audible underwater nearly a thousand miles away, and they may use these to communicate over long distances. ▶ The most diagnostic field mark is the unique *asymmetrical jaw coloring:* white on the right side, dark on the left. The light chevron on the back behind the eye is another good mark when visible. Some Fin Whales show two faint additional rostral ridges that could cause confusion with Bryde's Whale (previous page), but these are very faint and usually don't show well in the field.

BLUE WHALE *Balaenoptera musculus*

This magnificent animal is known to reach maximum lengths of 110 feet and weights of 200 tons. Many sightings of Blue Whales are made from boats that are less than two-thirds the size of the animals themselves. Babies at birth are more than 20 feet long and weigh at least three tons, and nursing young may gain 200 pounds per day. The whaling industry nearly drove these great creatures to extinction, with 360,000 killed in the Southern Hemisphere alone during the 20th century. Many populations still have not recovered, and some experts think they may never recover. ▶ Huge size, pale *blue-gray color,* and mottled pattern are distinctive. The belly sometimes looks yellowish because of algae growth. When seen well the head is broadly U-shaped. The raised fleshy ridge in front of the blowholes in rorquals, called the *splashguard,* is especially prominent in Blue Whales. The blow is rather narrow and tall, reaching heights of 30 feet. Dorsal fin is variable but usually small and set well back toward the tail. Dorsal fin and blowholes are seldom in view above the water at the same time. Blues raise their flukes when diving, whereas Fin Whales usually do not.

MASSIVE WHALES

tail
flukes

**Fin
Whale**

dorsal
fin

tail
flukes

**Blue
Whale**

dorsal
fin

breaching

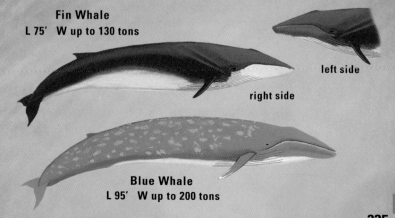

Fin Whale
L 75′   W up to 130 tons

left side

right side

Blue Whale
L 95′   W up to 200 tons

RIGHT WHALES

Bowhead and right whales (family **Balaenidae**) form a group of very heavy-bodied whales without dorsal fins, living mainly in cold waters. There is debate over how many species of right whales exist. Genetic studies show that the North Atlantic, North Pacific, and Southern Hemisphere populations have been separated for millennia and may constitute three species. The populations in our area, Atlantic and Pacific, are nearly identical, and we provisionally treat them as one species.

BOWHEAD   *Balaena mysticetus*

This whale of the Arctic thrives at the edge of the pack ice, insulated by a layer of blubber more than a foot thick. It uses its huge, arched skull for bashing through ice up to six feet thick — sometimes a necessity, as it may travel long distances under the ice and must surface to breathe. Like the Northern Right Whale, Bowheads were hunted to near extinction. There are five distinct populations of Bowheads, and four are highly endangered; only the population west and north of Alaska, estimated at about 8,000 animals, is doing well. Subsistence hunting by Inuit natives of that region does not appear to pose a threat. ▶ A short, heavy-bodied whale with no dorsal fin. The *mostly white lower jaw* should separate it from the Northern Right Whale, although the two species rarely overlap in range. Blow is a very tall V shape. The large hump near the blowhole and arched back form a double hump above water when Bowheads are on the surface.

NORTHERN RIGHT WHALE   *Eubalaena glacialis*

The name "right whale" has a grim background: whalers considered this the right whale to kill because it was slow-moving and rich in oil and baleen, and it floated when it was dead. This notoriety helped bring it to the verge of extinction. Northern Right Whales now number fewer than 400 individuals altogether. The Atlantic population is estimated at about 300, while the known Pacific population recently was an astonishingly low 13 animals. A mother and calf were spotted in 2002 in the Bering Sea, bringing some hope for the future. ▶ Recognized by large heavy shape, dark color, and lack of a dorsal fin. Roughened areas of skin on and near the head, called *callosities*, are often covered with dull whitish yellow cyamids (whale lice). Its blow is in a tall V shape. Might be confused only with the Bowhead, although their ranges barely overlap.

ENDANGERED WHALES

Bowhead

spout

tail
fluke

Northern
Right Whale

spout

Bowhead
L 55′ W 80 tons

Northern
Right Whale
L 50′ W 65 tons

The huge Sperm Whale (the only member of the family **Physeteridae**) and the two very small whales on the following page are quite different in size but are considered to be related. They are toothed whales, and all three species feed on squid, crustaceans, and fish in deep water. The most unusual characteristic that all three have in common is an oil-filled region in the head called a *spermaceti organ*. The function of this organ is still unknown, but some scientists speculate that it may help with diving or in focusing their sonar. Sperm Whales were heavily hunted in the 1700s and 1800s, when the waxy spermaceti was much in demand for use in making candles and later as an ingredient in cosmetics.

SPERM WHALE   *Physeter catodon*

The famous white whale of Herman Melville's classic *Moby Dick* was a Sperm Whale. (In fact, white Sperm Whales do exist, but they are rare.) Besides its literary claim to fame, this is a superlative whale in other ways as well. It has the largest head (more than one-third of its body), the deepest dives (to well over a mile below the surface), and the longest dives (up to two hours or even more at a time) of any whale. Sperm Whales have a single blowhole (not a double blowhole like the baleen whales) that is placed far to the left and at the front of the head, creating a blow that angles sharply to the left. On calm days, when the blow is not being shifted by wind, the blow alone can identify this species at great distances. Between dives, Sperm Whales may spend several minutes lying motionless at the surface, breathing to hyperoxygenate their blood. They feed primarily on squid, including some as large as 40 feet long. The large conical teeth of the Sperm Whale were once a prized object for whalers to carve scrimshaw — scenes of whaling etched in the surface of the teeth and then made visible with the addition of dark pigment to the etched areas. ▶ Easier to identify than most whales. The massive *rectangular head* and the distinctive left-angling blow make it recognizable even at great distances. The large triangular flukes, notched at the center, are usually raised high as the whale begins a deep dive. There is a small hump at midback instead of a dorsal fin.

SPERM WHALE

lunging
with mouth open

hump on back
in place of
dorsal fin

tail
flukes

breaching

Sperm
Whale

male L 48′   W 37 tons
female L 35′   W 17 tons

These two species (family **Kogiidae**) are very poorly known and are difficult to distinguish from each other. Neither is seen very often, but it is not clear whether they are genuinely rare or just easily overlooked. Both share the habit of slowly appearing on the surface and then simply sinking again rather than diving. When lying at the surface, they may even suggest a floating log at a distance. Dwarf and Pygmy Sperm Whales have a fold on the side of the head that looks like the gill on a fish; because of this pattern and the shape of their head, when stranded on shore they may be mistaken for sharks. Both species have a sac in the lower intestines that is filled with a dark liquid that they can eject when the whale is startled, much as a squid uses its "ink" as camouflage for its escape from predators. Plastic bags have been found in the stomachs of animals stranded on shore, and blockage by the plastic was evidently the cause of death in these cases.

As a measure of the similarity of these species, even scientists who study them are often unsure of which one they are observing at sea. Some stranded animals must be measured and the teeth counted before an accurate determination of species can be made.

DWARF SPERM WHALE   *Kogia simus*

The smallest of the toothed whales. Until 1966, this was thought to be the same species as the Pygmy Sperm Whale (below). ▶ Compared to Pygmy Sperm Whale, the dorsal fin is slightly larger, taller, and placed more toward center of back. Dwarf Sperm Whale may be more social; groups of up to ten individuals have been seen. The Dwarf Sperm Whale tends to live over or near the continental shelf, while the Pygmy Sperm Whale lives in deeper waters. Despite such differences, the two species are often impossible to distinguish, even for the observer who is lucky enough to see one of them.

PYGMY SPERM WHALE   *Kogia breviceps*

Widespread but poorly known; tends to be farther off-shore than the preceding species, usually traveling in groups of fewer than six. Apparently does much feeding in very deep water, taking much of its food from the ocean floor. ▶ Virtually identical to Dwarf Sperm Whale but slightly larger. The dorsal fin is smaller, shorter, and set a little farther back toward the tail.

SMALL SPERM WHALES

**Dwarf
Sperm Whale**

**Pygmy
Sperm Whale**

**Dwarf
Sperm Whale
L 7'   W 450 lbs**

**Pygmy
Sperm Whale
L 10'   W 800 lbs**

SOURCES OF FURTHER INFORMATION

This guide was designed for quick reference in the field. Wherever possible, we have tried to include additional points of interest about each species, but only so much can be crammed into a pocket-sized guide. Here are some places to go if you want more information.

Books: In the Peterson Field Guide series (Houghton Mifflin), *A Field Guide to the Mammals,* by William H. Burt and Richard P. Grossenheider (2nd edition, 1964), is somewhat out of date as to names and classification but still valuable. *Mammals of North America,* by Roland W. Kays and Don E. Wilson (Princeton University Press, 2002), has brief treatments of every species, including tooth and skull details for those that can't be identified in the field. For a more comprehensive reference, see *The Smithsonian Book of North American Mammals,* edited by Don E. Wilson and Sue Ruff (Smithsonian Institution Press, 1999).

For identifying mammals by their tracks and signs, three of our favorite references are *A Field Guide to Animal Tracks,* by Olaus J. Murie (Houghton Mifflin, 1974); *Tracking and the Art of Seeing: How to Read Animal Tracks and Sign,* by Paul Reszendes (Firefly Books, 1992); and *The Complete Tracker,* by Len McDougall (The Lyons Press, 1997).

A number of books treat specific groups of mammals or certain geographic areas. Here are some that we have found especially helpful. *National Audubon Society's Guide to Marine Mammals of the World,* illustrated by Pieter A. Folkens (Knopf, 2002), is useful worldwide, as is *Walker's Bats of the World,* by Ronald M. Nowak (Johns Hopkins University Press, 1994). Among many state and regional mammal books, we have especially referred to *California Mammals,* by E. W. Jameson Jr. and Hans J. Peeters (University of California Press, 1988) and *The Mammals of Texas,* by William B. Davis and David J. Schmidly (Texas Parks and Wildlife Department, 1994).

A scholarly classic is E. Raymond Hall's two-volume *The Mammals of North America* (2nd edition, Wiley, 1981, reprinted by Blackburn Press, 2001). And for the most comprehensive information available on a given species, the source is *Mammalian Species,* published by the American Society of Mammalogists. This ongoing project produces a thorough account of current knowledge for one species at a time, with 20 or more new accounts published each year, each one ranging from 2 to 14 pages. More than 700 accounts have been published, and eventually every mammal species in the world will be covered. For contact information, see below.

Web sites: The best place on the Web to get started in finding reliable information about mammals is the site maintained by the American Society of Mammalogists. This exemplary scientific society, responsible for many outstanding publications in print, also provides reliable information and links on the Internet. Find it at www.mammalsociety.org.

PHOTOGRAPHER CREDITS

This book would not have been possible without the cooperation of many outstanding photographers, who not only allowed us to use their photographs, but also gave permission to have those photographs altered for the sake of illustration. Plates are listed by page number (in bold), followed by a dash and the number of the image. Images on each plate are numbered sequentially. Read image numbers within each species from top to bottom and then left to right. The paintings of marine mammals were done by Kenn Kaufman.

David S. Addison/Visuals Unlimited: **151**-6

Bryan & Cherry Alexander/Seapics.com: **299**-1, 3

Dr. J. Scott Altenbach: **5**-5, 6; **260**-1; **263**-1, 2, 6; **265**-3, 6; **267**-3, 5; **269**-5, 10, 11, 12; **271**-2, 4, 5, 8, 9, 11; **273**-2, 5, 10; **275**-3, 4, 5, 9, 10; **275**-10; **277**-8, 9; **279**-4, 5, 7, 12, 13; **281**-8; **283**-2, 4, 5, 8; **285**-8, 9

Ronn Altig: **4**-7; **65**-3; **83**-5; **197**-3; **205**-5; **207**-5, 6, 7; **221**-4; **227**-1, 2; **232**-1; **235**-1, 6; **245**-8; **249**-3; **279**-10

Scot Anderson: **67**-6, 7

M. Andrea/American Society of Mammalogists: **219**-3

Robin Baird/Marine Mammal Images: **297**-6, 11; **315**-3; **319**-1, 5; **321**-1

Frank S. Balthis: **115**-2; **141**-2; **157**-1; **291**-8; **329**-2, 3

Bill Banaszewski/Visuals Unlimited: **113**-3; **127**-2

Roger W. Barbour: **4**-12; **181**-6; **185**-4, 5; **189**-3; **211**-6; **213**-5, 6; **217**-4; **221**-7, 8; **223**-2, 3; **225**-7; **229**-4; **232**-2; **239**-2, 3; **241**-1, 2; **243**-7; **247**-2; **249**-2; **251**-3; **257**-3; **259**-7; **265**-4, 5; **271**-10; **277**-2; **279**-2; **285**-7

Breck Bartholomew: **237**-2

Bill Beatty/Visuals Unlimited: **243**-8

Cathy Beck/Marine Mammal Images: **307**-4

Russell Benedict: **255**-4

Scott Benson/Marine Mammal Images: **321**-3

Hal Beral/Visuals Unlimited: **293**-4

Troy L. Best: **4**-5; **31**-10; **59**-3; **61**-2; **201**-5; **203**-3, 6, 7; **205**-1, 2

J. Betts/American Society of Mammalogists: **83**-1

Dean Biggins/U.S. Fish and Wildlife Services: **33**-6

Rick and Nora Bowers/ BowersPhoto.com: **2**-2, 3, 4, 8, 10, 12, 13, 14, 15; **3**-2, 4, 9, 10; **5**-9; **22**-1, 2; **23**-2; **7**-1; **8**-1; **15**-1; **20**-1; **27**-2; **29**-2; **31**-1, 9; **33**-2; **37**-1, 4; **38**-1; **39**-2; **41**-3; **43**-1, 3; **45**-2, 4; **47**-1, 2, 4; **49**-4; **53**-9; **57**-1, 4, 5, 6; **59**-1, 2, 4, 5; **61**-3, 4, 5, 6, 7, 8; **63**-4; **69**-1; **73**-1, 3, 4, 5; **75**-1, 7, 8, 9, 10; **77**-1, 3; **79**-1, 2; **81**-1, 2, 7; **85**-1, 2, 3, 5, 8; **87**-6, 7, 8; **89**-3, 4, 5; **91**-4, 5; **93**-2, 5, 6; **96**-1, 3, 4; **97**-7; **99**-4, 7; **101**-1, 2, 3; **105**-6, 7; **109**-1, 2, 3, 7; **111**-2, 3, 4; **117**-2; **119**-3, 6, 7, 8; **123**-5; **124**-1; **127**-6; **129**-1; **131**-5, 8; **133**-2, 3; **135**-6; **137**-1, 2, 4, 5; **139**-3, 7, 8; **141**-5, 7, 8; **145**-6, 8, 9; **147**-4, 5, 6, 7, 9; **149**-1; **155**-5, 6; **157**-2, 4, 5, 6, 7; **159**-1; **169**-1, 3; **171**-1, 2, 3; **173**-4; **187**-2; **195**-2; **223**-9; **237**-1; **263**-3, 7, 8; **267**-6; **269**-1, 3, 4; **271**-1, 3; **273**-1, 3, 7; **275**-7, 8; **277**-1, 3, 5, 7; **279**-11; **281**-1, 3, 4, 5, 6; **283**-9, 10; **285**-2, 4, 6; **286**-2; **289**-1, 6; **295**-2, 4

Tom Brakefield/Bruce Coleman Inc.: **297**-3

H. E. Broadbooks: **63**-1, 3, 5; **67**-5

Milo Burcham: **29**-8; **189**-2; **221**-1; **225**-4; **237**-3

Gary W. Carter/Visuals Unlimited: **167**-7

Carolyn Chatterton: **35**-5, 6

Budd Christman NOAA Corps: **295**-6

Herbert Clarke: **43**-4; **45**-1; **53**-6; **67**-1; **77**-5; **83**-6; **85**-4; **215**-3; **293**-5; **335**-3

Brandon D. Cole/Visuals Unlimited: **287**-2; **301**-6; **311**-1; **327**-2; **331**-1, 3

Lew Consiglieri/National Oceanic and Atmospheric Administration, National Marine Fisheries Service, Alaska Fisheries Science Center,

National Marine Mammal Laboratory: 299-5, 8

Gerald and Buff Corsi/Visuals Unlimited: 71-2; 93-1; 129-2; 131-6; 147-1, 3; 165-6; 291-6; 299-7, 9

Mike Couffer/Bruce Coleman Inc.: 205-3

Rob Curtis/The Early Birder: 65-2; 93-7; 115-5; 159-7; 163-2; 167-6; 279-9

Beth Davidow/Visuals Unlimited: 35-3; 101-4; 119-4, 5; 155-2; 331-4

James L. Davis/Visuals Unlimited: 289-3

Larry Ditto: 3-5, 14, 15; 31-3, 5; 75-4, 6; 87-5; 111-5, 8; 121-2; 125-1; 139-4; 148-2; 149-3; 151-3, 5; 153-4; 171-4, 6

Robert C. Dowler and Zane Laws: 179-5, 6

Michael Durham: 107-1; 169-2; 235-2; 245-1, 2

Patrick J. Endres/Visuals Unlimited: 159-4

Marc Epstein/Visuals Unlimited: 14-1

Cheryl A. Ertelt/Visuals Unlimited: 53-4; 135-4

M. B. Fenton: 4-13; 231-1, 2, 3

Fletcher and Baylis: 95-5

Richard B. Forbes: 61-1; 65-5, 6; 83-2; 183-3; 221-2, 3; 249-4, 5; 319-2

Richard B. Forbes/American Society of Mammalogists: 195-5; 249-1

John K. B. Ford/Ursus/Seapics.com: 327-4, 5, 6; 337-2

Mats Forsberg/Nature Picture Library, BBC Broadcasting House: 299-4

Gerard Fuehrer/Visuals Unlimited: 23-1; 25-1; 97-5; 123-4, 6; 131-7

Michael Gabridge/Visuals Unlimited: 169-5

John Gerlach/Visuals Unlimited: 2-9; 49-2; 53-2; 85-6; 115-1; 165-4; 205-4; 209-7; 257-8, 9

Francois Gohier: 299-11, 12, 13

Daniel W. Gotshall/Visuals Unlimited: 335-4

William Grenfell/Visuals Unlimited: 189-6; 245-6; 249-6; 257-8, 9

Bob Gress: 3-1, 16; 33-5, 8; 35-2; 65-1; 79-6, 7; 89-1; 96-2; 103-2, 5; 133-5, 6; 163-5, 6; 209-1, 2

J. Harris/American Society of Mammalogists: 207-4; 215-1

C. C. Hass: 105-8, 9, 10

J. D. Haweeli/American Society of Mammalogists: 37-5

Glenn Hayes/KAC Productions: 103-6

Virginia Hayssen: 201-1

Mack Henley/Visuals Unlimited: 29-7; 55-3

Richard Herrmann/Visuals Unlimited: 289-4

Wyb Hoek/Marine Mammal Images: 297-8, 9, 10; 337-3

John H. Hoffman: 45-5; 169-4

Ken Howard/Sea Images.org: 327-3; 339-3

John Hyde: 143-8

Cathy and Gordon Illg: 77-2; 79-5; 89-2; 91-2; 99-3; 117-3; 123-1; 127-1, 5; 143-4; 153-3; 165-7

Dr. Lloyd Glenn Ingles/© California Academy of Sciences: 63-2; 201-2, 3; 203-2, 4; 237-5, 8

Thomas Jefferson: 333-1

Benjamin Kahn/Seapics.com: 341-1

Bill Kamin/Visuals Unlimited: 13-1; 101-5

Darin Kamins/Marine Mammal Images: 333-2

Robin Karpan/Visuals Unlimited: 165-1

Douglas A. Kelt: 201-4

T. R. Kieckhefer/Marine Mammal Images: 315-5

D. R. Klein: 35-4; 219-6

G. Lagerloef/National Oceanic and Atmospheric Administration, National Marine Fisheries Service, Alaska Fisheries Science Center, National Marine Mammal Laboratory: 295-5

Greg W. Lasley/KAC Productions: 111-7

Tom and Pat Leeson: 2-5; 3-7, 12; 5-7, 11, 12; 33-4; 37-3; 41-8; 47-3, 5; 69-2; 81-8; 87-1, 3, 4; 91-1; 97-2, 3; 99-5, 6, 8; 105-2, 3; 109-4, 5; 111-1, 6; 115-3, 4; 117-4, 5; 119-1; 123-2, 3; 125-2; 127-3, 4, 7, 8; 129-3, 4, 5, 6; 131-4; 135-1; 137-3, 6; 139-2, 5, 6; 141-4; 143-1, 2, 3, 6; 145-1, 4, 5, 7; 147-2; 148-1; 149-5; 151-1, 2, 4; 153-1, 6; 155-4; 157-3; 159-2, 8; 161-1, 3, 4, 5; 163-4, 7; 165-5; 173-1, 2, 3; 286-1; 289-2, 7; 291-2; 301-3; 305-1, 2; 317-1, 2, 4

William Leonard: 217-3; 237-4; 257-4

David Liebman: 15-2; 243-5

Lindholm/Visuals Unlimited: 135-7

Irene Lindsey: 223-5

Gil Lopez-Espina/Visuals Unlimited: 169-1

Ken Lucas/Visuals Unlimited: 203-1

C. D. MacLeod: 323-1, 2, 3

John Marriott/wildernessprints.com: 3-11; 143-5

Steve and Dave Maslowski: 121-9, 10; 229-1, 2

Steve Maslowski/Visuals Unlimited: 2-6; 51-3; 105-4; 117-8; 123-7

Steve McCutcheon/Visuals Unlimited: 161-7

Joe McDonald: 4-14; 235-4; 237-6, 7

Joe McDonald/Bruce Coleman Inc.: 297-2

Joe McDonald/Visuals Unlimited: 29-4; 41-4; 51-1; 53-1; 103-3; 131-1; 159-3; 167-8; 297-1, 4, 5; 305-4

Mary Ann McDonald: 235-4

Mary Ann McDonald/Visuals Unlimited: 139-1

Diana McIntyre/Marine Mammal Images: 341-2

R. McLanahan/IFAW/Seapics.com: 339-4

Charles W. Melton: 2-11; 17-1; 55-1; 68-1; 71-7; 79-3, 4; 153-2; 165-2, 8; 167-1; 215-2

Anthony Mercieca: 3-13; 45-6; 49-1, 6; 55-2; 67-4; 68-2; 73-2; 75-5; 77-4; 81-5; 85-7; 93-3; 95-4, 6; 101-6; 105-1; 107-2; 121-1; 143-7; 149-4; 159-5; 161-2; 163-9; 167-2; 169-3, 6; 171-5; 181-7; 183-1; 195-3, 4

Peter L. Meserve: 201-6

Gary Meszaros/Visuals Unlimited: 251-1; 255-3; 295-1

Jack Milchanowski/Visuals Unlimited: 45-3

Sally Mizroch/National Oceanic and Atmospheric Administration, National Marine Fisheries Service, Alaska Fisheries Science Center, National Marine Mammal Laboratory: 319-3

C. Allan Morgan: 5-13, 14; 45-7; 81-9; 89-7; 113-4; 141-1, 3; 199-6; 287-1; 289-5; 291-5, 7; 293-1; 295-3; 301-2; 315-1, 2; 317-3; 331-2; 335-1, 5, 6

Arthur Morris/Visuals Unlimited: 135-8

John C. Muegge/Visuals Unlimited: 41-7; 153-7

R. W. Murphy/Royal Ontario Museum: 231-4, 5, 6

Phil Myers/www.animaldiversity.org: 53-8; 253-6

Allan G. Nelson: 3-3; 29-5; 55-4; 93-4; 95-2, 7; 113-2; 117-6

Michael Newcomer/Marine Mammal Images: 311-4

Mark Newman/Visuals Unlimited: 147-8

Michael S. Nolan/Seapics.com: 339-1

Glenn M. Oliver/Visuals Unlimited: 77-8; 145-3; 161-6

Oregon Zoo/Photo by Michael Durham: 29-9

James F. Parnell: 25-2; 31-2; 121-6

Michael Patrikeev: 4-16; 121-3; 243-9, 10; 251-4; 259-1

Brian Patteson: 309-3

Donald Pattie: 121-7, 8; 257-1, 2

Dean E. Pearson: 229-6

Robert L. Pitman/Seapics.com: 315-6

John V. Planz: 195-7

Rick Poley/Visuals Unlimited: 185-3

Fritz Polking/Visuals Unlimited: 301-1

R. G. Poulin: 221-5, 6

Roger A. Powell/Visuals Unlimited: 217-6

Todd Pusser: 303-1; 305-3; 307-1, 3; 309-1, 4; 311-2; 313-2, 3, 5; 315-4; 321-4, 5; 331-5; 333-3; 334-2; 339-2

Todd Pusser/Marine Mammal Images: 341-3

Michael Quinton: 29-3; 33-7, 9; 225-3; 246-2; 253-7

Roger Rageot/© David Liebman Nature Stock: 185-8; 246-1; 259-2

Betty Randall: 97-6; 121-4; 197-6

Gaylen Rathburn/U.S. Fish and Wildlife Service: 5-8; 301-7

R. L. and V. R. Rausch: 95-1; 219-4, 5

Ryan L. Rehmeier: 229-3; 259-6

Hans Reinhard/Bruce Coleman, Inc.: 171-7

Don Roberson: 65-4

Eda Rogers: 5-10; 297-7; 301-4; 327-1; 341-4

H. S. Rose/Visuals Unlimited: 131-3

Leonard Lee Rue III/Visuals Unlimited: 77-7

Mike Salisbury/Nature Picture Library, BBC Broadcasting House: 299-2

Larry Sansone: 29-6; 53-7; 57-2, 3; 64-3; 67-3; 71-3; 73-6, 7; 77-6; 131-9; 133-1, 4; 173-6

C. Gregory Schmitt and Marshall C. Conway: 31-6, 7, 8

Alisa Schulman-Janiger/Marine Mammal Images: 333-4

Alison M. Sheehey/NatureAli.org: 215-4

Dennis Sheridan: 203-5; 257-7

Dennis Sheridan/© David Liebman Nature Stock: 257-6

Paul W. Sherman: 83-3, 4

Ronnie Sidner: **285**-3

Lee H. Simons: **249**-7

Ann and Rob Simpson: **4**-10; **25**-4; **31**-2; **38**-2; **49**-3; **99**-2; **105**-5; **107**-5; **137**-7; **197**-1; **217**-7; **267**-1

Ann and Rob Simpson/Visuals Unlimited: **167**-3, 4; **225**-5; **253**-1

John Sohlden/Visuals Unlimited: **243**-1

Doug Sokell/Visuals Unlimited: **89**-6

Michael A. Steele: **47**-6

J. M. Sulentich/American Society of Mammalogists: **215**-5

Fiona Sunquist: **185**-9

Jack Swenson: **307**-2; **319**-5

Jack Tasoff: **67**-2; **95**-3

B. P. Tatum/Visuals Unlimited: **245**-5

Texas Parks & Wildlife © 2003/Glen Mills: **207**-3

Richard Thom/Visuals Unlimited: **153**-5; **271**-7

Michael Tove/Marine Mammal Images: **325**-2

Merlin D. Tuttle/Bat Conservation International: **261**-1; **263**-4, 5; **265**-1, 2, 7; **269**-2, 6, 8, 9; **271**-6, 12; **273**-4, 6, 8, 9, 11; **275**-1, 2, 6; **277**-4, 6, 10, 11, 12; **279**-1, 3, 6; **281**-2, 7, 9, 10, 11; **283**-1, 3, 6, 7; **285**-1, 5

John and Gloria Tveten: **3**-6; **4**-1, 2, 3, 4, 6, 8, 9, 11, 15; **5**-2, 4; **27**-1, 3, 4, 6; **29**-1; **31**-4; **41**-1; **33**-3; **43**-5, 6; **71**-1, 4, 5; **75**-2, 3; **97**-1; **103**-4, 7; **107**-4, 6, 7; **109**-6, 8; **117**-1; **141**-6; **149**-2; **165**-3; **177**-1, 2, 3, 4, 5, 6, 7; **179**-1, 2, 3, 4, 7, 8; **181**-1, 2, 3, 4, 8; **183**-4, 5; **185**-1, 2, 7; **187**-1, 3, 4, 5, 6; **189**-1, 4, 7, 8; **191**-1, 2, 3, 4, 5, 6; **193**-1, 2, 3, 5, 6; **195**-1; **197**-2, 4; **199**-1, 2, 3, 4, 5; **207**-1, 2; **209**-3, 4, 5, 6; **211**-1, 2, 3, 4; **213**-1, 2, 3, 4; **219**-1, 2; **223**-1, 4, 8; **225**-1, 6; **235**-3, 5; **239**-1, 4, 5, 6, 7; **241**-3, 4; **243**-3, 4; **253**-3, 4, 5; **255**-2, 5; **259**-4, 8; **267**-4; **279**-8; **293**-3, 6; **313**-1; **317**-5; **329**-1, 4, 5

John and Gloria Tveten/KAC Productions: **267**-2; **269**-7

Tom J. Ulrich: **33**-1; **37**-2; **41**-5; **43**-2; **51**-5; **81**-3, 4, 6; **93**-8; **97**-3; **113**-1; **117**-7; **121**-5; **225**-2; **291**-3; **293**-2

Tom J. Ulrich/Visuals Unlimited: **131**-10; **135**-5

U.S. Fish and Wildlife Service: **187**-7

R. W. Van Devender: **5**-1, 3; **181**-5; **189**-5; **193**-4; **217**-1, 2, 5; **229**-5; **233**-1; **243**-2, 6; **245**-3, 4, 7; **247**-1; **251**-2, 5, 6, 7; **253**-2; **255**-1; **253**-2; **257**-5; **259**-3, 5

Tom Vezo: **2**-1; **3**-8; **25**-3; **35**-1; **41**-2, 6; **49**-5, 7; **53**-3, 5; **71**-6; **87**-2; **91**-3; **99**-1; **103**-1; **117**-9; **119**-2; **131**-2; **145**-2; **155**-3; **159**-6

Dylan Walker/Seapics.com : **325**-1

Harry M. Walker: **37**-6; **115**-6; **155**-1; **163**-8; **173**-5; **291**-1, 4

Tom Walker/Visuals Unlimited: **135**-2, 3

James Watt/Visuals Unlimited: **313**-4

William J. Weber/Visuals Unlimited: **27**-5; **39**-1; **51**-2; **107**-3; **113**-5; **185**-6; **301**-5

Nancy M. Wells/Visuals Unlimited: **51**-4

Randall Wells/Marine Mammal Images: **321**-2

Hal Whitehead/Marine Mammal Images: **311**-3

Glenn Williams/Ursus/Seapics.com: **337**-1

Stephen L. Williams: **241**-5

Julia Witczuk: **197**-5

Jerry O. Wolff: **223**-6, 7

INDEX OF ENGLISH NAMES OF MAMMALS

You can tally your "life list" here by checking off the boxes in front of the names of mammals you've seen. A box is provided for each full species in the book, except for exotics that may not be fully established.

Antelope, see Pronghorn 164
Aplodontia, *see* Sewellel 234
Aoudad 168
☐ **Armadillo**, Nine-banded 108
☐ **Badger**, American 118
☐ **Bat**, Allen's Big-eared 276
☐ Big Brown 268
☐ Big Free-tailed 262
Brazilian Free-tailed, *see* Mexican Free-tailed Bat 262
☐ Buffy Flower 264
☐ California Leaf-nosed 276
☐ Cuban Flower 264
Cuban House, *see* Pallas's Mastiff Bat 264
☐ Eastern Red 278
☐ Evening 268
Ghost-faced, *see* Peters's Ghost-faced Bat 280
☐ Greater Bonneted 264
☐ Hoary 280
Indiana, *see* Indiana Myotis 270
☐ Jamaican Fruit 264
☐ Lesser Long-nosed Bat 284
Little Brown, *see* Little Brown Myotis 268
☐ Mexican Free tailed 262
☐ Mexican Long-nosed 284
☐ Mexican Long-tongued 284
North American Long-nosed, *see* Lesser Long-nosed Bat 284
☐ Northern Yellow 282

☐ Pallas's Mastiff 264
☐ Pallid 282
☐ Peters's Ghost-faced 280
☐ Pocketed Free-tailed 262
☐ Rafinesque's Big-eared 276
☐ Seminole 278
☐ Silver-haired 280
Southern Long-nosed, *see* North American Long-nosed Bat 284
☐ Southern Yellow 282
☐ Spotted 278
☐ Townsend's Big-eared 276
☐ Underwood's Bonneted 264
Underwood's Mastiff Bat, *see* Underwood's Bonneted Bat 264
Vampire, *see* Hairy-legged Vampire 280
Velvety Free-tailed, *see* Pallas's Mastiff Bat 264
☐ Wagner's Bonneted 264
Wagner's Mastiff, *see* Wagner's Bonneted Bat 264
Western Mastiff, *see* Greater Bonneted Bat 264
☐ Western Red 278
☐ Western Yellow 282
☐ **Bear**, Black 142
Brown, *see* Grizzly Bear 144
☐ Grizzly 144
☐ Polar 146
☐ **Beaver**, American 110
Mountain, *see* Sewellel 234

☐ **Beluga** 326
☐ **Bison**, American 160
☐ **Blackbuck** 168
Boar, European Wild, *see* Feral Pig 170
☐ **Bobcat** 138
☐ **Bowhead** 334
Buffalo, *see* American Bison 160
☐ **Caribou** 158
Chickaree, *see* Douglas's Squirrel 48
Chipmunk, Allen's, *see* Shadow Chipmunk 64
☐ Alpine 62
☐ California 66
☐ Cliff 56
☐ Colorado 58
☐ Eastern 52
☐ Gray-collared 58
☐ Gray-footed 60
☐ Hopi 58
☐ Least 52
☐ Lodgepole 62
☐ Long-eared 62
☐ Merriam's 66
☐ Palmer's 60
☐ Panamint 60
☐ Red-tailed 54
☐ Shadow 64
☐ Siskiyou 64
☐ Sonoma 66
☐ Townsend's 64
☐ Uinta 56
☐ Yellow-cheeked 64
☐ Yellow-pine 54
Chital 166
☐ **Coati**, White-nosed 100
☐ **Cottontail**, Appalachian 24
☐ Desert 28
☐ Eastern 24
☐ Mountain 28
☐ New England 24

Cougar, *see* Puma 136
☐**Coyote** 128
Deer, Axis, *see* Chital 166
    Black tailed, *see* Mule
      Deer 152
    Common Fallow 166
☐ Mule 152
    Sambar, *see* Sambar
      166
    Sika 166
    Spotted, *see* Chital 166
☐ White-tailed 150
☐**Deermouse**, Brush 180
☐ Cactus 180
☐ California 182
☐ Canyon 180
☐ Cotton 184
☐ Merriam's 182
☐ Northern Rock 182
☐ Northwestern 178
☐ Oldfield 184
☐ Pinyon 180
☐ Saxicolous 182
☐ Texas 178
☐ White-ankled 178
☐ White-footed 178
Dog, Prairie, *see under*
    Prairie Dog
☐**Dolphin**, Atlantic Spot-
    ted 306
☐ Atlantic White-sided
    310
☐ Bottlenose 304
☐ Clymene 308
☐ Fraser's 310
☐ Long-beaked Com-
    mon 304
☐ Northern Right Whale
    314
☐ Pacific White-sided
    310
☐ Pantropical Spotted
    308
☐ Risso's 314
☐ Rough-toothed 304
    Saddleback, *see* Short-
      beaked and Long-
      beaked Common
      Dolphins 304
☐ Short-beaked Com-
    mon 304
☐ Spinner 308
☐ Striped 308

☐ White-beaked 310
Donkey, Feral 172
☐**Elk** 156
☐**Ermine** 120
☐**Ferret**, Black-footed 118
☐**Fisher** 122
☐**Fox**, Arctic 134
☐ Gray 130
☐ Island Gray 130
☐ Kit 132
☐ Red 130
☐ Swift 132
Fur-seal, *see under* Seal
Gemsbok 168
Goat, Domestic 168
☐ Mountain 164
☐**Gopher**, Attwater's
    Pocket 238
☐ Baird's Pocket 238
☐ Botta's Pocket 234
☐ Camas Pocket 234
    Central Texas Pocket,
      see Llano Pocket
      Gopher 240
☐ Desert Pocket 240
☐ Idaho Pocket 236
☐ Knox Jones's Pocket
    240
☐ Llano Pocket 240
☐ Mountain Pocket 236
☐ Northern Pocket 236
☐ Plains Pocket 238
☐ Southeastern Pocket
    240
☐ Southern Pocket 236
☐ Texas Pocket 240
☐ Townsend's Pocket 236
☐ Western Pocket 236
☐ Wyoming Pocket 234
☐ Yellow-faced Pocket
    238
Groundhog, *see* Wood-
    chuck 90
Ground Squirrel, *see un-
    der* Squirrel
☐**Hare**, Alaskan 34
☐ Arctic 34
    Cape 34
    European 34
☐ Snowshoe 34
Horse, Feral 172
☐**Jackrabbit**, Antelope 30
☐ Black-tailed 30

☐ White-sided 30
☐ White-tailed 32
☐**Jaguar** 136
☐**Jaguarundi** 140
Javelina, *see* Collared Pec-
    cary 170
Kangaroo Rat, *see under*
    Rat
☐**Lemming**, Brown 228
☐ Northern Bog 228
☐ Northern Collared
    230
☐ Richardson's Collared
    230
☐ Southern Bog 228
☐ Ungava Collared 230
Lion, Mountain, *see* Puma
    136
    Sea, *see* Sea Lion
☐**Lynx**, Canadian 138
☐**Manatee**, West Indian
    302
☐**Margay** 140
☐**Marmot**, Alaska 94
☐ Hoary 92
☐ Olympic 94
☐ Vancouver Island 94
☐ Yellow-bellied 92
☐**Marten**, American 122
☐**Mink**, American 116
☐**Mole**, American Shrew
    244
☐ Broad-footed 244
☐ Coast 244
☐ Eastern 242
☐ Hairy-tailed 242
☐ Star-nosed 242
☐ Townsend's 244
☐**Moose** 154
☐**Mouse**, Arizona Pocket
    210
☐ Bailey's Pocket 210
    Brush, *see* Brush Deer-
      mouse 180
    Cactus, *see* Cactus
      Deermouse 180
    California, *see* Califor-
      nia Deermouse 182
☐ California Pocket 214
    Canyon, *see* Canyon
      Deermouse 180
☐ Chihuahuan
    Grasshopper 188

Chihuahuan Pocket 212
Cotton, *see* Cotton Deermouse 184
Dark Kangaroo 206
Deer, *see* North American Deermouse 176
Desert Pocket 212
Eastern Harvest 186
Florida 184
Fulvous Harvest 186
Golden 184
Grasshopper, *see* 188
Great Basin Pocket 208
Harvest, *see* 186
Hispid Pocket 210
House 176
Jumping, *see* 216
Little Pocket 210
Long-tailed Pocket 210
Meadow Jumping 216
Mearns's Grasshopper, *see* Chihuahuan Grasshopper Mouse 188
Merriam's Pocket 208
Mesquite, *see* Merriam's Deermouse 182
Mexican Spiny Pocket 212
Nelson's Pocket 212
Northern Grasshopper 188
Northern Rock, *see* Northern Rock Deermouse 182
Northern Pygmy 188
Northwestern, *see* Northwestern Deermouse 178
Oldfield, *see* Oldfield Deermouse 184
Olive-backed Pocket 208
Osgood's, *see* Saxicolous Deermouse 182
Pacific Jumping 216
Pale Kangaroo 206

Pinyon, *see* Pinyon Deermouse 180
Plains Harvest 186
Plains Pocket 208
Rock Pocket 212
Saltmarsh Harvest 186
San Diego Pocket 214
San Joaquin Pocket 214
Silky Pocket 208
Southern Grasshopper 188
Spiny Pocket 214
Texas, *see* Texas Deermouse 178
Western Harvest 186
Western Jumping 216
White-ankled, *see* White-ankled Deermouse 178
White-eared Pocket 214
White-footed, *see* White-footed Deermouse 178
Woodland Jumping 216
□**Muskox** 160
□**Muskrat,** Common 112
Round-tailed 112
□**Myotis,** California 270
Cave 272
Eastern Small-footed 268
Fringed 274
Gray 270
Indiana 270
Keen's 272
Little Brown 268
Long-eared 274
Long-legged 272
Northern 274
Northern Long-eared, *see* Northern Myotis 274
Southeastern 274
Southwestern 274
Western Small-footed 270
Yuma 272
□**Narwhal** 324
□**Nilgai** 168
□**Nutria** 110

□**Ocelot** 140
□**Opossum,** Virginia 102
Orca, *see* Killer Whale 316
Oryx, *see* Gemsbok 168
□**Otter,** Northern River 116
Sea 114
□**Peccary,** Collared 170
Phenacomys, *see* Heather Voles 226
Pig, Feral 170
□**Pika,** American 36
Collared 36
□**Pipistrelle,** Eastern 266
Western 266
Pocket Gopher, *see under* Gopher
Pocket Mouse, *see under* Mouse
□**Porcupine,** North American 108
□**Porpoise,** Dall's 318
Harbor 318
Possum, *see* Virginia Opossum 102
□**Prairie Dog,** Black-tailed 86
White-tailed 88
Gunnison's 88
Utah 88
□**Pronghorn** 164
□**Puma** 136
□**Rabbit,** Brush 28
European 34
Jack, *see under* Jackrabbit
Marsh 26
Pygmy 28
Swamp 26
□**Raccoon,** Northern 98
□**Rat,** Agile Kangaroo 200
Arizona Cotton 192
Banner-tailed Kangaroo 198
Big-eared Kangaroo 202
Black, *see* House Rat 190
Brown 190
California Kangaroo 200
Chisel-toothed Kangaroo 200

Rat *(cont'd)*
　Cotton, *see* 192
☐ Coues's Rice 190
☐ Desert Kangaroo 200
☐ Dulzura Kangaroo 204
　Fresno Kangaroo, *see*
　　San Joaquin Valley
　　Kangaroo Rat 202
☐ Giant Kangaroo 202
☐ Gulf Coast Kangaroo
　206
☐ Heermann's Kangaroo
　202
☐ Hispid Cotton 192
☐ House 190
☐ Marsh Rice 190
☐ Merriam's Kangaroo
　198
☐ Narrow-faced Kanga-
　roo 204
　Norway, *see* Brown Rat
　190
☐ Ord's Kangaroo 198
☐ Panamint Kangaroo
　204
　Roof, *see* House Rat
　190
☐ San Joaquin Valley
　Kangaroo 202
☐ Stephens's Kangaroo
　204
☐ Tawny-bellied Cotton
　192
☐ Texas Kangaroo 206
　Wood, *see under*
　Woodrat
☐ Yellow-nosed Cotton
　192
☐**Ringtail** 100
Sambar 166
☐**Sea Lion**, California 288
　Northern, *see* Steller's
　　Sea Lion 288
☐ Steller's 288
☐**Seal**, Bearded 298
☐ Gray 296
☐ Guadalupe Fur 290
☐ Harbor 296
☐ Harp 296
☐ Hooded 298
☐ Northern Elephant
　292
☐ Northern Fur 290

☐ Ribbon 298
☐ Ringed 298
☐ Spotted 296
☐**Sewellel** 234
Sheep, Barbary, *see* Auo-
　dad 168
☐ Bighorn 162
☐ Dall's 162
　Mountain, *see* Bighorn
　　Sheep 162
☐**Shrew**, Arctic 252
☐ Arizona 248
☐ Baird's 256
☐ Barren Ground 252
☐ Cinereus 254
　Common Water, *see*
　　Water Shrew 248
☐ Desert 258
　Dusky, *see* Montane
　　Shrew 256
☐ Dwarf 254
☐ Elliot's Short-tailed
　258
☐ Fog 256
☐ Gaspé 250
☐ Inyo 254
☐ Least 252
☐ Long-tailed 250
☐ Maritime 252
☐ Marsh 248
　Masked, *see* Cinereus
　　Shrew 254
☐ Merriam's 248
☐ Montane 256
☐ Mt. Lyell 254
☐ Northern Short-tailed
　258
☐ Ornate 256
☐ Pacific 256
☐ Prairie 254
☐ Preble's 248
☐ Pribilof Island 252
☐ Pygmy 254
　Rock, *see* Long-tailed
　　Shrew 250
　Sonoma, *see* Fog
　　Shrew 256
☐ Southeastern 250
☐ Southern Short-tailed
　258
☐ Smoky 250
☐ Trowbridge's 248
☐ Tundra 252

☐ Vagrant 256
☐ Water 248
☐**Skunk**, Common Hog-
　nosed 106
☐ Eastern Spotted 106
☐ Hooded 104
☐ Striped 104
☐ Western Spotted 106
☐**Squirrel**, Abert's 46
　Antelope, *see* 70
　Apache Fox, *see* Mexi-
　　can Fox Squirrel 44
☐ Arizona Gray 44
☐ Arctic Ground 80
☐ Belding's Ground 84
☐ Cascade Golden-man-
　tled Ground 72
☐ California Ground 76
☐ Columbian Ground
　80
☐ Douglas's 48
☐ Eastern Fox 42
☐ Eastern Gray 40
☐ Franklin's Ground 78
　Flying, *see* 50
☐ Golden-mantled
　Ground 72
☐ Harris's Antelope 70
　Kaibab, *see* Abert's
　　Squirrel 46
☐ Idaho Ground 82
☐ Mexican Fox 44
　Mexican Gray, *see*
　　Red-bellied Squirrel
　　46
☐ Mexican Ground 74
☐ Merriam's Ground 82
☐ Mohave Ground 84
☐ Nelson's Antelope 70
☐ Northern Flying 50
☐ Piute Ground 82
☐ Red 48
☐ Red-bellied 46
☐ Richardson's Ground
　80
☐ Rock 76
☐ Round-tailed Ground
　84
☐ Southern Flying 50
☐ Spotted Ground 74
☐ Texas Antelope 70
☐ Thirteen-lined
　Ground 74

☐ Townsend's Ground 82
☐ Uinta Ground 78
☐ Washington Ground 82
☐ Western Gray 40
☐ White-tailed Antelope 70
☐ Wyoming Ground 78
Tahr, Himalayan 168
☐**Vampire**, Hairy-legged 280
☐**Vole**, Beach 218
☐ California 222
☐ Creeping 220
☐ Eastern Heather 226
☐ Gray-tailed 222
☐ Insular 218
☐ Long-tailed 220
☐ Meadow 218
☐ Mogollon 222
☐ Montane 222
☐ Northern Red-backed 224
☐ Prairie 222
Red-backed, *see* 224
☐ Red Tree 226
☐ Rock 224
☐ Sagebrush 220
☐ Singing 218
☐ Sonoma Tree 226
☐ Southern Red-backed 224
☐ Taiga 218
☐ Townsend's 220
☐ Tundra 218
☐ Water 220

☐ Western Heather 226
☐ Western Red-backed 224
☐ White-footed 226
☐ Woodland 224
☐**Walrus** 300
Wapiti, see Elk 156
☐**Weasel**, Least 120
☐ Long-tailed 120
Short-tailed, *see* Ermine 120
☐**Whale**, Baird's Beaked 320
☐ Blainville's Beaked 322
☐ Blue 334
Bowhead, *see* Bowhead 334
☐ Bryde's 332
☐ Cuvier's Beaked 320
☐ Dwarf Sperm 340
☐ False Killer 312
☐ Fin 334
☐ Gervais's Beaked 322
☐ Ginkgo-toothed Beaked 324
☐ Gray 328
Hector's Beaked, *see* Perrin's Beaked 324
☐ Hubbs's Beaked 324
☐ Humpback 330
☐ Killer 316
☐ Long-finned Pilot 314
☐ Melon-headed 312
Minke, *see* Northern Minke 332
☐ Northern Bottlenose 320

☐ Northern Minke 332
☐ Northern Right Whale 336
☐ Perrin's Beaked 324
☐ Pygmy Beaked 324
☐ Pygmy Killer 312
☐ Pygmy Sperm 340
☐ Sei 332
☐ Short-finned Pilot 314
☐ Sowerby's Beaked 322
☐ Sperm 338
☐ Stejneger's Beaked 322
☐ True's Beaked 324
White, *see* Beluga 324
☐**Wolf**, Gray 126
☐ Red 128
☐**Wolverine** 122
☐**Woodchuck** 90
☐**Woodrat**, Allegheny 196
☐ Arizona 194
☐ Bushy-tailed 196
☐ Desert 194
☐ Dusky-footed 196
☐ Eastern 196
☐ Mexican 194
☐ Stephens's 194
☐ Southern Plains 196
☐ White-throated 194

QUICK METRIC CONVERSIONS

We regretfully had to leave metric measurements off the color plates, to keep those pages from becoming thickets of statistics. For those readers more comfortable with metric, here are some approximate conversions.

10 inches = about 25 centimeters
40 inches = about one meter
10 feet = about 3 meters
3 ounces = about 85 grams
7 pounds = about 3 kilograms
200 pounds = about 90 kilograms

Short index for KAUFMAN FOCUS GUIDE: MAMMALS OF NORTH AMERICA

(Some rare mammals, unlikely to be seen by most readers,
are excluded here but included in the regular index.)

Antelope ■ p. 164
Antelope Squirrel ■ p. 70
Armadillo ■ p. 108
Badger ■ p. 118
Bat ■ pp. 260–284
Bear ■ pp. 142–146
Beaver ■ p. 110
Beluga ■ p. 326
Bighorn ■ p. 162
Bison ■ p. 160
Bobcat ■ p. 138
Bowhead ■ p. 334
Buffalo ■ p. 160
Caribou ■ p. 158
Cats ■ pp. 136–140
Chipmunk ■ pp. 52–66
Coati ■ p. 100
Cottontail ■ pp. 24, 28
Cougar ■ p. 136
Coyote ■ p. 128
Deer ■ pp. 150–158, 166
Deermouse ■ pp. 176–184
Dolphin ■ pp. 304–310
Elk ■ p. 156
Ermine ■ p. 120
Ferret ■ p. 118
Fisher ■ p. 122
Flying Squirrel ■ p. 50
Fox ■ pp. 130–134
Goat ■ pp. 164, 168
Gopher ■ pp. 234–240
Ground Squirrel ■ pp. 72–84
Groundhog ■ p. 90
Hare ■ pp. 32–34
Jackrabbit ■ pp. 30–32
Jaguar ■ p. 136
Jaguarundi ■ p. 140
Javelina ■ p. 170
Jumping Mouse ■ p. 216
Kangaroo Rat ■ pp. 198–206
Lemming ■ pp. 228–230
Lynx ■ p. 138
Manatee ■ p. 302
Marmot ■ pp. 92–94
Marten ■ p. 122
Mink ■ p. 116
Mole ■ pp. 242–244

Moose ■ p. 154
Mountain Beaver ■ p. 234
Mountain Lion ■ p. 136
Mouse ■ pp. 176–188, 206–216
Muskox ■ p. 160
Muskrat ■ p. 112
Myotis ■ pp. 268–274
Narwhal ■ p. 324
Nutria ■ p. 110
Ocelot ■ p. 140
Opossum ■ p. 102
Orca ■ p. 316
Otter ■ pp. 114–116
Peccary ■ p. 170
Pig ■ p. 170
Pika ■ p. 36
Pipistrelle ■ p. 266
Pocket Gopher ■ pp. 234–240
Pocket Mouse ■ pp. 208–214
Porcupine ■ p. 108
Porpoise ■ p. 318
Possum ■ p. 102
Prairie Dog ■ pp. 86–88
Pronghorn ■ p. 164
Puma ■ p. 136
Rabbit ■ pp. 26–28, 34
Raccoon ■ p. 98
Rat ■ pp. 190–206
Reindeer ■ p. 158
Ringtail ■ p. 100
Sea Lion ■ p. 288
Seal ■ pp. 288–298
Sewellel ■ p. 234
Sheep ■ pp. 162, 168
Shrew ■ pp. 248–258
Skunk ■ pp. 104–106
Squirrel ■ pp. 40–50, 70–84
Vole ■ pp. 218–226
Walrus ■ p. 300
Wapiti ■ p. 156
Weasel ■ p. 120
Whale ■ pp. 312–316, 320–340
Wolf ■ pp. 126–128
Wolverine ■ p. 122
Woodchuck ■ p. 90
Woodrat ■ pp. 194–196